## *Collectors, have you ever wondered...*

- How to confidently collect more money?
- What to say on a collection call?
- How to diffuse fire-breathing, upset customers, and still collect the money?
- How to quickly overcome payment excuses and objections?
- How to convert more accounts into "Promises to Pay"?
- How to enjoy your job more?

## *Supervisors, have you ever wondered.....*

- How to motivate and lead your collection teams to new heights?
- How to get your new collectors "up-to-speed" quickly?
- How to move your experienced collectors to the next level?

## *Managers and business owners, have you ever wondered......*

- How to ensure more accounts pay on time?
- How does the West manage such low bad debt rates?
- How to ensure your staff are effective AND professional?
- How to minimize bad debt risk while doing business in Asia?
- How to raise your department's exposure to reflect the importance of the job they do?
- How to get your new team leads "up-to-speed" quickly?

This book answers these questions and more. It's full of creative, PRACTICAL ideas to strategically manage your firm's accounts receivables with techniques used in the West and in the Far East.

*Published by:*
ServiceWinners Publishing
1713 91st NE
Bellevue, Wa. 98004
USA

Orders at: orders@servicewinners.com
Website: http://www.servicewinners.com

**ISBN- 13: 978-983-42621-2-9**
**ISBN- 10: 983-42621-2-4**

**Perpustakaan Negara Malaysia**          **Cataloging-in-Publication Data:**
Coyle, Steven F., 1959-
Debt collections: stir-fried or deep-fried?/Steven F. Coyle
ISBN: 983-42621-2-4
1. Collecting of accounts. 2. Credit— Management. I. Title

658.88

Design & prepress by

RDC Publishing Group Sdn Bhd

Edited by: Faridah Noor Mohd Noor, PhD

---

**ATTENTION: Business Owners, Collection Managers, and Supervisors**

**Special sales:**

Purchases of this book in quantity are available for team awards, incentives or training.

**For more information, contact:**
ServiceWinners International Sdn. Bhd.
Email: orders@servicewinners.com
Website: http://www.servicewinners.com

## Rightful Copying

Up to 20 copies may be reproduced of any section in this book up to 20 pages without permission from the author as long as no charge is made for the copies.

However, please ensure the title of this book and chapter are on each page, and put my name on the front section.

Please share the ideas generated in this book with others in the credit profession. At the same time recommend they buy a copy!

If you need customized in-house seminars, please contact ServiceWinners International Sdn. Bhd. at http://www.servicewinners.com or +60-12-2000-998.

Seminars we offer :

| | |
|---|---|
| • Winning Collection Skills | • Advanced Negotiation Skills for Collections |
| • Proven Strategies in Managing Receivables | • Integrity @ Work (Business Ethics) |
| • Creative Thinking Skills | • Handling Hardcore Debtors |
| • Avoiding Friendly Fire: Working with the Sales People | • Credit & Collections for Sales People |

ServiceWinners International Sdn. Bhd.
Steven Coyle
Tel : +60 12-2000-998
E-Mail : steve@servicewinners.com
Website: http://www.servicewinners.com

Note: Any names used for customers and debtors are invented. If, in any case, I have used a real name, it's purely coincidental.

In this book, the words "credit" and "collections" are used interchangeably. If you see either of these two words- the other is implied. The exception to this rule is Chapter 2: In the Beginning There Was Credit, where credit is the chapter's sole focus.

# Acknowledgements

I want to thank everyone who answered my many questions. I'd especially like to thank my father, Terry Coyle, for his assistance on this book. To my editor, Dr. Faridah Noor Mohd Noor, for her excellent comments. I'd also like to thank my credit friends and colleagues from around the world who contributed to this book- they are:

| | |
|---|---|
| Argentina: | Richardo Cagnoni |
| Australia : | Neil Wood |
| Canada: | Tim Paulsen |
| Japan: | Steven Gan |
| Malaysia: | Andrew Gan, Barry Spencer, Nina Zainal, Tan Boon Wei, S. Santhirasegaran, Albert Khoo |
| Singapore: | Dominic Lee, Daniel Ord |
| Taiwan: | Jim Brown |
| U.S.A.: | Nick & Marianne Boechler, Bernice D'Arcy, Steve Akrish, Charles Klever, Michael Kinneman, John Ikazaki |

This book is dedicated to Credit and Collections professionals who – often quietly – contribute immensely to their organization's survival.

**Debt Collections:**

# Stir-Fried or Deep-Fried?

Asian and Western strategies to collect more money, reduce
bad debts and keep more customers

Steven F. Coyle, CCE

# TABLE OF CONTENTS

## Part I: Introduction

### *Did You Ever Think You'd Be Doing This?*
**Overview of the Credit and Collections Field**

Passion for Collections, "Collections is Not a Dirty Word, Employees' Primary Role, Organizational Disconnect, Importance of the Job, Where to Put the Credit Department?, Comparing the Collection Environments in Asia and the West, Collections Environments in Japan, Singapore, Taiwan, Australia and New Zealand, Hey Asia— Want to Save a Ton of Money?

## Part II: The Credit Field

### *In the Beginning There was Credit*
**Putting in Place Proper Credit Controls**

Writing a Credit Policy, Benefits of a Written and Agreed Credit Policy, Credit Policy's Contents, Policy's Writing Style, Creating a Useful Credit Application or Registration Form, Contracts, Approving and "Rejecting" Credit Submissions, Credit and Behavioral Scoring, How to Improve Your Credit Analysis Skills?, Signs of a Weak Credit Department

## Part III: The Collections Field

### *How Do We Do It and When?*
**Putting in Place Effective Collection Strategies**

Days Sales Outstanding (DSO) Comparison, Collection Strategies— Pre-emptive Stage, Collection Strategies—Early Stage, Collection Strategies—Mid-Stage, Collection Strategies—Late Stage, Signs of a Weak Collection Department, Importance of Reports

### *Written Communications*
**Effective Letters, Emails and Short Messages**

Collection Letters, Tips for Writing Collection Letter, Examples of Collection Letters (Asian and Western Styles), Collection Emails, Example of Collection Email, Short Message Service (SMS)

When to Use Agencies and Law Firms?, Monitoring Collection Agencies' Performance, Monitoring Law Firms' Performance, Auditing Collection Agencies and Law Firms

## Part VI: Leading Collection Professionals

### Chapter 18

### *"I've Been Collecting Before You Were Even Born!"*
**Leading a Collection Team**

Importance of Good Supervisors and Managers, Importance of a Share Departmental Vision, Getting Buy-in for Operational Processes, Motivating Your Teams, Building a Performance-based Work Environment, How to Recognize Good Perfomance?, Creating Incentive Programs, Yearly Performance Ratings, Promoting Open Communication, Promoting Fun!, Some Fun Ideas, Salary Scheme, Reducing Employee Turnover, Career Progression Scheme, Choosing Your Leadership Team, Managing Poor Performance: "The Dental Office"

## Part VII: The Future of Collections

### Chapter 19

### *What's Around this Corner and the Next?*
**Technical Advances in the Collections Field**

The Meaning of "New", Low Tech Solutions, Higher Tech Solutions, Revenue Collections and Debt Management System Profile: Profitera's *Power Collect*™, Future Technologies

### Chapter 20

### *Succeeding into the Future*
**Starting a Continual Learning Program for Yourself**

Importance of Continually Learning, From Knowledge to Wisdom, Recommended Books, Magazines, and Websites

### *Epilogue: The Diaper Incident*

### *About the Author*

### *Contact Information*

### *Appendix: Sample Scripts*

# Preface

As a collection manager, I often needed quick, practical ideas from others in the field. Sometimes I turned to books, but few were geared to the credit practitioner. Sure, there were plenty of books for students and professionals who needed to pass tests, but those kinds of books are usually bogged down with theories and formulas for calculating probabilities of payback. From experience, theories and formulas have collected me less money than having the right people, processes, and systems in place.

This book is written in a practical style for credit and collections people, at all levels, from new collectors to experienced managers. Its seven sections are divided as follows:

| Part | Section's Name | Target Audience |
|------|----------------|-----------------|
| I | Introduction | All Credit & Collection Professionals |
| II | The Credit Field | Credit Professionals |
| III | The Collection Field | Collectors, Collection Leaders & Future Leaders |
| IV | How to Become a Professional Collector? | Collectors |
| V | Fostering Alliances & Strategic Partnerships | Collection Leaders & Future Leaders |
| VI | Leading Collection Professionals | Collection Leaders & Future Leaders |
| VII | The Future of Collections | All Credit & Collection Professionals |

This book mixes collection practices from both Asia where I live, and from the West where Seattle is my original hometown. Collections people from both sides of the world can learn from each other.

I'm lucky being a collections consultant and trainer based in Asia. I'm able to devote time to a subject I enjoy while flying to interesting places. If you have any comments or questions about this book or about the field of collections, please feel free to contact me.

Terima kasih,

**Steve Coyle, CCE**     Phone: +60-12-2000-998

ServiceWinners International Sdn. Bhd.
E-mail: steve@servicewinners.com
Kuala Lumpur, Malaysia
Website: www.servicewinners.com

**Debt Collections:**
# Stir-Fried or Deep-Fried?

Asian and Western strategies to collect more money, reduce bad debts and keep more customers

*With special application for collection call centers, agencies, telcos, celcos, banks, finance companies, credit card centers, insurance companies, cable & satellite TV providers, tax departments, and Internet Service Providers*

Steven Coyle, CCE

# Part I:
# **Introduction**

# Did You Ever Think You'd Be Doing This?

**1**

*Overview of the Credit and Collections Field*

*Promises make debt, and debt makes promises.* – Dutch proverb

## After reading this chapter, you will be able to:

- Recognize the importance of the collections department

- Learn the primary role of a credit professional

- Evaluate where to place the collections department within your organization

- Compare Asian and western collection environments

## A Passion for Collections

Aren't you proud to be a bill collector?

If you had met me as a college student and told me that one day I would become a bill collector, I would have said, "No way, man." Of all the professions, bill collections would have ranked about 973rd on my list.

How about yourself? Did you choose collections or did collections choose you?

For most of us, I suspect the latter. Yet extending credit and collecting bills must be one of the oldest professions in the world. I bet humans have been borrowing things since the first harvest or the first hunt. And the lender probably received some kind of "promise" from the borrower.

| Og | : | *Urg, can I borrow your spear for the winter mastodon hunt?* |
| Urg | : | *Og, I'm not sure I can spare it.* |
| Og | : | *Please?* |
| Urg | : | *No, I need it.* |
| Og | : | *Urg, if I get a mastodon, I'll give you a leg.* |
| Urg | : | *Deal!* (Followed by joint head banging as shaking hands was unknown at this time). |

When I first began my career in collections it was a bit embarrassing. Friends, parents and strangers would ask, "So, what do you do for a living?"

That simple question caused all kinds of uncomfortable feelings within me. I didn't want to lie, but I sure didn't want to tell the truth either. It felt like I was holding a dirty secret. Eventually I mustered the courage to speak the truth, plus it's hard keeping track of different occpations if you lie and bump into the same person again.

"I'm a bill collector."

Their responses ranged from "You're joking, right?", to an uncomfortable, "Oh, I see." Dinner parties were the worst.

Nowadays, I handle that question easily. I give a one-two conversational knock-out punch. First, I answer the question confidently because I'm proud of what I do. I figure that if people feel awkward about my profession it's because they probably owe somebody money. Second, I follow up with a funny collection story.

I found it works. Soon small groups of people would encircle me wanting to hear more funny collection stories. Collections is indeed an interesting field. As my stories increased, so did the number of dinner party invitations.

Collections deals with life. We get our hands dirty. We hear stories. It's a job that allows us to interact with more groups within an organization than most other jobs. We deal with sales people to ensure the credit quality of their submissions is high. We share credit impacts with the marketing people before they roll-out new promotions. We meet with the I.T. department to ensure their systems allow us to touch more customers and process more money faster. We meet with the finance department to evaluate reports and statistics to forecast cash flow. We even contact our fellow employees for debts they owe the organization.

Senior management is concerned with our performance as it ties directly to shareholder performance goals. Chief Financial Officers are in regular contact to ensure the company is hitting its cash flow and expense targets.

By doing our job well, we give senior management something to brag about. We help them look good; which is the first rule in working for any boss. From their perspective, our role is to convert as many accounts receivable– which are simply "promises to pay"– into cash as quickly as possible.

## *"Collections" is Not a Dirty Word*

People treat bad debts like a taboo topic. Although we know we have them, we would rather not talk about them, thank you. However, if we ignore them, we cause more problems. Ask businessmen about their gross sales and few hesitate to share this information. Ask them their bad debt percentages and often you will be greeted with strange looks. Either they don't know or they feel uncomfortable sharing such downside information.

Mismanaging accounts receivable (A/R) causes companies to go bankrupt as cash returns are delayed. That delay is reflected in higher borrowing costs or worse – no one is willing to offer financing.

> **Tip:**
> A collections rule of thumb says you lose 2% of the value of the balance for every 30 days you let other people hold your money.

Not having cash, or mismanaging it, will cause companies to go bankrupt. According to a study commissioned by the U.S. Small Business Administration[1] the major reasons why companies go bankrupt are "Financing" at 28% and "Inside Business Conditions" at 27%. "Financing" includes high interest expenses, loss of financing or lack of financing. "Inside Business Conditions" include mismanagement of accounts receivable.

A similar study conducted by the U.K. based Association of Business Recovery Professionals found that some of the leading commercial causes for insolvency included lack of working capital / cash flow (11%) and bad debts (8%).[2]

Anyone who wants children needs to expect dirty diapers. The same is true for business. If you extend credit, expect bad debts. But, the nice thing about bad debts is, with proper credit controls, you can minimize them.

Bad debts don't get a lot of attention because they're not "sexy." Bad debts imply foreclosure, repossession, angry customers and nasty collectors. No one wants to get involved in such accounts.

Sales, on the other hand, are sexy. The word even sounds sexy: "Sexy Sales." Sales people have sales meetings, sales conferences and sales conventions. There are even sales "boot camps" where sales people go offsite to a resort and discuss sales techniques in between trips to the

---

1   Sullivan, Warren and Westbrook, *"Financial Difficulties of Small Businesses and Reasons for Their Failure"*, March 1999, <http://www.sba.gov> (4 June 2004), Office of Advocacy, U.S. Small Business Administration.

2   Association of Business Recovery Professionals, *"9th Survey of Personal Insolvency"*, 1999, <http://www.r3.org.uk> (3 July 2004), R3.

swimming pool. When was the last time you attended a "Collections Boot Camp"? In fact, when was the last time you ever attended any training in credit or collections?

Many sales people, like baseball players, are considered great if they get a "hit" 30% of the time. Whereas, if collection professionals achieved similar results, we would be off the team.

Sales and collections people have a lot in common. We both:

- Need many of the same skills to do our jobs effectively

- Ask busy people to part with their money

- Overcome objections while ensuring the overall experience for the customer or prospect was professional and pleasant

Both jobs aren't easy, yet they're similar.

## Employees' Primary Role

What's the primary role of employees for the organization?

When I ask that question to a room full of supervisors or managers, I normally hear, "To make our companies money." But is it our primary role as credit professionals?

Look at the top 50 companies in the Fortune 500 list of ten or twenty years ago. Many of yesterday's most successful companies have disappeared. How did it happen? Who would have thought companies like McDonnell Douglas, RJR Nabisco, Airtouch, Digital Equipment, Enron, Allied Signal, and Rockwell International would either disappear or become merged by larger forces?

The primary role of an employee is to ensure their employer's survival. It makes sense. If you believe organizations are living things created and run by living beings with the intent to grow, thrive and provide sustenance for its members; then its ultimate goal – like in nature itself – is survival. Just examine the root of the word "organization." The credit and collections function is an important organ within any organization. Without the organ functioning properly, the organism dies.

Companies disappear when the management is preoccupied with making money. As our sport coaches tell us, "Never take your eye off the ball." As a manager, if you're following your secondary role (making money), and your competitors are following the primary role, guess who's going to lose the game? This is especially so in today's work environment where we face competition both domestically and internationally. Andy Grove, co-founder of Intel, sums it up well : "Only the paranoid survive."

Many companies focus exclusively on sales. They think that by selling more they earn more. Instead, the focus should be on helping customers because if you don't help your customers, they won't help you.

Sales people have a difficult job getting people to buy, but a sale isn't profitable until the money is collected.

So, let's go back to the question: Where do bad debts come from?

Extending credit and experiencing bad debts are facts of life for businesses. Organizations bear credit risks in order to increase sales and stay competitive. However, the risks are manageable with proper strategies and controls in place. The key group that sets the drivers for effective debt management is an organization's senior management.

It's easy for the senior management to set unrealistic bad debt targets while launching aggressive sales programs with easy credit terms. When the bad debt numbers inevitably increase, fingers are pointed at the credit or collections department. But pointing alone doesn't fix the problem. Until senior management takes a firm stance on combating bad debt, its bad debt targets likely will never be achieved.

If a company has a banner sales year, should the sales department take all the credit? Did the sales department do it all themselves? Or did the engineering department help by designing good products, or customer service by providing good after-sales service, or marketing by creating excellent promotions? In fact, it's a team effort.

The same holds true for bad debts. The credit and collection department alone can't take full credit or blame for a company's bad debt levels. The sooner senior management recognizes this, the faster organizations will take control of their bad debts instead of the other way around. David and Martin Sher[3] write in How to Collect Debts and Still Keep Your Customers:

> Collection departments alone don't cause bad debts – bad management causes bad debts. You can't blame the doctor for the number of sick and ailing patients. You also can't necessarily blame your collection department for the large number of sick and ailing accounts.

## Organizational Disconnect

Many sales and credit professionals confide in me that the other party doesn't fully understand their business. Sometimes they will say that senior management doesn't fully understand the business, too. Usually, both the sales and the credit people are the ones who don't fully understand.

A customer-centric organization's top priorities should be (in order of importance):

---

3    David and Martin Sher, How to Collect Debts and still Keep Your Customers (AMA Publications) 1999.

1. Survival

2. Helping Customers

3. Earning Profits

4. Increasing Sales and Reducing Expenses

But often the focus of the sales and credit departments doesn't align with the organization's priorities:

| Priority No. | Organization | Sales Department | Credit Department |
|---|---|---|---|
| 1 | Survival | Increase Sales | Reduce Expenses (bad debts) |
| 2 | Helping Customers | Increase Sales | Reduce Expenses (bad debts) |
| 3 | Earning Profits | Increase Sales | Reduce Expenses (bad debts) |
| 4 | Increase Sales and Reduce Expenses | Increase Sales | Reduce Expenses (bad debts) |

Many sales and credit departments have only one priority. Is it any wonder there's a disconnect between these two groups and the organization? The sales and credit people point fingers at other groups for not knowing "what's really going on" when in fact they're the ones confused. It's at Priority 4 where sale's and credit's priorities are aligned with the organization's.

If your department's priorities are misaligned with your organization's, then you're missing the big picture. You're working in a silo.

Did you ever think that your top priority wasn't to collect money? Instead, concentrate your efforts on ensuring your organization survives, help your customers by providing excellent service, help your organization maintain profitability, and you will find yourself collecting more money than you have ever collected before.

## Importance of the Job

Collectors are corporate doctors. We take unhealthy, nearly dying and sometimes dead accounts and try to revive them. In our society, doctors are valued. When I see layoffs announced in newspapers, the affected groups are usually factory workers, middle management, R&D specialists, and sales and marketing people. I have never seen a layoff where doctors (or nurses for that matter) were targeted. I also rarely see layoffs where collectors were the primary targets. Organizations silently value their collectors, but it's up to us to highlight our importance within our organization.

We're doctors and we're jewelers. We manage one of the most precious assets in any company's balance sheet: accounts receivable (A/R). For many companies, A/R is the largest current asset, for others it is the largest asset. A/R is the "crown jewel." How well you guard this jewel determines the profitability and continued survival of both your organization and your career.

Finally, while others departments read reports and memos of this asset, we actually touch it every day. In fact, we touch the two most valuable assets of an organization: customers and money. With the growth of Customer Relationship Management (CRM) – where the customer becomes the central focus of an organization-- our organizational value should increase.

If you haven't already guessed, my method of collecting debts is CRM-based. It's customer-centric. I want the customer to see me as a partner, not an adversary. Will today's global collections professionals survive collecting otherwise?

## Where to Put the Credit Department?

In some organization's, the credit department is part of Finance or Accounting. In others, it's part of Customer Service or Marketing. In some, it's a stand-alone department.

There's no right or wrong answer; it depends on your business. If your organization is a consumer-based business catering to mass market consumers, like telecommunication companies (telcos), then perhaps Credit should reside in Customer Service. A company that wants to aggressively capture market share may put it in the Sales department. These are fine decisions, but I recommend against putting it in Accounting or Finance. These departments lack experience dealing with customers first-hand. They can cause customers to leave, and customers are our life-blood.

Senior management, with their overall understanding of the business strategy, is usually the most qualified group to determine the best fit for the credit department. Ideally, part of their decision-making process includes taking your views into consideration.

Dr. Barry Hutton, a professor at RMIT University in Australia, has written extensively on this issue. He suggests the credit department be a stand-alone department reporting directly to senior management, like an internal audit department. This way the department works cross-functionally to make its decisions wisely and impartially.[4]

---

4  Barry Hutton, "The Importance of Positioning," *Credit Management in Australia*, February 2003, 30-32; and "Are You Learning?", *Credit Management in Australia*, March 2003, 37-40.

Wherever your credit department is placed varies by an organization's needs. For me, I prefer the department residing with the sales or customer service departments. What other departments better understand customers?

Sales and credit are both part of the overall sales process. When I see credit and collections people in finance meetings, they often can't follow the conversation. They're unfamiliar with treasury's cash flow forecasts or the accounting people's problems with closing the monthly books, or the tax implications of purchasing certain assets. They're "fish out of water", but when credit or collections people attend sales meetings, they have plenty to say. Sales and credit departments are (like it or not) as the U.S./Canadian border reads: "Children of the same mother." We're both part of the sales process.

**Tip:**

If your organization places the credit department within the sales department, make sure both groups have joint KPI's (Key Performance Indicators). The sales people should have a component of their measurement determined by aging, bad debt and Days Sales Outstanding (DSO).[5] Conversely, the credit people should have a sales component added as a part of their measurement criteria.

## Comparing the Collection Environments in Asia and the West

A large chunk of my working life has been spent in Asia, primarily South East Asia. I would like to share my experiences looking at both western and Asian collection techniques. Both cultures can learn from one another.

This desire to learn is seen every day from my new hometown in Kuala Lumpur, Malaysia. In Kuala Lumpur– or "K.L" as it's known locally–you see Asians wearing the latest western fashions like Armani suits and Dona Karan outfits; while western business people sport the local batik and silk garments. Each side emulates the other. Even the young are involved whether it's Asians dressed as rappers or western backpackers wearing sarongs and sandals. Both sides can learn from the other.

One concept that's differentiates Asia from other parts of the world is the concept of "face." "Face" is a powerful driver in Asian societies.

---

5   Days Sales Outstanding: the number of days it takes the average debtor to pay that organization's invoice. Calculated many ways, but calculated here as Total Receivables / Total Sales x 365 days.

People will do just about anything to gain "face" and avoid losing "face." Losing one's temper loses face. Smiling gains face. Face is about maintaining the dignity and respect of one another. As a result, if you share a lousy idea with an Asian, unlike a Westerner, they won't comment that's it's a lousy idea. They will hint instead. If you give incorrect information, often you won't be corrected. In Asia, you learn to understand hints.

"Face" is a powerful tool to collect money. Asian debtors absolutely do not want to lose face.

I hope you, the reader, benefit from understanding how collections is done in other parts of the world. Although the collection environments in both are different, overdue debtors share similarities the world over. Debtors in every country have similar payment excuses and objections, and the responses and strategies used to overcome these obstacles are similar.

Some of the collection techniques used in Asia are illegal in North America. I will highlight those suggestions by recommending you seek legal advice. At the same time, I don't believe grafting 100% of the U.S.'s FDCPA (Fair Debt Collection Practices Act) to another country. Asia and the West operate in totally different environments. The West has an extensive credit bureau system where up-to-date, confidential information is reported to creditors via centralized databases. In Asia, these databases are either non-existent or else limited to small data-bases sharing old, negative data to a small circle of creditors within the same industry (like banks).

In Asia, it's common for collectors and collection agencies to make site visits at debtors' homes or workplaces. Calling or visiting after 8:00 pm, on public holidays and weekends is common. This is partially due to a lack of fixed phone lines and the horrendous Asian traffic jams. In developing Asian countries, many debtors don't have work phones, and rural debtors lack home phones.

Another reason why site visits are so important in Asia is due to a lack of an effective skip tracing system. Collectors visit debtors' previous addresses to gather information from the neighbors to determine where the debtor has skipped.

Asian collectors also face large numbers of third party payment excuses, " Don't call me for money, call (third party) who's suppose to pay." This is particularly troublesome on car loans.

The U.S., due to its extensive credit bureaus, has some of the lowest Days Sales Outstanding (DSO) and bad debt levels in the world. According to the U.S.'s Federal Deposit Insurance Corporation, the banking institutions it monitors have a total non-performing loan rate of less than 1%[6]. Ciaran Walsh in his book, Key Management Ratios, writes that the

---

6    "Stats At A Glance", 31 March 2003, <http://www.fdic.gov> (5 April 2004), FDIC QBP.

U.S. DSO level is under 40 days, while in the European Union it's over 80 and in Japan nearly 60.[7]

Non-performing loan (NPL) rates in Asia are higher than in the West. According to the *Taipei Times*,[8] the NPL rates for the following Asian countries are:

| | | |
|---|---|---|
| Philippines | : | 16 – 26% |
| Japan | : | 40% |
| China | : | 44 – 55% of GDP |
| Taiwan | : | 20 – 27% |
| South Korea | : | 7 – 14% |

In Malaysia, the NPL rate ranges from 6-7%.[9] The Central Bank of Indonesia reports Indonesian NPLs at 8%.[10]

America's bad debt losses and DSO levels are lower not because American debtors are saints, but because they're watched more. The credit "lights" are on longer and brighter. If an American pays slow or defaults on a bill, it becomes a negative mark on his / her credit record for up to seven years. In addition, good payment records are also captured.

If you visit Singapore, you will see one of the most orderly societies on the planet. There's no jay-walking, running traffic lights, toilets not flushed, spitting, and gum chewing. Singaporeans say, "Singapore is a 'fine' place." This is because the plain-clothes authorities pass out fines for these different transgressions. But observe Singaporeans once they cross the causeway into Malaysia and you will see a Dr. Jekyll- Mr. Hyde behavior change.

Ensuring the credit "lights" are on reduces overall delinquency rates and bad debt losses in any country.

Now, I would like to share brief views of the collections work environment in several selected Asian countries.

## Collections Environment in Japan

Steven Gan is an American who ran a collection agency in Japan called Advance & Associates. He has lived and collected in Japan for over ten years. He finds that Japan has a similar collections environment to SE Asia. He shares these glimpses on collecting in Japan:

1. *"For some prompt paying debtors, we send birthday cards as a token of our appreciation.*

---

7    Ciaran Walsh, *Key Management Ratios*, (Prentice Hall Financial Times, 2003), 93.

8    Christopher Lingle, *"Balancing risks and returns in Asia"*, 1 June 2003, <http://www.taipeitimes.com/News/edit/archives/2003/06/01/2003053537> (8 August 2003), Taipei Times.

9    *"Banking system remains healthy- Economic Report 2004/2005"*, 11 September 2004, New Strait Times, referencing data from Bank Negara Malaysia.

10   Central Bank of Indonesia's website at http://www.bi.go.id/bank_indonesia_english/monetary/banking_indicator/, (11 November 2004).

2. *Our collection manner is very polite (probably too polite). Sometimes I see the staff bowing to the debtors through the phone.*

3. *In Japan, we use a wide variety of collection letters and as much as possible try to customize the letter activity.*

4. *Legal action is almost never used as it protects mostly debtor rights.*

5. *There are approximately three credit reporting companies in Japan, but the data they supply is limited as not all companies contribute to it."*

## Collections Environment in Singapore

Dominic Lee is a Singaporean and managing director of Credit Management Consultancy (Asia) Pte Ltd. – a full service credit company and collection agency (see http://www.cmc.com.sg). Prior to running his own company, he worked at Citibank for many years. He shares the following challenges collection agencies face in Singapore:

1. *"Singaporean creditors mostly outsource 180+ day accounts only. For the most part, creditors don't treat their agencies as strategic partners.*

2. *Singaporean debtors are 'face conscious'. Collectors must be very sensitive to this fact when making collections calls. However, for the extreme hardcore case, this rule is ignored.*

3. *Most collection agencies aren't technology driven. Our agency has the only predictive dialer in Singapore."*

## Collections Environment in Taiwan

Jim Brown is an American running United Credit Services (see http://www.ucredit.com.tw). He is chairman of the Taiwan Financial Receivables Management Association – an association of credit agencies. He has this to say about the collections environment in Taiwan:

1. *"Consumer debt collection agencies in Taiwan tend to be large with eight or nine agencies employing between 150 and 400 collectors. There are over 40 registered companies providing full time debt recovery services—including field visits and legal support.*

2. *A major challenge we face here is strict data protection laws which prevent skip tracing or credit bureau support. In 2003, the Taiwan Financial Receivables Management Association (TFRMA) was established to promote a healthy collections environment, reduce complaints, and higher work standards among the agencies. The TFRMA members are to be ISO certified.*

3. *Commercial collections are generally handled by law firms, but there are no restrictions on the type of collections you do as long as your business is properly registered.*

4. *Debt portfolio sales have picked up recently with many banks selling off their NPLs (non-performing loans) to Asset Management Companies."*

## Collections Environment in Australia and New Zealand

These two beautiful countries have their own unique collections environment. Neil Wood is a collections expert "Down Under". He also regularly travels around the Asia-Pacific region on business. He runs Global Credit Solutions Ltd. based in Australia (http://gcs-group.com/). He has this to say about the collections environment in his area:

1. *"The biggest changes I have seen in the past twenty years across Asia Pacific are the legislation under which collectors work. Privacy legislation and data protection legislation enforced in the West have spread globally and impacted Australia and New Zealand on the collectors' ability to locate debtors who do not want to be located.*

2. *What were previously considered sources of public records such as electoral rolls, credit databases, reverse telephone search engines, court records, drivers license and motor vehicle registration have been closed to collectors."*

## Hey Asia, Want to Save a Ton of Money?

Asia could reduce its bad debt levels and make it easier to grant credit by implementing these next two recommendations:

### ❶ Creation of an extensive and accurate credit bureau system.

Western style credit bureaus that report both positive and negative payment behavior are less developed in Asia. Some countries have simple negative data-bases that report legal actions posted in newspapers, but many of the credit reporting agencies will expunge the record if the debtor satisfies the claim.

Some industries like phone companies and banks, share lists of charged-off debtors amongst others in the same industry, but not among outsiders.

One reason for Asia's lack of effective credit bureaus has to do with consumer privacy rights. Privacy rights, and especially the concept of maintaining "face", are strong.

The drawback in this thinking is that by protecting the poor paymasters from losing "face", the majority of prompt paying consumers suffer as they bear higher prices that vendors pass on due to higher than needed bad debt expenses. Good consumers also have difficulty getting credit as banks and other lending institutions are wary, thus loan sharks proliferate. Rarely will a month go by here in KL without a loan shark putting his business card in my mailbox, or car door handle, or under my wind-shield wiper. It's big business.

### ❷ Improve the efficiency of the legal system for creditors

In general, Asia's creditors need realistic protection. In the West, legal proceedings take a long time too, but in Asia it takes excessively long. As a result, many Asian creditors avoid the legal process, which the debtors take full advantage. Asian debtors, in general, are unafraid of legal action.

When I managed the collection department at a Malaysian company, my recovery rate on written-off accounts sent for legal action was 1%. The money recovered didn't cover the legal expenses. Still, it's important to send accounts for legal action as not sending them will send a more costly message to the market.

An exception to this legal inefficiency is Singapore. Singapore's legal system is automated and many of the forms can be downloaded and filed over the Internet.

## *Summary*

- The field of collections is a noble profession and a critical function of any organization.

- The primary role for a supervisor, manager or any employee for that matter is to ensure their organization's survival.

- The best fit for your collection department depends on the needs of your organization.

- Although the collections field is similar in both the West and Asia, you can't graft 100% of one onto the other.

- Two recommendations for Asia to save more money and extend more credit are:

  1. Creation of an efficient credit bureau reporting system

  2. Improve the efficiency of the legal system for creditors

# Part II:
# The Credit Field

# In the Beginning There was Credit

*Putting in Place Proper Credit Controls*

*Today there are three kinds of people: the have's, the have-not's, and the have-not-paid-for-what-they-have's.* – Earl Wilson

*If you don't have some bad loans, you aren't in business.* – Paul Volker

## After reading this chapter, you will be able to:

- Understand the importance of the Credit Department in an organization
- Write a credit policy
- Learn how to enhance your credit analysis skills
- Grasp the basics of credit and behavioral scoring
- Understand the importance of proper contracts
- Gain tips to ensure your Credit Department stays vigilant

## Introduction

Before discussing collections, it's best to first discuss the importance of the credit function in proactively filtering out high risk customers. A company's willingness to take on risk depends on the business goals set by its senior management. Once the risk level has been set and support given to the credit manager, steps can be taken by the manager to ensure the risk levels are achieved.

This chapter discusses how to maintain the necessary controls to achieve the risk levels set at your organization.

## Writing a Credit Policy

Policies, don't we just love them?

Whenever I hear the word "policy", I instinctively want to rebel. What is it about human nature that makes us dislike conforming to rules?

Yet, deep down, we understand that operating without a credit policy is dangerous. The few credit policy rebels I have seen didn't last long. Instead, many transferred to sales where some became great sales people.

If your credit department is operating without a credit policy, then you're operating on instinct. Which is a polite way of saying, you're gambling. And departments running on instinct are soon extinct.

Without a written credit policy, your applicants receive inconsistent treatment. One credit analyst "approves with conditions", while another analyst at a different branch "approves" the same applicant the next day. This leads to customer and staff complaints. The sales people start to act like defense attorneys who want their clients heard by the lenient judges.

A written credit policy, with agreement from sales and senior management, is a powerful tool for the credit manager. The policy supports the hard decisions you must make, especially those borderline credit decisions. The policy's requirements can be loose, tight or in between. It all depends on senior management's sales strategies and bad debt expectations. A new company wishing to capture market share will want a loose credit policy. An established company with high quality products and few competitors will want a stringent one. The policy will also be affected by external economic conditions. If the economy is good, the policy could be more relaxed. It's also affected by profit margins. If your margins are high, you will recoup bad debt losses faster, so the policy can be less stringent.

An overly tight credit policy is counter-productive as it limits sales and profits. You need to spend time analyzing, with other departments and senior management, the organization's ideal mix of sales, profits and bad debt levels.

The credit policy should make business sense. It should support maximum sales and profits within a logical risk level. The policy should inject into the organization a healthy dose of Vitamin C (credit). Companies with high Vitamin C take the time to evaluate credit risk as part of their decision-making process. This reduces the risk of launching programs that generate sales but without the required profit levels.

## Benefits of a Written and Agreed Credit Policy

1. Once the policy is approved by the head of sales, the sales department becomes your partner.

2. Credit applicants know where they stand. By standardizing credit requirements, there's less risk of customer complaints and supervisor calls. You present a united front to your customers.

3. The sales people and credit analysts know what's required to approve the deal. Correspondingly, there should be a reduction in the number of phone calls you now receive from sales

people asking basic questions. You can now simply refer them to the policy.

4. New hires have a shorter learning curve. Supervisors can make it mandatory for new hires to understand the policy. In addition, policies provide structure to new hires which reduces the chance of them picking up bad credit habits.

5. The policy increases your department's visibility. In organizational life, departments with low profile are soon outsourced. "Communicate or die." Once people know the importance of following the department's policies, the department's overall visibility increases as does your own.

6. Your internal auditors are happy. You're the guardian of the company's crown jewel, accounts receivable, by having a written and agreed credit policy in place, your auditors will feel more secure.

## Credit Policy's Contents

The length and detail of the policy depends on your senior management's strategy. However, try keeping the policies as brief and as easy to read as possible. Include examples in your policies to make the policy easy to apply.

Here are some suggestions to include in your credit policy:

### 1) Executive Summary

The policy starts with an overview that senior management reviews and agrees to without having to read all the contents.

### 2) Credit Department's Vision and Mission

Keep the vision short but inspirational. Link it to the company's vision. The mission is more detailed as it describes the steps taken to achieve the vision. Involve people in the creation of both the vision and the mission to increase "buy-in."

An example of a vision could be:

*To become a world-class credit control department*

Now your mission will state the steps the department will take to become "world-class."

### 3) Policy's Goals

Credit policies strive to maximize sales while minimizing bad debts and the cost of managing the accounts receivable. The value placed on each of these goals varies with each company. The goals should be detailed, ideally with targets, numbers and timelines.

## 4) Credit Requirements

This will be the main section of the report. It lists the required documents that credit applicants, customers and sales people must submit to the credit department. The policy will have different credit requirements for new applicants versus existing customers who are looking to increase their credit lines.

You could also include:

- Required documents from applicants such as a credit application, last two or three year's financial statements, bank references, bank statements, work references, trade references, copy of driver's license or passport, pay slip stubs, utilities bills. Again, credit requirements for new applicants are different from credit line increase requests from existing customers.

## 5) Credit Investigation Process

This explains what the credit analyst must do with the information submitted by credit applicants or sales people. The depth of the investigation depends on the amount of credit being requested, and whether the creditor is a secured creditor or a trade creditor that requires faster credit decisions.

For a business applicant, the following requirements could be investigated:

- Minimum number of years in business
- Average bank balances
- Previous financing experience
- Credit bureau report on the business and principals
- Credit score
- Trade and work references
- Minimum down payment and maximum term requirements based on equipment age, type and seller
- Minimum key financial ratio standards
- Minimum net worth
- Applicant's contact numbers and addresses

A consumer applicant's requirements are similar except also include:

- Minimum years at present address

- Minimum monthly salary
- Minimum number of years at current employer
- Certain demographic details

### 6) Levels of Authority (LOA's) for Credit Approvals

Up to what level can junior credit analysts approve deals? Senior analysts? Supervisors? Credit manager? Senior management? Set reasonable LOA's. If too low, bottlenecks will develop which slow the approval process. If too high, serious mistakes will occur. Consider working with your finance or internal audit department in setting your LOA's.

### 7) Exception Handling Process

How will you handle those credit requests that fall outside your policy? Perhaps the applicant fails your credit analysis, but the applicant is a V.I.P? This is especially important in Asia. Or, what happens if the customer won't submit all the credit documents requirements because s/he is a government minister? What happens if the CEO advises you to approve unconditionally an applicant who was already "approved with conditions"?

**Tip:**

Any exception handling should be in writing. This protects you if the exception becomes a written-off account. You will have an answer when the auditors question you on how such a customer could ever get credit in the first place. At the same time, avoid looking like you don't trust senior management, instead send them a brief note explaining you will do as instructed AND you will keep the person posted if the account becomes a problem. Keep a copy of that note in the file.

### 8) Dispute Resolution Process

How will the company handle credit decisions that are disputed by the sales department? Will the final arbitrator be the CEO? Managing Director? Credit Manager?

### 9) Criteria to Evaluate New and Existing Customers' Credit Line Requests

Setting credit lines isn't 100% science; there's also a lot of "art" involved as we're trying to predict future payment behavior.

You should be able to answer these questions before setting credit lines:

- What information will be required from existing customers?

- How deep will the credit analysis be?

- Will the staffs' LOA's apply both to new and existing customers? Or, will they have higher LOA's for existing customer accounts with payment history greater than six months?

## 10) Payment Terms and Fees.

What are your payment terms? 30 days? 14 days? What happens if corporate customers request longer terms? Do you give early payment discounts or rebates? In Asia, giving consumers a rebate for paying within 14 days or for signing up for automatic debit is common. Are there late charges or collection charges?

From personal experience in Asia, offering discounts and rebates works. My former employer got 25% of its customer base to take advantage of these incentives. As the collection manager, I didn't have to devote limited resources to a large chunk of the customer base.

In collections, too often we use disincentives in our field. Why not use more incentives?

## 11) Deductions

When can employees give customers deductions? When can customers take deductions? What are the limits? Is there a report tracking who issues the deductions, the value, and their type so that your organization knows where its short-comings lie?

## 12) Departmental Operations

This section gives an overview of the department's functions and Key Performance Indicators (KPI's) such as:

- The length of time it takes to receive a credit decision after the required documents have been submitted

- Departmental organization chart and job descriptions

- Key departmental work values like confidentiality and integrity

## 13) Credit Holds

When will credit holds take place? What is the notification process to the affected customer and salesperson? For multiple account holders, do credit holds take place on all accounts or only the ones in default? What are the requirements to lift a credit hold? Who lifts a credit hold?

### 14) Annual Credit Review Process

This ensures you actively manage your A/R portfolio. Each year, the credit department must actively review its largest creditors. This exercise leads to uncovering potential bad debt problems and avoiding future surprises. It also leads to proactively increasing a firm's credit line without being asked (ideally this should be automated). The annual review is conducted like a normal credit investigation for a new client. The review's results should be shared with the salesperson and senior management.

### 15) Examples

This section brings your policy to life. It provides credit scenarios so that the reader can better understand your policy. It gives the reader an idea of the whole process.

### 16) Common Questions & Answers

A Q&A section helps reduce the number of calls you get from sales people.

## Policy's Writing Style

Few of us enjoy reading policies, so the level of detail must be decided with the reader in mind. Too much detail and credit analysts start thinking like robots and hide behind the policy. Too little and the policy doesn't have clarity. Mention to the reader that the policies are merely guidelines. The reader should exercise judgment when analyzing deals.

Some suggestions when writing your policy:

- Keep it as short and pain-free as possible.

- Use bullet-points.

- Use diagrams and flowcharts.

- Use simple language. Credit lingo like DSO (Days Sales Outstanding) must be explained as many of your policy readers are sales people.

- Write it in a "Let's Make the Deal Happen" theme. This shows the sales people that you don't work in the "Reject Department."

- Review your policy. It's a living document and must be continually updated.

Will a credit policy solve all your bad debt problems? Will it make the credit and sales departments hand-holding best friends? No way! Still, it will save you from many problems.

## *Creating a Useful Credit Application or Registration Form*

Creating a useful credit application or registration form is tough, especially in mass market industries such as telcos, credit cards, and cable TV companies. Credit people want the application form to be as detailed as possible to help in the evaluation process. The collections department wants a lot of contact details in case the debtor becomes overdue. On the other hand, the sales and marketing people want the form to be as brief as possible – usually one page – to make it easy for the applicants to complete.

Think twice about accepting applicants who only have P.O. Boxes as addresses or who lack a contact number. I usually require them to give a physical address or a message contact number, I have had some applicants play dumb about giving this information. Again, think twice if you want these type of future customers. If it's tough to get information out of them now, just wait when they become overdue.

Get as much information as you can from your applicants. Rarely will they be as forthcoming with new information after you approve their credit request. Some credit folks believe the form should be called a "Sales Application Form". This way the credit reviewer's mindset is geared to approving the deal versus rejecting it.

Whatever you decide to call it, here are some details you may want to include:

- Name

- Social security number (U.S.) or Identification number (Asia)

- Business identification number (for business applicants)

- Ownership status (for business: sole proprietorship, partnership, corporation)

- Age (plus other pertinent consumer demographic information)

- Length in business

- Accounts payable name, direct contact number, and email address

- Billing address

- Ship to address

- Corporate address

- Physical address (if P.O. Box is used)

- Length at home address

- E-mail address

- Telephone contact 1
- Telephone contact 2 (cell phone or message number)
- Fax number
- Employer's name, address, contact number
- Salary
- Employment start date
- Credit card types and account numbers
- Credit references and contact numbers (business applicants)
- Desired credit limit
- Bank references
- Work references (business applicants)
- Personal references
- Financial statement information
- Contact of nearest relative or friend
- Applicant's signature and date (stating what was provided is "true and correct")
- Sales person or dealer / agent who made the sale
- Signature area giving permission to contact bank and trade creditors to release the applicant's balance and payment records

It's best to check with your legal team on what information you can legally require from your credit applicants.

## Contracts

Contracts are usually drawn up after the credit analysis has been performed and the deal is approved. It's important to understand a bit of the Terms and Conditions (T's & C's) within your organization's contracts- even if it's boring. Ask yourself, do the T's & C's support the collection process when you pursue legal action? Of course, the best people to pose your questions and recommendations are the lawyers who created your firm's T's & C's.

Ask yourself whether your organization's T's & C's allow it to :

- Charge late fees?
- Charge other types of fees: bounced cheque, suspension, legal?

- Add a "cross-default" clause to cross-tie multiple accounts that have the same debtor name?

- Clearly define the payment terms and credit period?

- Define the dispute / credit waiver process?

- Call the contract in default immediately ("acceleration clause") once it goes overdue or for other serious breaches such as lack of insurance on financed equipment, or bounced cheques?

- Temporary suspend the account? Some contracts only allow for permanent disconnection or termination.

- Hold the signatory personally liable if s/he was unauthorized to sign for the company?

- Share the customer's account details and payment record with other creditors?

## *Approving and "Rejecting" Credit Submissions*

Avoid using the "reject" option when analyzing credit submissions. If you reject too frequently, the sales people will view you more like the company's "chief deal executioner" rather than as a credit professional. Instead, use two positive credit decision choices:

a. Approve

b. Approve with conditions

By giving people positive choices ("approve" and "approve with conditions"), you allow **them** to reject **you**. I'm suggesting this for practical reasons.

1. You will get less "bad mouth" from customers.

2. If you reject too often, the sales people will find ways to go around you

Nobody likes being rejected; whether it happens on romantic dates or for credit applications. I distinctly remember the time I was rejected by a credit card company because I was a foreigner. It still bugs me. For some reason I can't remember when I was approved for credit, though. People have egos. We all think we're great. Who's the first person you look for when you look at a group photo? We take rejection personally, especially sales people, so avoid doing it.

"Approve with conditions" achieves your goals of reducing risk levels. An "approve with conditions" could ask for:

- Larger down payment
- Shorter credit term
- Higher interest rate
- Lower credit limit
- Additional guarantors or collateral
- Cross-tying of related accounts
- "All inclusive" receivable or equipment liens

## Credit and Behavioral Scoring

Once your policy is in place, you're ready to begin extending credit, but extending credit is both an art and science. Are we ever 100% sure our customers will pay us back? Credit and behavioral scorecards are tools that bring more science into the credit granting process.

Scorecards assist in issuing faster credit decisions and conducting more targeted collection actions on those accounts identified as "high risk." Credit and behavioral scoring is especially needed in Asia where well-developed credit bureaus are non-existent.

The scorecards can be changed to reflect current economic conditions or new senior management strategies. For example, the approval scores could be lowered to allow for more risk if the economy is improving or if the competition is capturing market share.

## Credit Scoring

Credit scoring takes place at the point of entry. The scoring model requires a certain benchmark to be achieved before the deal is approved. If the score is too low, then "approve with conditions." Credit scoring calculates the odds of repayment. Here are some hypothetical scores:

| Point Score | What it signifies | Credit Decision |
|---|---|---|
| 401-500 | = 1 out of 200 customers won't pay | Automatic approval |
| 301-400 | = 1 out of 100 won't pay | Assistant Manager's approval needed |
| 201-300 | = 1 out of 50 won't pay | Credit Manager's approval needed |
| 101-200 | = 1 out of 25 won't pay | Credit G.M.'s approval needed |
| < 100 | = 1 out of 10 won't pay | CFO's approval needed |

The scorecards are created by analyzing a sample of accounts that includes good paymasters, poor paymasters and written off accounts to determine the key factors for paying or not paying. The factors could include:

- Demographics (e.g. marital status, rent vs own)
- Length of time as a customer
- Length of time at employer or in business
- Salary
- Financial ratios
- Type of goods or service bought
- Level of deposit

As an illustration, "marital status" is an important factor for the furniture business as they find married people have a higher probability of payback versus single people.

After evaluating the factors that best predict payment behavior, points (weight-age) are assigned to each factor to create the scorecard. The scorecards can be created and scored manually or automatically. It's a good idea before rolling out a credit scoring system to first run a large sample of your good paymasters, poor paymasters, fully paid off accounts and written off accounts through it to check its accuracy. Try a sample size in the hundreds (ideally a few thousand).

Although credit scoring brings more science into your credit decision process, the creation of the scorecards is an art. The scorecards (and scores) need constant tweaking to ensure their validity. Seek legal advice to ensure your scorecard complies with local laws.

Having a valid credit scoring model saves a credit department time in doing in-depth credit reviews on new applicants. It also allows the collections department to focus on candidates that have medium to high probability for delinquency or default. The collection department will set a more aggressive collection treatment for accounts with low scores during their first six months as a new customer. After six months, decide if the accounts will be re-scored since the initial credit scores lose their value over time.

## Behavioral Scoring

Behavioral scoring takes place once the applicant becomes a customer. It assigns scores based on the customer's payment behavior. Behavioral scoring is more complicated than credit scoring. It should be performed automatically via a behavioral scoring system.

Behavioral scoring calculates the probability of receiving a payment. This score is updated daily or at each customer's bill cycle or installment due date. The system calculates points based on the timeliness of payments. The score also considers negative factors like bounced cheques and credit card chargebacks.

For example, if a long-time customer is overdue at day 50, but habitually pays at day 70, he may still have a good behavioral score. Whereas another long-time customer who's overdue at day 40, but who habitually pays at day 35, may receive a worse score and be considered "high" risk.

This type of scoring looks at a client's monthly spending habits. If a customer habitually spends $400 each month on his credit card statement over several years, then suddenly hits $3,000, it triggers an alarm to focus on that account.

While credit scoring allows you to focus on potential defaulters at the point of entry, behavioral scoring allows you to focus on actual slow paymasters who need prodding to collect payment. You can create different collection treatments and call campaigns based on customers' behavioral scores.

Behavioral scoring is used to monitor current spending and to evaluate customers' requests for credit line increases. It's a powerful tool, especially for credit cards companies and telcos that see customers' monthly usage go drastically up or down. With the greater acceptance of behavioral scoring, collection departments are shifting their strategic focus from aging-based receivable management to score-based ones.

For modern organizations, behavioral scoring can be used as a way to increase customer satisfaction. Usually collection departments punish customers for slow payment, but with a behavioral scoring system we could actually reward those customers with good payment history. Why not send those customers with good behavioral scores a "thank you" card or small token? How often is the collections department looked upon as an integral part of the total sales process? We can now actively court our good paymasters to encourage them to buy more. In turn, are good customers will feel valued which can lead to higher satisfaction and retention levels.

**Tip:**

Credit and behavioral scoring systems are expensive. One way to convince senior management of their value is to highlight how the systems can be expanded to customer service, sales and the marketing departments. The customer service department can use scoring to predict which customers' are at the highest risk of leaving; while the sales and marketing departments can target which type of customers have the highest probability of buying a new product the company is offering.

## Tip:

If there is no way your organization would pay for a scoring system, then create a basic one yourself. Classify your customers into two categories: Good and Bad Paymasters. Then classify "bad" paymasters as any account with any of the following characteristics: Bounced cheque within the last six months, credit hold within last six months, new account (less than six months old), and any other criteria you believe is relevant. For these types of accounts use a more aggressive collection treatment.

## *How to Improve Your Credit Analysis Skills?*

When I want to learn about something say, Harley Davidson motorcycles, I immerse myself in the subject. I will visit dealerships, talk with Harley owners, attend conventions and if I'm brave enough- visit a biker bar.

If you want to improve your credit analysis skills, spend time analyzing your past credit decisions. Are they still good credit risks? Yes? No? Why? Would you make the same decision again?

Look for commonalities in your organization's written-off accounts. Was the initial credit decision based on sound judgment at that point in time?

Some commonalities to look for would be:

- How long was it from the time the written-off customers obtained credit did they stop paying?

- What was the size of their last three bills before defaulting?

- Do many of the accounts lack good addresses and contact numbers?

- Are there more write-offs from a particular sales promotion, rate plan or customer group?

- Do more write-offs come from a particular dealer, region, salesperson or credit analyst?

- Was an extensive credit investigation done on the accounts?

- Were the accounts actively contacted by the collections department?

This information helps improve your credit application forms and requirements. By regularly analyzing written-off accounts, you will be able to give factual data to senior management on changes you desire in your organization's credit granting process.

For example, perhaps the "No Down Payment" promotion increases write-offs more than it increases profits. By analyzing the cost and benefits of the promotion, you will be able to show senior management that you're proactively managing the company's receivables. It also re-sets the company on a course for more profits.

Ideally, this write-off analysis should be automated. Some collection systems allow for "Champion Challenges." A Champion Challenge allows you to set aside a sample group of accounts to test a new credit or collection treatment (the challenger). The system runs aging reports on the overall customer base and the sample group. After 60-90 days, compare the two groups' aging. If the sample group's aging and bad debt levels improve, then consider using that treatment for the larger customer base.

## Signs of a Strong Credit Department

Once your credit policy has been written and approved, credit housekeeping becomes easier. Still, you need to work with your department to stay ever vigilant on accepting a proper level of risk.

Here are some tips to ensure your department doesn't get surprised too often by poor credit risks:

- **Welcome calls for new customers**
  These calls increase customer satisfaction, reduce fraud while ensuring customers receive their first bill. Welcome calling is used by mass market creditors who go through a limited credit filtering process. Welcome calling helps determine if the customer actually exists. If you lack manpower to make the calls, consider calling the high risk accounts first. Another idea is to outsource this function as the calls are simple to make.

- **Welcome cards for new customers**
  Send all new customers a quick card or kit. If it comes "returned to sender" there may be a problem. Make sure your department's address is listed as the sender.

- **Annual credit reviews on your largest creditors**
  By taking the time to do annual reviews, the credit department avoids being surprised when firms stop paying due to cash flow issues, bankruptcy, or other problems. You will avoid being the last creditor to know.

- **Perform regular commodity checks**
  You will ensure that the equipment still exists, is in good condition, is in the location where it's supposed to be, and hasn't been sold.

- **Visit new large business applicants (site visits)**
  This helps in many aspects, but most importantly, you discover if the company exists.

- **Chargebacks on future commissions for first payment defaults**
  If you rely on sales people or dealers, consider having a commission chargeback policy for new sales that never pay within the first 90 days of credit being extended. This improves the quality of their submissions to include multiple phone numbers and a physical address instead of a post office box.

  Better yet, tie commissions to the accounts' aging. For example, if the account pays net 30 days, the sales person receives 100% of his/her commission. If it pays 31-60 days, then 98%, and so on. You need to set the percentages based on your work environment.

- **Perform annual total A/R risk reviews**
  Evaluate if your firm is too heavily involved in one sector or in just a few customers. What would happen if that sector crashed? Remember the oil sector in the 80's, or the Japanese property sector in the 90's? What would happen if a couple of your largest customers went bankrupt? What would happen if your largest customer(s) withheld a payment due to a major dispute?

## *Summary*

- Before extending credit to future customers, companies need to create a written and agreed credit policy.

- The terms and conditions of a contract should support the collection process.

- Credit and behavioral scoring are powerful tools available to credit managers that help you make faster and more accurate credit decisions.

- Improve your credit analysis skills by using hindsight on your previous credit decisions. Study written-off accounts for commonalities that will help you foresee a future bad debt.

- An active credit department proactively manages a firm's accounts receivable portfolio, especially on large accounts. Key activities it should consider doing:

  ☑ Welcome calling

  ☑ Welcome letters

  ☑ Annual credit reviews on at least the largest customers

  ☑ Commodity checks

  ☑ Site visits

  ☑ Commission chargebacks

  ☑ Annual credit risk review on the company's
     A/R portfolio

Part III:
# The Collections Field

# How Do We Do It and When?

**3**

*Putting in Place Effective Collection Strategies*

*We fail more often by timidity than by over-daring.* – David Grayson

## After reading this chapter, you will be able to:

- Understand the importance of Days Sales Outstanding (DSO)

- Calculate DSO

- Focus your limited resources on the right accounts

- Develop collection strategies based on the aging of the accounts

- Write a collection policy

- Identify warning signs when a collection department is not "vigilant"

## Introduction

Establishing the right collection treatment for the right customer group plays a big part in your overall bad debt and Days Sales Outstanding (DSO) levels. The treatments should reflect senior management's desires for the company's operating results.

The collection treatment is determined by:

- How aggressive is senior management for sales?

- How aggressive are they in preventing bad debts?

- How aggressive are they in maintaining high customer service ratings?

- Are the customers based in Asia or the West?

A company wanting to increase its market share by 20%, while drastically improving its customer satisfaction level, will find it difficult to also achieve an aggressive low bad debt target.

How do you set collection treatments? When do you decide to do certain collection activities? These are the topics in this chapter.

## Days Sales Outstanding (DSO) Comparison

One factor investors use to evaluate a company's success is to analyze how quickly the company converts its credit sales into cash. The faster the cash is received, the faster a company can use it in its operations. It also usually means the company is well-managed.

In Chapter 2, Days Sales Outstanding (DSO) was defined as the average number of days it takes to a firm to convert its accounts receivable into cash. There are many formulas used to calculate it, but the one used here is the simplest:

**DSO = Total Accounts Receivable / Credit Sales During Period X days in period**

For example, Malaysia's largest cellular service provider is Maxis Mobile. According to its 2005 annual report, total accounts receivable were RM595.7m and sales were RM6,370.8m[11]. Their yearly DSO was :

$$\frac{RM595.7}{RM6,370.8} \text{ x 365 days} = \textbf{34 days.}$$

Right or wrong, DSO is one of the main determinants used in evaluating a collection department's performance. The ability to reduce DSO even a few days has a positive impact on a company's cash flow.

For example, Durians Unlimited Bhd. is a fictitious Malaysian canned durian exporter. It tried exporting its product to traditional western supermarkets, but it flopped as the consumers found the fruit's flesh and odor disgusting. However, sales and A/R are booming in Asian supermarkets.

The results show that DSO this year increased three days from last year. What is the effect of these three days?

**Table 1:**   Durians Unlimited Bhd. Year End financial Results (in thousands)

|  | This year | Last year |
|---|---|---|
| Credit Sales (thousands RM) | 5,000 | 4,280 |
| Total A/R (thousands RM) | 521 | 410 |
| Days in year | 365 | 365 |
| DSO (days) | 38 | 35 |

11   Note: Maxis doesn't break out credit sales. As a result, we'll use the total sales figure.

What would be the value of this year's accounts receivable if the company had maintained last year's DSO level of 35 days?

If annual sales are RM5,000,000, then daily sales are 5,000,000/365 = RM13,700. So the effect of the three day delay is **RM41,100** (RM13,700 x 3 days).

Those extra three days delayed Durians Unlimited Bhd. from collecting RM41,100 sooner. The effects of delays in collecting accounts receivable include:

- **Higher collection costs.** You may need more resources to handle the larger number of overdue accounts.

- **Higher interest charges.** You may need to borrow due to a short-term liquidity problem.

- **Higher bad debt expenses.** The longer an account ages, the less chance you will have of ever collecting the debt.

- **Poorer credit rating.** You may need to delay payment to others.

- **Lost interest income.** The organization's money could be generating interest in a bank.

- **Lower sales.** Overdue customers buy less than current customers.

- **Lower share price.** DSO is a "managerial efficiency ratio." If outside investors see a firm's DSO level increasing, the firm's share price could be affected.

"Time is money." The longer your receivables remain uncollected, the higher the price you pay. Good collection managers, with proper A/R management processes and systems in place, make significant impacts to a business' financial health. Bad collection managers also make an impact.

There's no "silver bullet" to reduce your firm's DSO level. Proper receivable management requires a strategy of combining multiple, small actions and constantly tweaking them over time to reduce bad debts. Bad debt is reduced by drops, not buckets. It's a drop here, a drop there but over time the savings are significant. Receivable management involves many small actions that lead to great results. It's like the saying:

> Question : How do you eat an elephant?
> Answer  : One bite at a time.

## Collection Strategies

Collection strategies shouldn't commence once the account goes overdue, nor when the first call is made. It starts right at the credit application process.

The four stages of a collection strategy are:

1. Pre-emptive stage

2. Early stage

3. Mid stage

4. Late stage

## Collection Strategies: Pre-emptive Stage

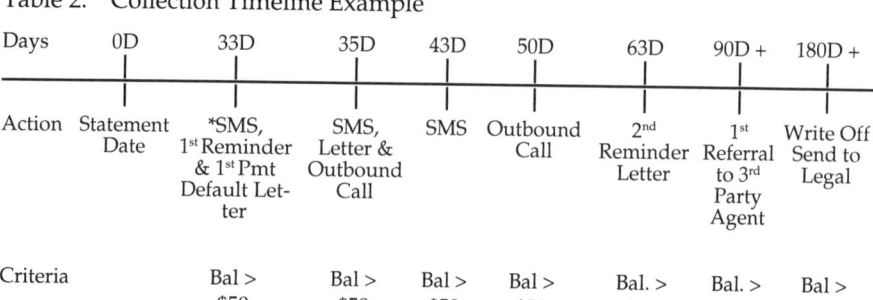

> *Victorious warriors win first and then go to war, while defeated warriors go to war first and then seek to win.-- -*
>
> Sun Tzu, *The Art of War*

Similar to the importance of having a credit policy, a collection policy is also needed prior to starting collection activities. This policy details an orderly sequence of actions at specific times to prompt customers for payment. Usually these actions start off mild and then escalate. However, for new customers who become overdue, sometimes called "first Payment Defaults" or "Non-starters", the first collection actions are usually firm.

The collection policy is easier to write than the credit policy as it consists mostly of timelines for the various customer groups and the actions that take place during that timeline. The timeline starts at day 0 and ends at the write-off / legal stage, usually at 180-210 days. If your firm sells its write-offs to debt purchasers, then your treatment will end later.

Table 2: Collection Timeline Example

| Days | 0D | 33D | 35D | 43D | 50D | 63D | 90D + | 180D + |
|---|---|---|---|---|---|---|---|---|
| Action | Statement Date | *SMS, 1st Reminder & 1st Pmt Default Letter | SMS, Letter & Outbound Call | SMS | Outbound Call | 2nd Reminder Letter | 1st Referral to 3rd Party Agent | Write Off Send to Legal |
| Criteria | | Bal > $50 | Bal > $50 | Bal > $50 | Bal > $50 | Bal. > $50 | Bal. > $200 | Bal > $500 |

*SMS: Short Message Service (text message received via customer's cellular phone)

Similar to the credit granting process, the collection treatment needs to be more lenient for certain groups like corporate and VIP accounts.

Corporations' accounts payable departments often have payment terms which are much longer than your organization's credit terms.

Besides corporate accounts, there are usually different collection treatments for VIP accounts, royalty, and politicians. Credit card companies have different treatments based on customers' average monthly spend, payment behavior and length of service. It is critical to sort your accounts by different customer types and each customer type will have a different collection treatment. Some collection treatments will be more aggressive than others.

Some ways to sort your customer types will be by:

- ☑ Industry
- ☑ Product
- ☑ Length as a customer
- ☑ Dealer / Salesperson
- ☑ Behavioral score
- ☑ Location
- ☑ Balance
- ☑ Consumer
- ☑ VIP
- ☑ SME
- ☑ Corporate
- ☑ Government
- ☑ Secured
- ☑ Unsecured

No matter how many different treatments you devise, consider treating all new customers the same until the first payment is made. This means creating a "First Payment Default" treatment that activates quickly if the customer goes past due. Once a payment is made, the customer then joins the normal collection treatment based on the customer type. Or, better still, create another treatment for customers with less than six months of service. Upon reaching the seventh month with timely payments, the customer joins the normal customer group.

By watching first payment defaults and new accounts closely, you set a serious tone with your new customers. You want them to understand that you take payment seriously. You want them to know that you **fully expect full payment on time**.

Psychology plays a big part in the field of collections. We want to reward our customers who pay on time and extinguish negative behavior that leads to slow payment. It's easier extinguishing negative behavior early than later. Anyone with children will agree. Changing a toddler's behavior is easier than changing a teenager's.

Humans are creatures of habit. As debt collectors, we need to ensure our collection treatment reinforces positive payment habits. In Asia, where it's more difficult to locate skipped debtors, your collection treatments need to be even tighter. You need to maintain steady contact with your debtors if you want to get paid.

**Tip:**

Avoid sharing the collection policy's specifics with other departments. Otherwise, you will feel as if you're quarterbacking a football team when the opposing side knows every play you're going to call.

Sales people will ask you about the specifics of the company's strategies so that they can inform their customers. Think twice before releasing this information. These prying questions come in the following guises:

- "How long can a customer go before collections does anything?"
- "How long do you wait before repossessing a customer's equipment?"
- "When do you refer accounts to external collection agencies?"
- "What overdue amounts do you refer for legal action?"
- "What percent of the balance will you accept for a settlement?"

## Importance of a Collection Policy

Some companies have a separate policy for credit and another for collections, others combine them. Since the policy will be given to a handful of people outside your department, it's usually shorter and targeted to those people.

It includes:

1) Executive Summary

2) Collection Department's Vision or Mission

3) Policy's Goal and Objectives

4) **Main Content**
This section contains the various collection treatments by customer group, rate plan, promotion or however you segregate your customer types. It will also include a write-off policy and when to turn accounts over to external agents and legal firms.

5) **Exception Handling Process**
The policy should discuss when there are exceptions to the treatment, and who is authorized to withhold the collection action. You will also need to decide if accounts in good standing will be negatively affected if they have a related account in overdue status.

6) **Departmental Operations**
Show the departmental organizational chart and the function of each collection team. Include job descriptions.

7) **Common Questions & Answers Regarding the Policy**

## Collection Strategies – Early Stage

According to ACA International, an association of credit and collection professionals based in the U.S., receivables sent to external collection agencies at 60 days achieved an average recovery rate of 26%, while accounts sent at 180 days had an average recovery rate of 16.5%.[12]

In my Asian work experience, 60% is considered an excellent recovery rate for 90 day accounts, 20% at 120 days and low single digit rates thereafter. Time is the enemy of collection managers. Start your strategies on your receivables early. The longer you wait to start, the less chance you have of collecting.

Psychologists use the term "recency." The longer you wait after a payment to collect the next payment, the "recency" of the payment event diminishes, and so will your chances of getting the debtor to repeat the positive payment behavior.

Early stage accounts are defined here as 1-60 days delinquent. Here are some tips to focus on these account types.

## Use Your Resources (especially time) Correctly

Successful A/R management has a lot to do with successful time management. When an account goes overdue, there's a limited amount of time where there's a high probability of payment. If we don't act before the "window" closes, we will have squandered our chances of collecting the full balance.

---

12 ACA International, "Declining Recovery Rate by Age at Time of Placement- 2003 Top Collection Market Survey", 36.

Follow the 80/20 Rule. Normally, 20% of your customer base contribute 80% of your delinquency problems. So, as collection professionals, avoid spending excessive amounts of time on the 80%. These accounts could include current accounts, fraudulent accounts, refuse to pays, and accounts greater than 120 days overdue. Instead, give the current accounts to customer service, the fraudulent ones to the fraud department, and the refuse to pays and greater than 120 day accounts to collection agencies and legal firms.

Focus most of your resources on the overdue customers with the highest possibility of paying after a collection contact. Sort the accounts by rate plan, location, balance, length of service, intention to pay (behavioral scoring), and any other factors important for you.

## Make It Easy for Debtors to Pay

Whenever I call a sales hotline the number is almost always a 1-800 number. The phone rings once or twice and a sales person picks up. I order the product and pay with my credit card. It's simple.

But, I'm amazed how difficult some collection departments make it for their customers to pay their bills. They don't have 1-800 numbers. They don't accept payments over the phone. They don't even have a voicemail system if the collector is away from his/her phone. Customers call and get busy signals or no answers. Why is this so?

Besides offering customers congestion-free 1-800 numbers and the ability to pay with a credit card, organizations need to offer other convenient payment options like:

- Post offices
- Third party dealers or sales agents
- Banks, ATMs
- Supermarkets and gas stations
- Cheque over the phone
- Internet
- Western Union
- Automatic credit card debiting

By providing multiple payment channels, you help reduce the customer traffic into your organization's sales and customer service centers. This helps their frontliners to focus on selling.

## Utilize Your Collectors Well

Do you want your best collectors collecting early stage accounts, or do you want your new and average performers collecting those accounts? Perhaps you want your best collectors collecting high balance and VIP accounts?

You need to strategize your collection teams. Ensure the front-end collection team, the team that handles the early stage delinquent accounts, is the largest team. You don't win basketball games by keeping your team down by your basket. You need a strong offense.

Ensure your teams are collecting during the peak calling times, usually in the morning until lunch hour. Fishing is best in the morning. Don't have collectors doing administration matters during peak calling times. In Asia, many collection departments peak calling times is after 8:00 p.m. on weekdays and all day Saturday and Sunday.

An especially good time to call overdue Chinese customers is a few weeks before Chinese New Year (January / February). Many Chinese believe that going into the New Year with last year's debts brings bad luck. Some debtors respond to collection calls at this time, especially if the call is coming from a Chinese collector. However, don't be surprised if many debtors will risk bad luck and use their money instead for their festive season preparations.

The same applies for many Muslim debtors who will want to pay their debts during Ramadan- the month-long period of fasting, prayers, alms-giving and atonement- in preparation for the holiest holiday in the Islamic year: Eid ul-fitr. Using Muslim collectors to call overdue Muslim debtors is particularly effective in Indonesia, Malaysia and Brunei where there are Muslim majorities.

In Asia, cash flow problems due to the multiple festive seasons are a frequent payment excuse used throughout the year.

## Supervise Your Teams Well

Collection supervisors are key players in the smooth running of any collection department.

Here are some questions to evaluate their effectiveness:

- Are your supervisors actively managing their teams?

- Are the supervisors spending too much time in meetings and away from their teams?

- Do the supervisors frequently communicate and coach their teams?

- Do the supervisors monitor when the collectors log-in and log-off during the work day? Do the supervisors view the collection system to measure their team's productivity during the day?

- Do the collectors receive daily stats on how much they have collected both individually and as a team?

- Are collectors able to view other individuals' and teams' statistics to see how they fare in comparison?

- Do you and your supervisors reward positive behavior?

- Do you address and extinguish negative behavior?

The complicated task of leading people is covered in more detail in Chapters 18.

## Use Grandma to Collect

Put in place "grandma" processes in your policies. These processes follow the same principle grandma used. Grandma's principle is: *"You can't have a cookie until you finish your vegetables."*

Don't allow customers to get future services until they first take care of any overdue amounts. At a minimum, you should require a Promise to Pay (PTP) from the customer before granting what they desire.

For example, if a customer wants a change of due date, they will receive it after paying off the open balance. In some billing systems you need to create a new account. Customers, over time, forget about paying the old account with the old due date. They will even dispute the amount by saying that the old balance was already taken care of when the new account was created. Memories are short in this age of information overload.

## Automatic Notification When Credit Line is Exceeded

Send a warning- ideally automatically – when customers reach 70-80% of their credit threshold. Upon hitting 100%, the system should auto-matically place a credit hold on the account. Industries where customers' monthly usage fluctuates, like power companies and telcos, need to track unbilled usage.

For large accounts, a warning should also be sent to the salesper-son. Depending on your senior management strategies, you may want to put in a buffer. For example, instead of the system placing a credit hold on an account at 100% of reaching the credit line; perhaps place the hold at 110%?

In organizations with credit limit alert systems, bad debt is significantly reduced. Many Asian telcos bar or suspend more lines due to exceeding credit limit than for overdue bills. Such proactiveness allows them to have low Days Sales Outstanding (DSO) and bad debt levels.

## Support Cross-tying of Accounts

This allows you to affect "good" accounts with negative collection actions if they're related to accounts in a default status. It avoids scenarios where new accounts are approved while your company is repossessing or suing customers on other accounts.

Centralize your IT system so that if a customer walks into any service outlet, s/he won't be extended more credit when there are balances owning at other stores.

## Leave Effective Messages

Leave effective LMTC's (left message to call). Normally, half a collector's calling time is spent leaving messages. A LMTC should generate one of two things:

1) Payment
          *or*
2) Call back

Unfortunately, ineffective collectors are sometimes afraid to ask third parties to take messages. Or, they pass control of the call by meekly asking, "Can you take a message for (customer's name)?"

Message-takers are notoriously lazy and respond with, "Just call back after lunch." The collector then calls back after lunch and the customer is now in a meeting.

Instead, the next time you call and someone informs you the customer is away, say:

*"Oh, then I'll just leave a message. Please have him/her call........."*

It works.

Some collectors work so fast that they leave vanilla-flavored messages on voicemail systems or answering machines. There's no life to them. They're easy to delete and forget. Instead, try leaving a slightly stronger, different message. You get customers calling to complain about your message, but I would much prefer an angry call from a seriously overdue, difficult-to-contact customer, than no call at all.

Here's an effective LMTC script for an answering machine or voicemail system. It also helps if you use a serious, confident tone when leaving this message:

*This is an urgent call for Mr. / Ms. Customer, please call (collector's name) with (your organization) before 4:59 pm today. My number is 1-800-XXXX. Again, my number is 1-800- XXXX. Thank you.*

You will find customers who have never returned your calls before, now calling you back immediately and saying things like, "What's this stupid 4:59 p.m. thing?" Or, "How dare you speak to me like that."

> **Tip:**
>
> In many parts of the world it's illegal to release information about an individual's account to third parties. However, in some instances you can release information to the spouse. It's best to check with an attorney in your location regarding what kind of information you can or can't reveal in a message.

## Collection Strategies – Mid Stage

The longer an account ages, the less strategies you have to address its non-payment. Mid-stage delinquent accounts are defined here as 60-120 days delinquent. Here are some mid-stage strategies to consider:

- Send stronger SMSs, collection letters and LMTCs.
- Alert sales to assist in the collection of the debt.
- Suspend services. Enact credit holds. Affect related accounts.
- Alert senior management for delinquent corporate accounts. They can assist in their collection.
- Make site visits asking for payment.
- Bill late fees.
- Accelerate sending certain files such as skips (untraceable debtors) or "refuse to pay" accounts to external collection agencies or law firms. Don't waste time on such accounts.

## Collection Strategies – Late stage

Late stage accounts are greater than 120 days delinquent and near write-off. Old debts are like cancer, you need to excise them from the body as quickly as possible. If you determine they're uncollectible, quickly turn them over to agents and legal firms. You're rated on how well you manage accounts receivable. Expending resources on late stage accounts takes precious resources away from early stage delinquent accounts that have a higher probability of payment.

Here are some late stage strategies to consider:

- Involve sales and senior management
- Refer accounts to agents and legal firms
- Disconnect services
- Repossess equipment
- Report to credit bureaus and negative databases, if not already done so
- Start legal action

## Signs of a Weak Collection Department

Similar to the credit department, the collection department must stay vigilant once its collection policy, treatments and strategies are in place. Here are some possible signs when a collection department becomes sleepy:

- **Weak collection treatments**

Customers receive collection letters and calls advising of tough, negative actions that never materialize. Whenever you launch a new treatment or tighten an existing one, customer complaints will increase. Debtors don't like the new change to their payment routine, however, if the treatment is fair, stay firm. After a couple of weeks the complaints usually reduce and after a month they nearly disappear.

> **Tip:**
>
> Alert your senior management before enacting any drastic change in your collection treatment.

- **Late collection treatment**

Many debtors pay not because it's the right thing to do, but because it's the least painful thing to do. If you don't start the "pain" until it's too late, then many debtors embolden themselves to default. They might have paid had you been more assertive earlier, but now that you have allowed them to go overdue for several months; they tend to think that you're not serious. To them, the debt is also higher and looks insurmountable.

Collections has the one-third rule:

☑ **One-third of our customers pay without being asked.**

☑ One-third pay if they know they're being watched (collection letters work).

☑ One-third won't pay unless you ask.

Look at your own aging and decide if it's true.

Many debtors need to know you're watching their account the day it goes overdue or exceeds its credit limit. They're surely watching you. If your collection treatment is slow, your A/R "jewel" will begin to resemble a chunk of coal.

- **Credit terms not enforced**

Sometimes the creditor doesn't hold the customer to the agreed credit terms. For example, late charges, suspension fees, blocked credit card fees, or other fees that were supposed to be charged weren't charged. Customers soon learn there are no teeth in your collection treatments. In fact, you're rewarding slow payment behavior.

- **Unrewarded prompt payment**

On the other hand, creditors who don't reward customers for early payment, direct debit, or 12 months of consecutive timely payments are taking customers' good payment history for granted. Rewards could be in the form of cash, discount vouchers for future sales items, or even a simple thank you card. The collections field needs to consider using more incentives in the collection process in this era of Customer Relationship Management.

- **Poor relations with external collection agencies and legal firms**

Some creditors treat their collection agents and law firms poorly, which is a mistake since these parties are our business partners. Creditors need to devote adequate resources to serve these business partners. By helping them, the quality of your company's receivable portfolio improves.

## *Importance of Reports*

Accurate reports are needed to set accurate strategies. I believe in the old saying: "Nothing gets done unless it's measured." A collection manager needs to have accurate reports showing correct aging status, bad debt levels and Days Sales Outstanding (DSO) levels. Only with correct reports are future strategies and collection treatments effectively planned.

Aging reports should show the company's overall receivables picture and the aging breakdowns by various customer groups such as:

- Sector

- Customer group

- Product

- Rate plan

- Promotion

- Behavioral score (will show if your scorecard is valid)

- Location

- Salesperson

- Third party agent or dealer

- And any other factor important to your company

Aging reports should be generated by the collection system after each bill cycle. They should show both aging and flow rates. In most organizations, the finance department provides monthly summary reports to show the company's overall aging, DSO and bad debt levels. Ask them to provide bad debt and DSO levels broken down by individual customer groups, rate plans, locations or however your organization breaks out its customers.

On a daily basis, you need reports showing how much money was collected yesterday and month to date. You need to know how much was collected by each collector, the number of people away from your department due to illness / vacation / other reasons. The number of calls made or received, number of Promises to Pay (PTP's), and number of PTPs kept (or that paid) as a percent of the total number of PTPs received.

The right reports save time and increase efficiency. The wrong reports do neither. Often we get wrong reports, and it's tempting to blame the I.T. or finance departments. But often the reports were wrong because the users (collections) didn't take the time to think through what information they wanted to receive.

Take the time to design useful reports. I know it's boring, but it will make your job easier knowing the "true" situation of the A/R portfolio. Accurate reports ensure that your organization's "crown jewel" stays shining.

## *Summary*

- Reducing a firm's DSO level will result in added savings.

- Receivables, like bananas, start off green and solid but over time turn brown, black, and soft. It's important to maximize your limited resources quickly before too many spots start appearing on your bananas.

- Before starting the collection process, it's a good idea to know what you're going to do at each stage of the delinquent account. This entails having a collection policy in place. Once the policy is in effect, concentrate your resources in the early stage accounts as your chances for payment are greater.

- Keep your collection treatments confidential. The treatments are the many techniques you use to collect payment. Avoid sharing them openly. Constantly tweaking your treatments to adjust to changes in the economy, senior management's strategy, or any serious deterioration in your aging portfolios.

- Ensure your collection department stays "vigilant" by:

  ☑ Having firm but fair collection treatments

  ☑ Having prompt collection treatments

  ☑ Enforcing credit terms

  ☑ Rewarding prompt payment

  ☑ Treating its external collection agencies and legal firms as business partners

  ☑ The best way to measure the success of your strategies, and your own effectiveness as a strategist, is to ensure you get accurate reports.

# Written Communication

**4**

### *Effective Letters, Emails and Short Messages*

*Easy reading is damn hard writing.*– Nathaniel Hawthorne

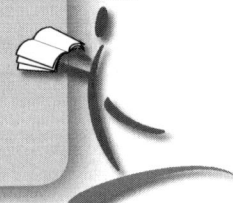

**After reading this chapter, you will be able to:**

- Learn some tips on writing effective collection letters, emails, and SMSs

- Study some examples of collection letters, emails and SMSs

## *Collection Letters*

Collection letters are likely the most sensitive correspondence your organization sends its customers. Their style is completely unlike sales, marketing or customer service's nice correspondence. One unprofessional collection letter ruins years of carefully built up goodwill.

Collection letters aren't your most effective collection tool, but they do have their advantages. Such as:

- They're cheap.

- They remind and motivate some debtors to pay.

- They trigger phone calls if the customers didn't get a bill.

- They're waiting for the customers when they return from work.

- Letters stamped "Return to Sender" alert creditors of customers who have moved or skipped town.

- They act as a paper trail during legal proceedings. (Note: They will also hurt you if they violate the law).

For companies catering to a mass market consumer base, the letter generation and mailing process should be automated or outsourced. Devote your resources to calling overdue customers, not mailing letters.

## *Tone of Letters*

The collection letters' tone depends on the age of the debt.

| Delinquency of the debt | Letter's tone |
|---|---|
| 1. Early stage delinquency: | "Polite reminder." |
| 2. Mid stage delinquency: | "Let's work together to solve this problem." |
| 3. Late stage delinquency: | "Last chance. Meltdown imminent. Need immediate action." |

With a behavioral scoring system in place, you can also tailor your collection letter's tone to the behavioral score. If you find a customer with a good score, but in the mid-stage delinquency range, then perhaps a hard toned letter is unnecessary. If you find a customer with a poor score, but in an early stage delinquency, the reverse could be true.

Some customers with excellent scores don't need letters at all until they reach a certain long term overdue status. This helps avoid upsetting some of your best customers. If you treat all your customers the same (based on the age of the debt), you risk damaging customer relations with some of your longest, most profitable accounts.

## *Tips for Writing Collection Letters*

Collection letters are extremely sensitive. Care needs to be taken in their composition.

Some writing tips:

1. Be brief. Nobody enjoys getting or reading collection letters. Get to the point, fast. Use short sentences with simple, everyday language. Avoid legalese.

2. What's In It For Me? (WIIFM). Explain the benefits the customer gets by paying the debt.

3. Advise how to pay. List some easy payment methods, phone numbers and locations.

4. Personalize it. Use the customer's name. Use your name. Sign it either yourself or via a computer signatory system. Personalized letters make more of an impact than letters stamped, "This is a computer generated reminder no signature is required."

5. Make it visual. Use lots of white space between paragraphs. For the Letter 2 (L2) and Letter 3 (L3), add a bit of color. Stamp "Urgent" in red on the front of the envelope, put the amount in bold. A collection letter's main message is delivered upon its receipt, not its reading.

6. Consider couriering the letter to send a more powerful message, especially for large balance accounts.

7. Consider printing on double-sided paper. One side is the collection letter; the other side the bill summary.

8. Beware lawyers. Ensure your legal department reviews all letters you send out, but avoid having your lawyers write them. Their expertise is insuring the letters' legality; your expertise is in the communication.

9. Beware the corporate communications department. These people specialize in maximizing good publicity for your organization. They don't specialize in crafting effective collection letters to generate payment. The corporate communications department's goal is to do "damage control", whereas your letters' goal is to do "controlled damage."

10. Avoid treating all customers the same. If your organization doesn't have a behavioral scoring system, then you tie the collection letters' tone to both the age of the debt and the length of service the customer has spent with your firm. This will reduce the number of complaints from long-time, valuable customers upset at receiving a strong collection letter because for some reason they're overdue this one time.

## *Pet Peeve About Collection Letters*

Many collection letters, especially Asian collection letters, read as if they were written by robots with no intention of the letter ever being read. The last thing a collection letter should be is boring. Please use creativity in writing your letters. Make them stand out from the rest and you will likely be paid first. If you're serious to take the time to write effective letters, more debtors will take you serious and write you more cheques.

Hallmark Cards now has a line of collection cards. Diners Card, one of America's largest credit card companies, uses them. The collection card has a nice nature picture on it with the following message :

---

*'I don't know about you, but I find that life often takes sudden turns, many times without warning. Please know that at Discover Card we understand life's unexpected detours and are dedicated to serving you in any way we can. Give us a call so we can work through this together.'*

---

## *Examples of Collection Letters (Asian and Western styles)*

Ideally, your debt management system should determine what language the customer prefers to receive his / her correspondence in: English, Malay, Chinese or any other languages your customers' speak. But, if you lack such a system, I have attached some bi-lingual collection letters examples.

(COMPANY LETTERHEAD)

Letter 1
Early stage (**L1 Asian**)

August 1, 200_

Tan Choon Ngor
No. 58, Jalan PJS 9/28
46150 Petaling Jaya
Selangor DE, Malaysia

Re: **OVERDUE ACCOUNT**
Account number / *Nombor akaun*:    2.68327
Invoice date / *Tarikh invois*:    June 24, 200_
Overdue balance / *Baki tertunggak*:    RM402.36

Dear Ms. / Puan: Tan Choon Ngor

Thank you for your business, however, we have not yet received your loan installment of **RM402.36.** / *Terima kasih di atas bisnes anda, walau bagaimanapun, kami masih belum memerima bayaran ansuran pinjaman anda sebanyak RM402.36.*

Please make payment today to avoid late charges that are accruing on a daily basis. / *Sila buat bayaran anda hari ini untuk mengelakkan caj kelewatan yang dikira berdasarkan asas harian.*

If your payment has crossed this reminder, please accept my apologies and ignore this letter. / *Jika anda telah membuat bayaran sebelum menerina notis peringatan ini, pohon ribuan maaf dan sila abaikan surat ini.*

Regards / *Yang benar,*

V. Jaya
Recovery Specialist (03-5638-5689)

You can pay at / *Anda boleh bayar di*:
- Any of our 125 service outlets
- Shell petrol stations
- E-pay: www.goldencollections.com.my

- POS Malaysia
- Pay-by-phone: 1-800-989-5455
- Northern Bank
  ATM machines

(COMPANY LETTERHEAD)

August 1, 200_

Letter 2
Mid-stage (**L2 Asian**)

Tan Choon Ngor
No. 58, Jalan PJS 9/28
46150 Petaling Jaya

**Urgent Payment Reminder! / Peringatan Pembayaran Segera!**

Account number / *Nombor akaun*:     2.68327
Invoice date / *Tarikh invois*:          June 24, 200_
Overdue balance / *Baki tertunggak*:    RM658.64

Dear Ms. / Puan: Tan Choon Ngor

Is there a reason / *Adakah kerana*:

Why you have not paid your arrears?
*Mengapa anda tidak membayar hutang anda?*

Why you have not written or telephoned me?
*Mengapa anda tidak menulis surat atau menelefon saya?*

Your account remains OVERDUE for **RM658.64**. Please pay the total amount TODAY to release the credit hold placed on your account. / *Akaun anda menunjukkan TUNGAKKAN sebanyak **RM658.64**. Tolong buat bayaran sepenuhnya HARI INI.*

Failure to pay the above amount will result in your account being issued to our external collection agency for recovery of the debt and additional charges. / *Kegagalan membayar amaun tersebut akan menyebabkan akaun anda dihantar kepada seorang Permunggut Hutang untuk mengutip hutang tersebut dan caj-caj tambahan.*

If you are unable to pay the overdue amount, please contact me TODAY at 5638-5689 for a repayment plan. / *Sila hubungi saya pada HARI INI di talian 5638-5689 jika anda menghadapi kesulitan kewangan supaya satu pelan pembayaran boleh dirancangkan.*

Thank you for your prompt action. / *Terima kasih di atas permerhatian anda yang segera.*

Yours sincerely / *Yang benar*

V. Jaya
Recovery Specialist (03-5638-5689)

You can pay at / *Anda boleh bayar di*:
- Any of our 125 service outlets
- Shell petrol stations
- POS Malaysia
- Pay-by-phone: 1-800-989-5455

(COMPANY LETTERHEAD)

August 1, 200_

Letter 3
Late stage (**L3 Asian**)

Tan Choon Ngor
No. 58, Jalan PJS 9/28
46150 Petaling Jaya

**VIA: REGISTERED MAIL**

**Prevent Legal Action / Elakkan Tindakan Undang-Undang**

Account number / *Nombor akaun*:     2.68327
Invoice date / *Tarikh invois*:     June 24, 200_
Total Balance Due / *Jumlah Baki Tertunggak*:   RM700.00

Dear Ms. / Puan: Tan Choon Ngor

We have tried to work with you to resolve the outstanding balance on your account. However, the balance of **RM700.00** still remains unpaid. / *Kami telah cuba berusaha dengan anda untuk menyelesaikan baki tertunggak bagi akaun anda. Walau bagaimanapun, baki sebanyak **RM700.00** masih belum dibayar.*

Please pay this amount by August 10, 200_ to prevent your account from being sent for legal action. This may result in additional charges to you. / *Tolong bayar baki ini sebelum 10 Ogos, 200_ untuk mengelakkan akaun anda dihantar untuk tindakan undang-undang. Ini akan menyebabkan lebih kos kepada anda.*

In addition, your account will be: / *Tambahan, akaun anda akan:*

☞     Reported as a "WRITE-OFF" in the industry's negative data base. / *Dilaporkan sebagai "WRITE-OFF" di dalam pengkalan data-base negatif industri.*
☞     Experiencing a permanent service disconnection. / *Menghadapi perkhidmatan yang diputuskan selama-lamanya.*

If your payment is not made before that date, actions will be taken to collect this balance without further notice to you. / *Jika bayaran tidak dibuat sebelum tarikh tersebut, kami akan mengambil tindakan yang sewajarnya untuk mengutip baki tersebut tanpa notis selanjutnya diberikan kepada anda.*

Yours sincerely, / *Yang benar,*

V. Jaya
Recovery Specialist (03-5638-5689)

You can pay at / *Anda boleh bayar di*:
- Any of our 125 service outlets        - POS Malaysia

(COMPANY LETTERHEAD)

August 1, 200_                                    Early stage (**L1- Western**)

Initiatives Inc.
78 S. Ogden Way
Salt Lake City, Ut. 68235

RE:                          Account Number:  2.65796
                             Invoice date:        June 24, 200_
                             Overdue balance:  $451.65

Dear Mr. Pratt:

TIME....

There is so little of it around these days.

Please take a little time today to pay the outstanding balance of **$451.65** to save more time and late charges later.

I thank you for spending your time reading this short note and I look forward to receiving your payment.

Sincerely,

Ron Jones
Financial Service Representative
602-555-5555 (direct line)

PS: To save time every month while enjoying a $5 monthly discount, sign up for direct debit payment at any of our service locations or via our website at: www.servicewinners.com.

You can pay at:

- Western Union
- Credit card over the phone: 1-800-989-5455
- Check over the phone: 1-800-999-1111
- E-pay: www.payment.com

(COMPANY LETTERHEAD)

August 1, 200_                                    Early stage (**L1- Western**)


Initiatives Inc.
78 S. Ogden Way
Salt Lake City, Ut. 68235


RE:                          Account Number:  2.65796
                             Invoice date:        June 24, 200_
                             Overdue balance:  $451.65


Dear Mr. Pratt:


Thank you for using our services, however your payment of **$451.65** has not yet arrived. Please make payment today to avoid any interruption in your service.


You may want to sign up for direct debit facilities and enjoy a $5 rebate off each month's bill. Just visit any of our 50 service centers to enroll or sign-up at our website: http://www.servicewinners.com.


I look forward to receiving your payment. Please accept my apologies if this letter crosses in the mail with your payment.


Sincerely,


Ron Jones
Financial Service Representative
602-555-5555 (direct line)


You can pay at:

- Western Union
- Credit card over the phone: 1-800-989-5455
- Cheque over the phone: 1-800-999-1111
- E-pay: www.payment.com

(COMPANY LETTERHEAD)

September 1, 200_                          Mid-stage (**L2- Western**)

Initiatives Inc.
78 S. Ogden Way
Salt Lake City, Ut. 68235

RE:                                      **OVERDUE Account Status**
                                         Account Number:   2.65796
                                         Invoice date:       June 24, 200_
                                         Overdue balance:   $600.00

Dear Mr. Pratt:

Despite repeated notifications and telephone calls, your payment of **$600.00** has not been received. Unfortunately, your service has been temporarily suspended until payment is made.

Please make payment today to reinstate your service and avoid referral to our external debt collection agency.

If you are unable to make full payment, please call me immediately at 602-555-5555 to make suitable payment arrangements.

I look forward to receiving your payment to bring your account back to its previous up-to-date status.

Sincerely,

Ron Jones
Financial Service Representative

You can pay at:

- Western Union
- Credit card over the phone: 1-800-989-5455
- Cheque over the phone: 1-800-999-1111
- E-pay: www.payment.com

(COMPANY LETTERHEAD)

October 1, 200_                          Late stage (**L3- Western**)

Initiatives Inc.
78 S. Ogden Way
Salt Lake City, Ut. 68235

**VIA: REGISTERED MAIL**

**LEGAL PROCEEDINGS IMMINENT**
Account Number:  2.65796
Invoice date:        June 24, 200_
Total balance due: $650.00

Dear Mr. Pratt:

Over the last several months, we have tried to work with you to resolve the outstanding balance on your account. However, the balance of **$650.00** still remains unpaid.

Please pay this amount today or call me at 602-555-5555 to avoid permanent disconnection of service and having your account referred for legal action.

I am sure your intentions are to make good on your obligations. By making a payment today, you demonstrate those good intentions.

Sincerely,

Ron Jones
Financial Service Representative

You can pay at:

- Western Union
- Credit card over the phone: 1-800-989-5455
- Cheque over the phone: 1-800-999-1111
- E-pay: www.payment.com

## Collection Emails

To date, collection reminders are rarely sent via email. This may be partly due to legal issues. Another reason may be its newness and fear of acceptance. Email has its benefits and it's particularly useful in Asia where the postal service is unreliable.

## Tips for Writing Collection Emails

Writing collection emails should follow the same tips as for collection letters. It's merely a different format.

Some words of warning. Avoid allowing collectors to send out their own collection emails as some of their notes will sound unprofessional and result in legal action against your organization. Instead, have standardized, legally certified, professional emails built into your debt management system that are automatically sent out at different times during the collection treatments. In addition, the collectors need some standardized emails that they send "ad-hoc" when required. One such email is the "thank you for the payment" email.

Here's an example of a collection email my wife received from an accounting association. I liked it because it uses lots of white space and is direct. It also mentions the negative action that will befall the debtor if payment isn't received.

The creditor's name has been changed.

From:      Joe O'Connor- Membership Dues (joe@xyz.com.uk)
To:        Tan Choon Ngor (choon@servicewinners.com)
Subject:   FINAL DUES REMINDER
Date:      25 June 2006, 10:55:35 +0000

Dear Ms. Tan:

Payment for your 2006 annual subscription is now past due. The amount is **100.00 sterling.**

If you have already paid, please ignore this reminder. If you have not paid, please do so without delay.

Failure to do so by August 31, 2006 will result in your name being removed from the registry.

Payment by credit or debit card can be accepted through the subscription department's email address: subscription@xyz.com.uk or by fax at +44-98-5668-533.

Please include your reference number, card number and expiry date.

Regards,

Joe O'Connor

## Short Message Service (SMS)

In Malaysia, 90% of the population has a mobile phone. A great, inexpensive and convenient collection communication method opens up: SMS.

Collection calls and letters make some customers irate. SMSs reduce the number of customer complaints since the message is sent unobtrusively. The messages can be read after important meetings, job interviews or blind dates. Most people still enjoy getting SMSs. The same can't be said for calls and letters.

It's easy to broadcast your SMS messages. There are mobile data companies that send SMSs to the customers' cell phone numbers that you supply. Generic or customized SMS messages can be sent. Some examples:

**Generic:**

"Pls pay your (creditor's name) overdue bill today or call us at 1-800-XXX-xxxx. Pls disregard if you have just paid. Thank you."

**Customized:**

"Pls pay your (creditor's name) overdue bill of ($amount) today or call us at 1-800-XXX-xxxx. Pls disregard if you have just paid. Thank you."

Like collection letters, you send an SMS1, SMS2 and SMS3. For low balance accounts, consider using SMS broadcasts as one of your main collection actions in order to save resources. And, like collection letters, have your legal department review them to ensure their legality.

For VIP and other such accounts, consider eliminating the chance of an upset customer receiving a collection letter and instead rely mostly on SMSs for early-mid stage delinquency ranges.

Magistrate's courts in England and Wales send SMSs to people evading fines or falling to appear in court. The messages warn that if they don't comply, they will face further action, like jail. In their first SMS trial to 150 offenders, they found 75% of them paid immediately.[13]

---

**Tip:**

Some creditors send proactive SMS payment reminders three days before the payment is due. This is sold to the customer as a free billing service. The alert gives customers the option of paying via their credit card by simply replying to the message.

---

13   New Strait Times reporting on Rueters article, "Beep, beep... 'U.O.US': Using SMS to reel in British fine defaulters", 30 December 2005.

## *Summary*

- The effective use of collection letters, emails and SMSs will help you collect more money.

- Collection letters are cheap and do motivate some debtors to pay.

- The tone of a collection letter is usually based on the age of the debt.

- Behavioral scoring systems allow you to send letters based on scores rather than just the age of the debt.

- Tips for writing collection letters:

  ☑ Be brief

  ☑ Use "What's In It For Me?"

  ☑ Advise how to pay

  ☑ Personalize it

  ☑ Make it visual

  ☑ Courier letters for large balance accounts

  ☑ Consider double-siding printing collection letters

  ☑ Use lawyers to ensure your letters are legal, but beware of allowing them to write the letters

  ☑ Avoid using the corporate communications department altogether

- When sending collection letters, avoid treating all the customers the same. Your high value, long-standing customers require different letters, or letters sent at different times.

- Collection emails and SMSs are effective methods in motivating debtors to pay.

# Value of an Overdue Debtor

**5**

*We Can't Live without Them*

*Revolve your world around the customer and more customers will revolve around you.* – Heather Williams

## After reading this chapter, you will be able to:

- Receive an overview of "Customer Relationship Management"
- Understand the value of an overdue debtor
- Analyze the profit impact a collector has on your firm

## Overview of "Customer Relationship Management"

Customer Relationship Management (CRM) concerns itself with placing the customer at the center of the organization. The customer becomes the primary driver for the organization's strategies, instead of money. The more we know about our customer base, the better chance we will have of keeping them satisfied and buying. CRM organizations study their customers' demographics, spending habits, and satisfaction levels.

Collections people play an important part in CRM since we're in touch with customers (and their money) every day. Our collection data can be recorded in various CRM software systems to provide additional information about our customers.

I like Dominos' pizzas. I like them so much that I'm a Dominos gold card member. I have probably spent RM20,000 on their pizzas, and I will likely spend another RM20,000 before I die. According to CRM principles, my gross sales "Customer Lifetime Value" to Dominos is RM40,000. The value could be even higher if I say good things about Dominos to others. That is, provided, Dominos keeps me happy.

## CRM Story – Dominos Pizza

It was a hot and humid Friday night in Kuala Lumpur. I needed two Dominos beeferoni pizzas. I called their toll-free sales number, and my call was quickly and courteously handled. The young man said that my total bill would be RM60. Since I'm a corporate trainer, I decided to test his CRM principles. I told him I had only RM40 in my pocket. The agent knew I was a Gold Card member. He also saw the total amount of money I had spent over the years. I asked him to extend me RM20 credit and I would pay the balance on my next purchase.

Did he extend this Gold Card customer RM20?

No.

Does it make sense to treat your best customers like all rest? How often have we rejected valuable customers' request for small credit limit increases? How often have we rejected high-spending customers' requests for a few extra days to pay the bill?

## Cost of an Overdue Customer

Looking at it from a broader perspective, doesn't it also make sense to treat your overdue customers well? Overdue customers cost your organization a fortune. First, the organization had to spend money to acquire them. That entailed advertising costs, paying sales commissions, and offering discounted promotions and freebies. Second, once the customer enters you database, the organization needs to maintain the account by purchasing billing systems and paying customer service people.

In contrast, most collectors view overdue customers as a nuisance when they should be viewing them as gold. Overdue customers will turn a collection department from a cost center to a profit center. At one of my former employers, the revenue earned from late charges, reconnection fees, "cheque over the phone" fees, and miscellaneous fees paid the yearly cost of a 90-staff collection department, twice. At credit card companies their "best" customers are those who regularly run mildly overdue.

It's a fact that most overdue customers eventually pay their bills. It's a small minority that gets written off, yet many collection departments let the minority set the rule. We treat all overdue customers as "bad" people. For cellular service providers, it normally takes 12 months before any profits are made from the average customer. Why would you want to chase these people out of your organization by treating them poorly?

## A Collector's CRM Impact

Each day collectors call many customers. What's the financial CRM impact if collectors make poor quality collection calls?

Let's imagine one poorly trained collector who collects consumer accounts in an organization with a gross profit margin of 25%. The average customer in this organization has the following statistics.

- Incurs RM100.00 a month in charges or RM1200.00 yearly gross sales

- Stays with the organization for three years

What's the gross profit to the organization if the above conditions stay constant over the next three years? We won't use a discount factor.

$$25\% \times RM1200.00 \times 3 \text{ years} = RM900.00$$

In this case, the average debtor has a gross profit Customer Lifetime Value of RM900.00. What's the total value a collector "touches" each day? Each week? Each year? Let's assume s/he contacts only 40 customers a day:

|  |  | Gross profit impact |
|---|---|---|
| 40 customer calls x RM900.00 each | = | RM36,000 per day |
| RM36,000 x 5 days | = | RM180,000 per week |
| RM180,000 x 47 work weeks | = | RM8,460,000 per year |

Of course, some overdue customers are follow-up accounts that could be called more than once. Let's say 50% are follow-up calls, so reduce the yearly value by half to **RM4,230,000**.

If your average collector is touching customers worth RM4.2m in **gross profits** each year, do you care? If you have a team of 10 collectors, they're touching customers with a gross profit value of RM42m. Are they trained to touch this kind of value?

Run the Customer Lifetime Value numbers for your industry and your collection team. Don't be surprised if the value your collectors touch is much higher.

## Summary

- The field of Customer Relationship Management and the importance of Customer Lifetime Value impact collections.

- It's difficult and expensive bringing in new customers and retaining them as customers. Avoid allowing the collectors to chase them out the door.

- Collectors touch two of an organization's most important assets: customers and money. Are they trained to touch these assets?

# You Will Do It
# Our Way

## 6

*\*Strategies in Managing Corporate and Government Accounts*

*"We cheat the other guy and pass the savings on to you."* - Banner across the bar at Chilkoot Charlie's Saloon in Anchorage, Alaska

### After reading this chapter, you will be able to:

- Evaluate six causes of corporate and government delinquency
- Learn seven strategies to combat their delinquency

## Corporate and Government Collections is a Different Animal

Whether in Asia or the West, collecting from corporate and government accounts is a completely different animal than collecting from consumer and small business accounts. In this chapter, the word "corporate" refers to both corporate and government customers as the processes used in both are similar.

Many collectors dread collecting from corporate accounts and going through the lengthy process to get paid. Many corporates have the money; it's just that you have to go through hell to get it.

When consumers and small businesses fall overdue, it's usually due to a reduction in cash flow, job loss, or poor economic factors. The reason is usually cash-based. Although corporate accounts fall overdue for similar reasons, the more prevalent reasons are due to service and process issues.

Some of the **service** issues that delay corporate payments include:

1. Dissatisfaction with the quality or quantity of the goods or services delivered (or undelivered).

*\*More corporate collection tips are included in chapter 10.*

2. Dissatisfaction with the salesperson or account manager servicing the account.

3. Dissatisfaction with the pricing.

Some of the **process** issues that delay corporate payments include:

1. Customer has "take it or leave it" payment terms policy. This is especially true for blue-chip corporations who require their suppliers to act as bankers.

2. Customer is unable to adapt to your organization's billing cycle, billing system, or bill format.

3. Customer has an ineffective payables system.

4. Customer's employees or ex-employees committed the company to debts they were unauthorized to commit.

Let's examine how to tackle these causes.

## Service Causes of Corporate Delinquency

**1. Customer is dissatisfied with the quality or quantity of the goods or service delivered (or undelivered)**

Consumer and small business accounts use the same objection. You need to investigate these complaints promptly while they are still fresh and relatively easy to solve. If you wait to resolve it, the customer might still default because of other issues that pop up after this initial issue has been solved.

Your corporate accounts are valuable and any issues need quick resolution. In most cases, you will need to work with the salesperson or account manager to rectify the complaint. Don't be stingy with deductions, provided it hasn't been abused by the client in the past.

**2. Customer is dissatisfied with the salesperson or account manager servicing the account**

These complaints are difficult to handle because they lead to in-fighting between collections and sales. It's especially difficult in companies where the emphasis is on getting new sales instead of account management.

Unfortunately, guess who ends up handling these complaints? (You already know).

As a collector, I often heard customers say, "Your sales guy promised us we'd get......" Supposedly they were promised something that they never received. Sometimes these disputes stretch unresolved for months or even years. It's especially difficult to resolve if the sales person is no longer employed with the organization. It's important your collection policy has a process to handle such disputes. You don't want to make the customer suffer for your organization's internal issues.

### 3. Customer is dissatisfied with the pricing.

This dispute is often related to the sales person. The customer will claim certain prices were promised. They may insist certain items should be tax-free. Again, resolution involves investigating with the sales people and others.

## *Process Causes of Corporate Delinquency*

### 1. Customer has "take it or leave it" payment terms

Many corporate customers pay late simply because they can. They are so financially strong that they dictate their own payment terms. Wal-Mart is one such example.

In some large organizations, the accounts payable staff are trained in the art of delaying payment; it's called cash management. They are pressed to increase profit margins just like the rest of us. They use the interest float as much as possible. The corporates know that if they keep your money a bit longer than normal, they reduce their interest expenses and pass the savings to their customers. It's a competitive advantage.

Corporate clients are our most lucrative accounts, but they cause headaches if mismanaged. In a way, we're to blame. We don't charge them late fees, we don't refer them to collection agencies, and we don't send them for legal action. There is little incentive for them to pay on time. If you treat corporate clients like princesses, they are going to act like princesses.

When you ask corporate accounts for prompt payment, they give many reasons why it's difficult to pay on time. Although, somehow they are able to pay their taxes or other critical creditors on time.

Ingram Micro is the world's largest wholesaler of computer hardware like disk drives, mouses, and key pads. Its 2005 annual sales was $22.6b. Their primary customers are corporate customers. Ingram Micro's gross profit margin for the last five years hovers at 5%. With such low profit margins they are unable to allow corporate accounts long payment terms. Ingram Micro's Days Sales Outstanding (DSO) level over the last five years is in the low 30-day range. Ingram Micro's corporate clients pay them quickly because Ingram Micro requires them to do so.

You may say Ingram Micro can wield this power because they're big and can dictate terms to customers. Wrong. The computer whole-sale business is extremely competitive. Ingram Micro has been able to weather the economic storms in the I.T. industry by having a tough collections policy. Companies who do business with Ingram Micro know the company will be around. Their tough collections policy allows them to operate with virtually no debt and pass the interest savings onto their customers through lower prices. Similar competitors, with easier payment terms, have gone bankrupt.

Tetra Pak is one of the world's leading drink packaging companies. Their clients are corporates. Ricardo Cagnoni was the Malaysian operations finance director. He has done corporate collections both in the West and in Asia. He and his team created a strategy to deal with slow-paying corporate accounts. They call the strategy, "Draw the Line."

Once Tetra Pak delivers its quality products to their corporate customers, they no longer take any payment excuses. This strategy has helped them reduce Malaysian corporate Days Sales Outstanding from 88 days to 33; which is comparable to their North American operation's level. This strategy is now being rolled out throughout their other Asian and European operations.

Here are some highlights of the "Draw the Line" strategy:

1. Give credit talks to customers. Advise them of the agreed payment terms and what will happen if they exceed the terms.

2. Involve the senior finance manager in collections. S/he makes field visits to delinquent corporate accounts' managing directors and finance managers to show the seriousness they attach to slow payment.

3. Clearly state (and mean it) that you will commence a negative action like stop deliveries or late charges unless the payments are settled. Often this catches corporate accounts by surprise as few of their creditors do this. Your bill now takes priority over others.

4. Send an official letter mentioning that the legal department will be involved if payment is not forthcoming.

5. Close monitoring. Once the negative behavior is extinguished, monitor the account closely – even for the slightest deviation from the payment terms. You want them to know you're always watching.

Richardo believes one of the reasons this strategy was successful in Asia is due to the concept of "face" and the avoidance of embarrassment when a stop-order happens due to the debtor's slow payment. By involving the corporate customer's senior management, lower level administrative payment obstacles are reduced. The customer's admin people will heed your requests for payment much faster than other creditors since they don't want your senior management contacting their senior management about their payment process.

> **Tip:**
>
> Understand you corporate accounts' payable processes and take advantage of this knowledge. At one Fortune 500 company, they pay invoices 60 days from the invoice date, provided the invoice is received before the 5th of the month. A collection colleague of mine needed to get his bills paid faster than 60+ days. By understanding the account payable process, every time the client ordered work, he would immediately raise an invoice on that date. Then, when the work was completed, usually 60 days later, he would submit his invoice before the 5th of the month. He is now able to collect his money 15 days from submitting the invoice.

## 2. Customer is unable to adapt to your organization's billing cycle, billing system or bill format

What are your company's bills like? Do they suit your corporate clients' needs? Or is the client supposed to adapt to your bills? You will know if you have this problem if you hear your collectors say, "I'm sorry about that, but that's how our bills are; now when will you be paying?"

Your corporate accounts are your largest and most profitable accounts. Why make it difficult to do business with you? Billing should be easy and customized to your biggest clients' needs so that you get paid faster and book more of their business. If my biggest corporate customer wants me to print a pink elephant on the upper left hand corner of my invoice with a message, "Go, Seattle Sonics!", I will do just that.

> **Tip:**
>
> Try asking your I.T. department for help customizing bills and see what they say. Good luck! They may tell you that the change will cost a million bucks. Don't you believe it. If your billing system can't make slight changes according to corporate customers' requests, then you need a new billing system (*or new IT staff*). This is especially true when certain corporate clients request you to add a simple thing, such as a purchase order number, to the bill.

Scott Tweedy, as head of corporate collections at a major U.S. celco, was able to eliminate a large corporate receivable problem by simply adapting his company's bill format to the format requested by his corporate customers. His solution was to add a P.O. field and number to the bill summary page. He did this manually.

### 3. Customer has an ineffective payables system

Sometimes when corporate clients become delinquent it has nothing to do with complaints, lack of cash, or the bill's format. It's due to poor processes within the corporation itself to track and pay the invoices it receives.

There could be several reasons why your bill is unpaid:

- Signatory out of town with no back-up signer designated
- The bill is sitting in a pile in the back of the office
- The bill has been lost

These process problems often require site visits to your corporate accounts' A/P departments. You may even find yourself giving them advice on how to resolve their payable bottlenecks. We must visit our largest corporate customers every year. The more we know about them and their processes, the better chance we will have of getting paid before other creditors.

### 4. Customer's employees or ex-employees committed the company to debts they were unauthorized to commit.

Some A/P departments will say that the unpaid debt is caused by a current or ex-employee who didn't have permission to commit the company to the debt in the first place. Instead, they will blame the creditor for approving the credit request. It may be true, but it needs to be investigated.

- How long has the account been in existence?
- Who's been paying the bill?

If A/P has been paying this now disputed bill, then hold firm on the open balance. If the user has been paying, then try to get payment from A/P because surely they have been reimbursing the user each month. If A/P says they never reimbursed the bill, then pursue the user- if locatable and if your terms and conditions allow it.

If the A/P department was aware of this matter and even made payments on the account, then consider affecting other related accounts that aren't in default status. Be careful when doing this. First check the Terms and Conditions to see if it provides for cross-tying of accounts. You should also do a cost benefit analysis as you could be jeopardizing your entire business relationship for this one invoice. Is it worth it? Keep the account manager, legal officer, and senior management updated before doing this action.

## Strategies to Combat Corporate Delinquency

### 1. Establish Close Relationships with Your Customers

If you believe that people generally pay people they like, then you need to get out of the department minimum once a month to meet your top corporate clients. In fact, weekly is even better. These field trips will endear you to your sales people and your customers. You will learn more from these trips then the hours spent reading dry credit reports and financial statements. When clients tell me they have problems collecting from their corporate accounts the first question I ask them is, "Do you regularly have face to face meetings with your corporate clients?"

Besides learning from you customers, you can educate them on your credit terms. You will also see the mistakes that the sales people make out in the field. What appears as a small mistake promised to the customer then will develop into a nasty problem months later. You can now educate the sales people on the correct responses to customers' credit questions. You are proactively reducing the number of future customer complaints and improving the quality of your sales peoples' interactions with their customers. You're working smart.

**Tip:**

Ensure your firm's credit application requires that the customer or sales person notate who is the accounts payable contact and ideally their boss. You will need their name, direct telephone number, and email address. Corporate collectors spend an inordinate amount of time just trying to find the right "Person In Charge" (PIC) for payment.

### 2. Use Your Best Collectors

Corporate collections is complex. It requires collectors to have detailed account reconciliation skills in addition to the normal collection skills. It requires your best collectors. If the collectors in your organization don't receive business cards, then give them to the corporate team since they deal with high value accounts.

In some collection departments, before a collector becomes a corporate collector, s/he must first excel in handling consumer accounts. Corporate collectors should be smart and presentable. When they visit a corporate client, you need to feel confident that they will present your department in a good light. They should arrive prepared with the necessary invoices and account summaries.

Corporate collectors are great role models in any collections department. Poorly performing collectors will listen to the advice given by a corporate collector more than from a supervisor. When there are supervisory openings in your department, the first people to consider filling them should be the corporate collectors.

If a corporate collector is failing to perform to the required standards of the position, s/he needs to be warned, and if performance continues to deteriorate, then move the collector to a less important team. Corporate collections is too important a task to delegate to a poor or even average performer. Your corporate collectors – and their customers – make a significant contribution to you and your department's overall success.


## 3. Give Credit / Collection Talks

When sales people ink up deals with large corporate clients, someone from credit or collections should be present to meet his/her accounts payable counterpart in the organization. The main purpose is to give a friendly "credit talk."

The credit talk should explain to the new client the credit terms they have agreed to. The talk includes:

- How to qualify for any credit discounts or rebates?

- What are the payment terms and due dates?

- What happens if bills aren't paid within the payment terms?

- When do late charges take effect?

- What happens if there is a dispute on the goods or services?

- How does the deduction process work?

- Who to call if they run into cash flow problems?

- What you require for your annual credit review?

- Who to call to increase or decrease a credit line?

You also want to understand their payables process :

- What requirement do they have of you?

- When do they require the bills? Any special format?

- To whose attention should the bills go?

- Who's your Accounts Payable contact? And, who's the A/P contact's supervisor?

- Will they be taking any early payment discounts?

The more you know about their peculiarities and processes, the better chance you will have of preventing them from becoming delinquent. If you don't have formal credit talks with big, new corporate clients, you are opening yourself up for future unpleasant surprises.

In cases where a credit talk isn't cost effective, either due to the size of the account or the location, the credit department should mail the new A/P contact an overview of the agreed credit terms and payment requirements. The welcome letter should also give the telephone number and name of the collector managing their account.

It's a good idea for sales people to hear the credit talk. It teaches them what to say to customers who tell them their payments will be delayed. You also increase the chance of receiving the proper documentation when they submit the customer's credit application.

## 4. Involve Others

Advise sales and senior management before initiating any significant negative actions against corporate accounts like:

- Credit holds

- Suspension of service

- Repossession

- Legal action

Often, sales and senior management will assist in the collection process to avoid such actions from occurring.

## 5. Show Your Tooth First

If faced with a corporate client where a negative collection action is needed, consider affecting only a few of their accounts. Perhaps don't show all your teeth at once. Instead, show just one. Your goal is to send a strong message that non-payment will result in a negative action, but at the same time minimizing damage to such an important account.

Often, after the initial negative signal is sent, future payments become prompt- until they forget the earlier message and another signal needs to be sent. Performing initial negative actions that still allow the customer to operate their business will get their attention, and cause less stress on both sides. Holding tough does shake payments loose from the money tree, and your calls will be answered quickly the next time you call them.

## Corporate Collection Story

It was nearly midnight when my cell phone rang. The caller was a telephone technician desperately trying to please an upset corporate client. The client was a major hotel in Kuala Lumpur that was 180+ days delinquent. The hotel had broken several promises to pay and it was time to interrupt one of their many trunk lines (approximately 30 lines) due to non-payment. We could have interrupted their total phone service but chose instead to just interrupt their room to room phone lines. The collection action was strong enough to get a payment the next day, but weak enough to prevent severely damaging their business.

## 6. Contact Their Boss

If your accounts payable contact is difficult to work with, breaks promises, or pays extremely late; consider contacting their boss. Explain the problem you're having to their supervisor. Ask for the supervisor's assistance on this problem and if the problem reoccurs.

If the supervisor is willing to help you in the future, then the next time you're A/P counterpart delays payment for an excessive amount of time, you can rightly say:

> "Mr. / Ms. Accounts Payable, Mr. / Ms. (supervisor's name) told me
> to contact him / her directly the next time this problem happened.
> I'd rather not bother him / her over this small matter. When will you
> be making the payment?"

When dealing with corporate clients, it pays to be the "squeaky wheel".

## 7. Provide Quality Products or Service Supported with Excellent Customer Service

Sales and customer service people do a fine job. However, from time to time, a minority of them provide lousy after-sales service. Some customer service people are more concerned with average talk time and the number of calls answered, then whether their customers were satisfied with their service. Some sales people put a greater focus on booking new business than servicing existing clients. If the sales people are rewarded more for booking new business than servicing the old, then they're innocent. Senior management is guilty. The sales people are only doing what they're rewarded to do.

In such cases, often it's the corporate collector who picks up the ball and fixes the problem.

The collection manager decides if it warrants contacting the sales manager. From personal experience, I report poor account management service. Sales managers need to know if a major account is upset. But, I take it upon myself to own the problem. It's too important a problem to wait for sales to resolve. However, you first need to ensure that senior management empowers you to issue the necessary waivers, deductions, or discounts to solve the disputes and collect the payment. Check your collection policy to ensure you're authorized.

Properly servicing your 80 / 20 customers and collecting their large payments is one of the few "quick wins" in reducing your organization's DSO level and improving overall aging.

## 8. Reward Positive Behavior

Corporate accounts give us an opportunity to use positive actions to reward our good high-balance paymasters.

**Tip:**

Next time one of your corporate clients has consistently paid promptly, consider sending the A/P contact a personalized thank you card or small gift. These "low maintenance" corporate accounts should be remembered. You're showing them that you value their timely payments.

Consider rewarding those clients that used to have an ineffective payables system, but are now paying you on time. Perhaps, they took your advice and got their payable problem under control? Likely it was difficult to fix. A small token of appreciation to the person who fixed this bottleneck will be well-received.

## 9. Generate Detailed Aging Reports

Each corporate collector needs a detailed aging report of his / her account portfolio. Corporate clients should also be provided with a copy of their aging whenever it's required. These aging reports serve two purposes:

1) Old debts have poor memories and corporate debts can get quite old. It's important that the corporate collector continues to highlight the open invoices to his / her A/P counterpart.

2) You want to ensure your aging figures reconcile with theirs. This will reduce the chance of billing disputes later.

Generate detailed aging reports by salesperson to see if certain sales people have a significantly higher percentage of corporate clients overdue 90 days or more. Often, this is due to poor account management. If so, it needs to be highlighted as it will lead to customers leaving your organization.

## *Summary*

- Unlike consumer and small business accounts, corporate accounts usually become delinquent due to service or process issues, not lack of cash. The reasons for the delinquency are due to :

  1. Customer has a "take it or leave it" policy on payments.

  2. Customer is unable to adapt to your billing cycle, system or bill format.

  3. Customer is dissatisfied with the quality of the goods or services delivered.

  4. Customer is dissatisfied with the sales person who is servicing the account.

  5. Customer has an ineffective payables system.

  6. Customers' employees or ex-employees committed it to debts they were unauthorized to commit.

- Strategies to combat corporate delinquency:

  1. Establish close relationships with your customers.

  2. Use you best collectors.

  3. Give credit and collection talks when new corporate clients enter your organization.

  4. Involve others, especially sales and senior management, when a corporate client is delaying payment.

  5. Show your tooth first. Be prepared to launch a token negative action to show you're serious about the payment.

  6. Call your A/P counterpart's boss. Explain the problems you face in getting payment from their A/P department and ask for the boss' assistance.

  7. Provide excellent customer service, and if necessary, account management duties.

8. Reward positive payment behavior that your corporate clients demonstrate.

9. Generate detailed aging reports by corporate clients and by salesperson. This will allow all parties to be aware of any aging.

## Part IV:
# How to Become a
# Professional Collector?

# The Role of Collectors

*What Do Collectors Really Do?*

*Work while you have light. You are responsible for the talent that has been entrusted to you.* – Henri Matisse

### After reading this chapter, you will be able to:

- Understand the primary role of a bill collector

## *The Genesis Question*

There's a famous bar and nightclub in Anchorage, Alaska, called "The Fly By Night Club." The bar is owned by Mr. Whitekeys or "Keys" for short. The Fly By Night bar serves more kinds of beers than just about any bar in Alaska. If you order a Budweiser beer, American's number one selling beer, Mr. Whitekeys will sell you a Bud at a premium over any other beer. He figures that if you lack the creativity to choose from such a vast array of tasty, specialty beers, then you won't flinch at paying the "Bud Tax." He makes a fortune off the "Bud Tax."

Now, I would like to pose the "Genesis Question" to you. I call it the Genesis Question because your answer, whichever way you do answer, drives your overall philosophy of bill collections. In Chapter 1 we looked at the primary role of an employee. Now, I would like to ask you a question that on the surface looks easy to answer, but please take a moment and think creatively. Avoid stating the obvious.

**Genesis Question**: What is the primary role of a bill collector?

If your answer was, "To collect bills", or "To collect money", buy two copies of this book as a form of "Bud Tax." The primary role of a collector is not to collect bills or even money. I have met art collectors, stamp collectors and bill collectors. Two of them actually amass those items and display them on their walls or in stamp books at home, but I have yet to see framed bills decorating the walls of a bill collector's home.

**The primary role of a bill collector is to <u>help</u> customers.**

This belief is an integral part of my customer-centric collections philosophy.

Historically, bill collectors were hired to collect money. It was a simple and straight-forward job done in the days of less competition and less pressures on profit margins. Their collection tools included harassment, threats and perhaps even force since they operated without oversight. In ancient Rome, a creditor could even chain his debtor for 60 days and if the bills remained unpaid, the creditor had the right to sell the debtor as a slave or even kill him.

Today, collections is a matter of helping customers solve their problems in order to get back your money. Their problems are your problems. Any unprofessional collection techniques will cause valuable customers to take their business and bad "word-of-mouth" experiences elsewhere. Even the U.S. Internal Revenue Department's mission statement reflects a customer-centric collections philosophy:

> *To provide America's taxpayers top quality service by helping them understand and meet their tax responsibilities and apply the tax law with integrity and fairness to all.*[14]

Helping debtors also applies to Asia. The economic progress South East Asia has undergone is astounding. They have had some of the world's fastest growing economies over the past few decades. Millions of people have been lifted out of poverty in a relatively brief period of time. Incomes have doubled or tripled. Unfortunately, the understanding of how to manage the extra income is lacking. As a result, Asian collectors spend a larger part of their time explaining to debtors about basic payment terms. Debt education and counseling is a large part of their job.

Today's collectors truly help debtors. On the other hand, loan sharks don't help. In Asia, there are many types of loan sharks. The Chinese loan sharks are called "Ah Longs", the Indians "chettiars." These people constantly compete for customers. You will find their business cards everywhere. Each will emphasize their readiness to help you get out of a financial mess. They then list several cellular prepaid numbers to call. They want to *help* you so badly that they even make house calls.

---

14   "Mission Statement", <http://www.irs.gov> (1 May 2005), Internal Revenue Service.

In KL, a business associate of mine had a brother sign over his house for a RM2,000, two-week loan. After two weeks the loan increased to RM4,000. The brother couldn't pay. The loan shark happily threatened to take the house. My business associate came to his brother's rescue by negotiating a RM20,000 payment to get the loan settled and documents returned. The reason the brother didn't ask his own brother for the money was because he was afraid of losing "face." He would have pre-ferred to lose his house for a RM2,000 loan than to lose "face."

Providing debtors with help is a powerful tool in collecting money because most collectors don't offer this tool. In Asia, most collectors act like the enemy rather than as a partner. They also view overdue customers as the enemy.

## Do You Like Being Sold To?

Do you like buying from sales people who are only concerned about making a sale?

No? Why?

Because we don't like being sold to.

We want to be treated as people; the same applies to customers. By treating customers as people; you will collect more money. The old saying: "You scratch my back; I'll scratch yours" applies to overdue customers, too.

Do customers like paying bill collectors who are only concerned about taking their hard-earned money? In Asia, such collectors are called "money faces". And nobody likes "money faces". And it's easy to break promises to money-faced collectors.

Do you truly think you're the only person calling that debtor for money? There's a good chance that you're one of many all asking for his limited funds. But, if you call with an approach of trying to help, and the other collectors don't, who would you pay if you were the debtor?

In sales, they teach new sales people that prospects only buy from people they like. A hybrid of this rule applies to collections as well. Debt-ors pay people they like. If debtors don't like you, they're going to pay someone else.

Convincing collectors, especially experienced ones with ingrained work habits, that their primary role is to help customers is a tough sell. Like most of our customers, some collectors' brains have been stained by the words "bill collector." The words conjure up confusing images. Many of us need a paradigm shift in our thinking. The "iron fist" style of collecting is gone.

Making the paradigm shift and accepting the view that collectors' primary role is to help people will garner you benefits. You will :

- Collect more money

- Collect more money faster

- Get in less disputes

- Retain more customers

- Look forward to work

- Finish the day with a greater sense of purpose

## *Helping Customers*

If customers hear sincerity in your tone and language, there's a greater chance for payment. The goal on each customer contact is to help prevent a negative action from occurring. We're trying to make our customers' lives less stressful. We give them a little stress now to elicit payment, but by doing so now we prevent more stress later.

If your collection style is that of a "Cowboy Collector" and you jump into conversations with guns ablazin', demandin' payment and sayin' what you're gonna do if they don't pay, then you're gonna lose the customer, partner.

As a customer, it's easy to get into disputes with someone who they know doesn't care about them, especially if the nature of the call is a collection call. But it's tough arguing with someone trying to help. You're no gunslinger. Put the gun down. Get off the high horse. Take off the spurs. You will soon see yourself getting into less oral gunfights. Remember, we're just trying to help people- that's all.

If a customer says, "You don't care about me, all you care about is my money." You rightly respond with, "Mr. / Ms. Customer, I'm just trying to help prevent (negative action) from occurring." Although we help people, we're not charity workers. We won't be paying the bills our-selves. We can only help those who help themselves. And how do cus-tomers help themselves? By paying. Paying is the by-product of helping.

Let's admit it. Customers have something that we want; otherwise we wouldn't be calling or tracking them down. At the same time, we have something they want, though they don't always realize it. We give them peace of mind. As collectors, our job is to educate customers on the peace of mind they will enjoy if they pay their bills on time.

Most overdue customers eventually pay, but what about those who refuse to pay? For them, our job is to explain the consequences of their decision so that they make an informed decision. We alert them of the benefits of paying and the dangers of defaulting. Our primary role is to help customers, but we need to recognize that not all customers want our help.

These are the types of negative actions we try to help our customers avoid:

- Collection calls
- Collection letters
- Credit holds
- Suspended or disconnected service
- Site visits
- Lost business
- Repossessions / foreclosures / auctions
- Negative credit reporting
- Lost reward points (providing you have a reward scheme)
- External collection agencies
- Additional fees and charges
- Related accounts being affected
- Legal action
- And many others...........

**Tip:**

Helping customers does not necessarily mean giving them more time to pay. Financial problems cause enormous stress to most people. Allowing customers to pay minimum amounts as late as possible just prolongs their stress. Instead, if you truly want to help your customers, then collect as much as possible as soon as possible. By reducing customers' debt levels, you reduce their stress levels. You will help them more.

## Summary

- The primary role of a collector is to help customers.

# Asking for the Money

## 8

*Collection Skills*

*The secret of joy in work is contained in one word - excellence. To know how to do something well is to enjoy it.* – Pearl S. Buck

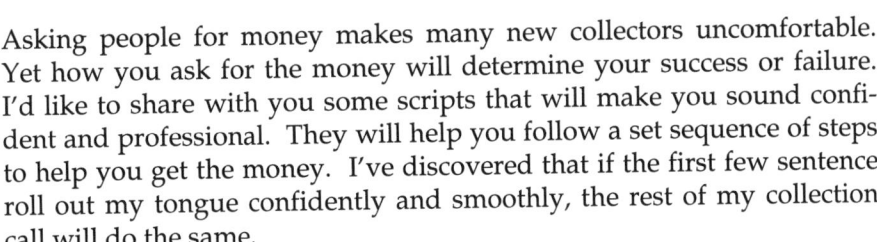

**After reading this chapter, you will be able to:**

- Understand the importance of scripts in a collections environment
- Learn the steps of a collection call
- Recognize the importance of a positive attitude when collecting money
- Learn the traits of a top collector

Asking people for money makes many new collectors uncomfortable. Yet how you ask for the money will determine your success or failure. I'd like to share with you some scripts that will make you sound confident and professional. They will help you follow a set sequence of steps to help you get the money. I've discovered that if the first few sentence roll out my tongue confidently and smoothly, the rest of my collection call will do the same.

## Scripts

When I mention the importance of using scripts, collectors roll their eyes and tell me only robots use scripts. I guess I'm a robot, then. People have knee-jerk reactions to the word "scripts", yet they love to go to movies where all the actors use scripts. Collectors who don't use scripts and want to "collect on-the-fly" sound just like that. They sound unprepared, unprofessional and weak as a fly.

## *Scripts' Advantages:*

### Scripts Buy You Time.

In an era of predictive dialers, where little if any review time is given before the call is connected, scripts give you precious seconds to scan the account while speaking with the customer.

### Scripts Make You Sound Confident and Professional.

Once memorized, your script sounds so natural that people won't know it's a script. First impressions are important in collections, whether face to face or over the phone, and a confident opening gives customers a stronger impression of you. Scripts are especially important for new collectors to feel and sound confident.

Collectors who dislike scripts don't understand their benefits. Instead, they try to create new scripts for each call and the result is a lot of "ums" and "ahs." In fact, I bet most of us already use mental scripts, it's just that they're informal.

Instead, I would like to formalize your scripts. Here are some examples, please customize them to your environment:

## *Script Examples*

Scripts should be short and simple. I use three simple scripts for the three key parts of a collection call:

1. Asking for the customer

2. Asking for the BIF (Balance in Full)

3. Reconfirming the agreement

### Script 1. Asking for the Customer:

For this first script, I have listed some options based on the delinquency of the debt. Personally, I use script 2a for nearly all my calls at all delinquency stage, though my tone will change.

Outbound call 1: (early stage account): *"Hello, I'd like to speak with (customer's name), please."*

Outbound call 2a: (early or late stage) : *"Hello, let me speak with (customer's name), please."*

Outbound call 2b: (late stage): *"Mr / Ms. (customer), please."*

Outbound call 2c: (late stage debtor who is hiding): *"(Customer's first name)?*

## Tips for "Asking for the Customer" scripts :

- Decide beforehand if you will use "Mr." or "Ms." Sometimes formality tips off the call receiver that you're a bill collector.

### Script 2. Asking for the BIF:

When asking for the money, use words that show you assume that the payment WILL be paid versus that it CAN be paid. Set high expectations for your debtor. I don't always get BIF, but if I don't ask for it then I never get it. If you don't get BIF, fine, often you will get the next best. In contrast, collectors who call asking for only the oldest bill are not true collectors in my book. They are merely "reminders".

> *"I'm calling to confirm the balance of (full amount) will be paid today for the (type of business) account."*

## Tips on "Asking for BIF" scripts :

- If a recent bill has just run and the debtor likely won't have it yet, I will ask for the overdue balance to reduce the chance of the customer getting upset. Later, after I get a Promise to Pay (PTP), I will mention which months it pays and also advise the debtor of the new bill. Sometimes, after hearing that there's a new bill coming, some customers will pay more.

### Script 3. Reconfirming the Agreement

Before ending every call, it's important to summarize what has been agreed (or disagreed) to reduce miscommunication and broken promises.

> *"Mr. / Ms. Customer, I'll note your account that you'll pay (amount) by (date), correct?"*

## 6-Steps of a Collection Contact

There are six key steps in a collection contact. Of the six, the greeting and the closing are simple, thus you are left with just four steps to learn well.

I've created **Coyle's Collection Pyramid** as a powerful job aid to visualize each of the six steps. This icon makes it easier to follow the steps during live collection attemps. When customers are busy firing excuses at you, it's easier simply glimpsing a picture versus reviewing heavy text-based job aids.

Read the next section and match each step with the appropriate icon. The sequence starts at the top and goes left to right.

## Coyle's Collection Pyramid

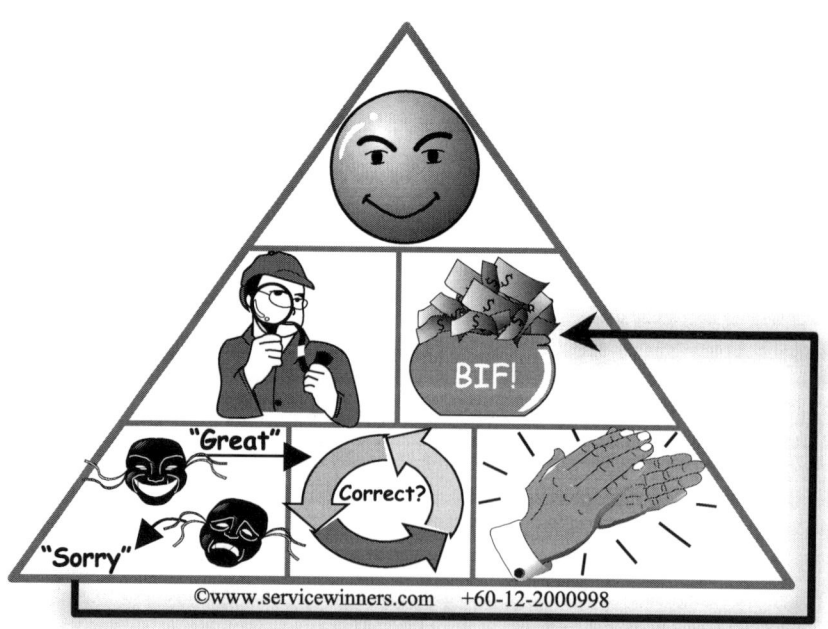

©www.servicewinners.com   +60-12-2000998

## Breaking It Down Step by Step

### Step 1: Opening (top of the pyramid)

Firmly but politely ask for the customer. However, if you're calling a late-stage account that has been avoiding you, use a friendly, mysterious tone. This technique works especially well if the customer is of the opposite gender.

## Step 2: Identify the customer first and then yourself.

New collectors have a problem at this step. After they ask for the customer, hardcore debtors will often screen their calls by asking, *"Who's this?"*

The collector replies, *"This is Steve with ServiceWinners."*
The other party then says, *"Oh, Mr. Customer's not here, bye."*

Game over.

This is especially frustrating on late-stage accounts where you have left countless messages on answering machines and received no call backs. Then, suddenly, you FINALLY reach a human on the other end of the phone line only to have that person "escape."

**Tip:**

Collecting debts is like playing poker. Don't reveal your poker hand first! Have the call receivers identify themselves first. If you're calling a debtor named "Bob" and the suspect asks, "Who's this?" You can respond with your first name, or use more creative techniques such as saying, "Bob, how are you doing?" Then wait for his response.

## Step 3: Ask for the BIF (Balance in Full).

If you don't ask, you don't get. I cringe when I hear collectors say, "When will you be paying the oldest bill?" These collectors aren't even playing poker. They're merely taking orders. The customer is in control. These collectors are breaking the cardinal rule in collections :

### Reinforce positive behavior, extinguish negative behavior.

At times, I have heard surprised customers cheerfully inquire, "You mean I don't have to pay the whole bill each month?" What the collector has just done is taught the customer a new bad habit.

Asking for Balance in Full (BIF) saves time. If the customer agrees, then you have just saved yourself a future call to collect another partial payment. Collectors who focus on partial payments rarely hit bonuses and are lucky to even hit their target. Of course, you won't BIF every time, but asking for it increases your negotiating power and size of the PTPs you do get.

Some collectors believe that asking for the current bill is unreasonable. I see it differently. I look at it as providing good customer service. The debtor can either pay it now or wait to pay when it's due, but I'm at least going to offer the option now to save the person time later.

**Step 4: Handle the positive or negative response.**

**If a positive response:**
Reward the customer with a positive word(s) such as "great", "thanks", "good", "marvellous", "terima kasih", "super", "bagus", "shiok", "you've done the right thing." Don't overdue it, just sincerely and quickly reinforce the positive behavior. I offer positive reinforcement even if customers offer lousy payment arrangements. For me, any payment offer is a positive behavior. In such instances I say, "Thank you for the offer, however, the amount needed to hold your account is RMXXXX."

**If a negative response:**
Use a key but neglected word in the collector's tool chest: "sorry." On difficult calls or those where the customer has a problem, the word "sorry" works wonders. It diffuses upset customers. It resolves disputes. It collects money. If you don't like that word, say, "I understand".

But besides saying "sorry", you will also need to exit the Pyramid since the Pyramid is a money pyramid and customers won't pay you as long as they have excuses or unaddressed problems. Leave the Pyramid, address the excuse or dispute, then resume the conversation at Step 3: Ask for the BIF. If part of the problem is in paying the full balance, then ask for the next largest amount.

We will cover excuses and upset customers in the next chapter.

**Step 5: Summarize the agreement.**

On each collection contact, your goal should be to get some type of agreement. We may not always get a PTP, but we should get an agreement, even if it's to disagree. Often the call ends with an agreement to pay. If so, reconfirm the dates, amounts, and payment method. Clarity reduces the chance of a future broken promise.

**6: Closing: Thank the customer and document.**

Politely bid the customer goodbye and document the agreement. Some collection departments "brand" the image of their company at the close. E.g. *"Thank you for doing business with XYZ Company."*

**6-Step example (Easy PTP)**

> Customer:   "Hello."
>
> Collector :   "Hello, let me speak with Mr. Tan, please."
>
> Customer:   "This is Mr. Tan."

Collector : "Hello Mr. Tan, this is Steve with XYZ Bank. I'm calling to confirm the balance of RM5,000 will be paid today for the credit card account."

Customer: "Oh yes, it will."

Collector : "Great. I'll note your account that you will pay RM5,000 today, correct?"

Customer: "Yes."

Collector : "How will you be paying that?"

Customer: "I'll pay at the Kuala Lumpur main branch."

Collector : "Great, thank you. Bye."

Customer: "Bye."

## 6-Step example (Difficult PTP)

Customer: "Hello."

Collector : "Hello, let me speak with Mr. Tan, please."

Customer: "This is Mr. Tan."

Collector : "Hello Mr. Tan, this is Steve with XYZ Bank. I'm calling to confirm the balance of RM5,000 will be paid today for the credit card account."

Customer: "No, I can't. I'm having cash flow problems."

Collector : "Sorry to hear that Mr. Tan, however, you need to pay RM5,000 to avoid your credit card from being terminated." *

Customer: "Oh. OK, I'll make the payment."

Collector : "Great. I'll note your account that you will pay RM5,000 today and I will hold the card's termination, correct?"

Customer: "Yes."

Collector : "How will you be paying that?"

Customer: "I'll pay at the Kuala Lumpur main branch."

Collector : "Great, thank you. Bye."

Customer: "Bye."

*Usually after saying this debtors will negotiate the amount and the date it needs to be paid. In this example, for brevity sake, the customer will pay BIF.

## *You Are What You Think. The Importance of Attitude.*

Nutritionists say, "You are what you eat."

Descartes, the father of modern philosophy wrote, "I think therefore I am."

I believe, "You are what you think."

Top collectors are good collectors because they know they can do it. I have no doubts in my mind that I will succeed in collections, but when it comes to carpentry I'm lousy. I'm a lousy at carpentry because I've convinced myself that I have two left hands. My mind is full of doubts. No matter if I attend carpentry school for ten years, I will never be able to build things from wood.

Collections, like sales, requires a positive attitude to succeed. Before making any collection call or visit, your attitude should be:

*"I fully expect full payment today."*

If you expect anything less, you'll get it.

When you enter your collection calls with a positive attitude and high expectations, you will achieve more at the end of the day. Every day we expend effort arriving to work on time. What do you do?

- You set the alarm clock the previous night

- You wake up (sometimes reluctantly)

- You make ourselves look and smell nice

- You fight traffic, or stand in a crowded subway, or bus

Do you make all this effort to arrive at work to just collect partial payments all day?

NO WAY!

When I'm collecting, I'm asking for Balance in Full (BIF). I want the whole thing. I want the triple scoop ice cream cone with nuts, whipped cream and the banana. If it's possible to ask for a fourth scoop, I will ask for it.

If the customer offers me anything less than BIF, I act politely shocked. If the customer promises to pay later than today or minimum tomorrow, I act surprised.

A research study[15] on school children showed the importance of setting high standards on actual performance. The researchers separated 406 children into two random groups. Both groups received the same standardized math test. In one group, their teachers read the standard instructions for the test. In the other group, before reading the standard instructions, their teachers read the following:

---

15    Steven M. Brown and Herbert J. Walberg, "Motivational Effects on Test Scores of Elementary Students", *The Journal of Educational Research*. 86 (1993), 133-136, Heldref Publications.

*"It is really important that you do as WELL as you can on this test.*
*The test score you receive will let others see just how well I am doing in*
*teaching you math this year.*

*Your scores will be compared to students in other grades here at this*
*school, as well as to those in other schools in Chicago.*

*That is why it is extremely important to do the VERY BEST that you can.*
*Do it for YOURSELF, YOUR PARENTS, AND ME."*

(Capitalizations are the researchers')

The researchers found that the average test score for the students who didn't receive the message was 14% lower than the students who got the motivational message. The researchers described the effect the message had on the test scores as "moderately large."

Give your customers a boost by setting high expectations on them. Some will strive to delight you. Let other collectors set low expectations on their debtors and experience higher broken promise rates, but not you.

The importance of setting high expectations also applies to supervisors setting high expectations on their collection teams. If you think your team is composed of a bunch of losers, believe me, they won't disappoint you. Guaranteed.

When I train collectors, the easiest part is imparting new knowledge and skills. The tough part is changing attitudes. How do you convince people to change a collection style that has taken years to form, especially if the style has allowed them to attain a mediocre level of success?

Dear reader, how do I change your attitude?

Having a positive attitude and setting high expectations for yourself and your customers will help you collect more money. People are attracted to positive people. They're repelled by negativity. People pay positive collectors more than the negative ones.

## Setting High Expectations on Customers

One wintry day, I made a collection call to a customer in the frozen American state of Minnesota. The account had an overdue balance of $500. It was a cell phone bill and the customer's line was going to be terminated that day if payment wasn't forthcoming. The account had many broken promises. From the notes on the account, the previous collectors wrote that this debtor was a loser, but for some reason I decided to give her a last call anyway. When I called her, to my surprise, I found her to be polite and friendly, perhaps too friendly.

Like most debtors, she wanted more time to pay. I asked for the full balance. We politely negotiated back and forth. She wanted more time, I wanted more money in less time. Eventually we agreed that she would pay 100 dollars a day to the Minneapolis sales office for five straight days, so by Friday she would be current. In return, I wouldn't disconnect her cell phone number. She understood that if she missed even a single payment, the line would be permanently disconnected due to the extensive history of broken promises.

I didn't expect she would keep her commitment, but I made sure she didn't know that.

Later that afternoon I got a call from an upset Minneapolis branch manager. He said, *"Steve, why the hell did you send a prostitute to my office?"*

Frankly, I had no idea what the guy was talking about. *"I'm sorry, what did you say?"*

He said, *"There's a prostitute named Wendy standing here wearing a cheap rabbit fur coat, and a miniskirt, in freezing weather. I can't believe you send us such customers. It's embarrassing. It makes our office look bad."* He added, *"And her coat reeks of marijuana."*

I didn't know what to say. I just advised him to be expecting her for the next four days. And, sure enough, each day she walked in with a $100 bill. By Friday, she had paid her final installment and the branch manager called to inquire if I would be sending her the next week. When I told him "no", he was disappointed. Once he got to know her, he found her to be a great person.

## Collections Physics TEST: "For Every Action there is an Equal an Opposite Reaction"

For this test, I'd like you to go to your workplace tomorrow morning and do the following:

1) Smile and say a lively, "Good Morning!" to the next person who walks past you. What was his or her reaction and response?

2) Now say a low-energy, "Good morning" to the next person. Did you get a dead response? You probably did because you sounded like a loser.

The same applies in collections. Who wants to discuss overdue payments with losers? Who wants to pay losers? Attitude is the single most important factor to be successful in collections. My attitude and the one I would like to instill in you is:

> *I fully expect full payment today.*

You are what you think.

## *Traits of a Top Collector*

There's a nice memory tool that quickly sums up the traits of a top collector.

| | |
|---|---|
| **C**ontrol | A top collector stays in control. There are times in the conversation where a customer takes control. That's OK if it's temporary, but a top collector will eventually bring the customer back to the matter at hand: the debt. |
| **A**ttitude | A positive attitude will help you and your customers hit new heights. |
| **S**kills | A top collector needs to quickly display the "hard" skills needed to do the job. They know scripts; understand the organization's collection system; know the "6-Steps of a Collection Contact", and the department's policies and procedures. These are the functional skills needed to do the job well. |
| **H**uman Touch | These are the interpersonal skills you have learned throughout your life. From experience, it's easier to train a nice collector to be firm than a firm collector to be nice. The experts say that your expertise in human skills determines you E.Q. (Emotional Quotient). Those with high EQ usually get promoted faster. |
| | Collectors with well-developed human skills listen more. They empathize. They aren't afraid to use the word "sorry", and when they say it they mean it. Such collectors experience less oral battles with customers because they relate to them as humans. |

**Check Point**: Are you a **C.A.S.H.** collector? Is your department full of C.A.S.H. collectors?

## *Summary*

- Scripts save you time. They make you sound more confident and professional.

- The easy 6-Steps of a collection contact are:

   1) Opening: Ask for the customer

   2) Identify customer first, then self

   3) Ask for the Balance in Full (BIF)

   4) Handle the positive or negative response

   5) Summarize the agreement

   6) Thank the customer and document

- A positive attitude determines how successful you will be. My friend, Dalwi Lee, believes: "What you think is what you get."

- Traits of a C.A.S.H. collector are:

   ☑ Control

   ☑ Attitude

   ☑ Skills (functional skills)

   ☑ Human Touch (interpersonal skills)

# Diffusing Time Bombs, Excuses and Objections

*How to Handle Difficult Debtors with Confidence*

*Now a promise made is a debt unpaid….–* Robert Service

*Some people use one half their ingenuity to get into debt, and the other half to avoid paying it. –* George D. Prentice

## After reading this chapter, you will be able to:

- Value overdue customers
- Handle the most common payment excuses and objections
- Handle broken promises
- Diffuse upset customers by using the A.U.S.E. technique
- Learn which words to use and avoid when collecting money
- Examine your "hot buttons" to stay cool with customers

## O-V-E-R-D-U-E  D-E-B-T-O-R-S

How do you feel when you hear those words? The words contain all kinds of negative emotions. What do you think about people who don't pay their bills on time?

When I ask collectors that question I hear them use words like: "deadbeats", "bad", "wrong" and "flakes". They will personalize it and say things like, "I don't like them" or worse, "I hate them."

To me, people who don't pay their bills on time are great. Without them, I would be out of a job. We need them more than they need us. They're our rice bowl.

Credit card companies "love" customers who don't pay on time. Most card companies earn at least 18% annual interest rates. In 2003, American credit card holders paid "$43.1 billion in late fees, over-the-limit fees, finance charges and other fees, up from $39.6 billion...."[16]

If you have a negative perception of debtors, change it. You won't be successful if you don't like your customers. It's also hard trying to help someone whom we consider "bad."

## Discover the "Why" of the Non-payment

Collectors do a good job asking debtors "When?" and "How much?" questions, but one of the most important questions to ask is "WHY?"

*"Why hasn't the payment been made on time?"*

Collectors avoid "why" questions because they lead to long-winded stories, but if you're uncertain about the true causes of the non-payment, you will waste more time later dealing with crazy excuses and broken promises.

A professional athlete and his wife taught me the value of asking, "Why?" The athlete's yearly salary was $800,000. He had an overdue bill of about $1,000. I imagined he could easily pay it.

Each time I spoke with him, he would give me a Promise to Pay (PTP) that would later break. And I never asked him "why?" One day I reached his wife and I finally asked her "why?" She said, "Steve, we're flat broke. My husband's a cocaine addict and he's been suspended from the league. We're about to lose our house." Once I knew the "why", I immediately sent the account to legal.

By asking customers, "why?", you're attempting to get to the truth. "Why?" gives people a chance to talk, and the more they talk, the more they reveal. Once you understand their "why?", you have a better chance of designing a workable payment plan.

It also feels great discovering the real reasons for customers' non-payment because only then will you offer the best solution. However, to get to the truth, you sometimes have to listen to a story or two.

## Tips for Handling Excuses

Some debtors play delay games like, "I never got a bill." "Someone else pays the bill." "Call back I'm busy." "Yeah, yeah, I'll pay you. Are we done?"

Unfortunately, many collectors play along, which is a mistake because the debtor is a pro at these games. You're the amateur. When

---

16  "Credit card fees cost Americans billions", Reuters, as reported by the New Strait Times, 2 January 2004.

you sense a customer is playing a game with you, politely express your reservations by "naming the game". Your goal isn't to get the customer upset. Your goal is to get to the truth in order to create a workable payment solution.

When I sense a game is being played, I say, "Mr. / Ms. Customer, may I speak frankly with you?" So far, I have yet to hear "no" to that question. I then politely share my doubts with them.

## Common Excuses

Once you decide you're not going to play games with debtors, you're now ready to call them and ask for payment. Get ready for their excuses. It's important to create a list of your most common excuses and memorize your responses to each. Customers who use excuses frequently are looking for chinks in your amour. Show them you're ready by having effective responses.

I will now list some common excuses and some responses as a guide. Please customize them to fit your industry and work environment.

1. "I never got a bill."
2. "I have no money."
3. "Someone else pays the bill."
4. "The computer is down."
5. "Cheque signatory is overseas / out of town."
6. "I don't need your goods or services."
7. "I'm busy, call back later."
8. "I don't care."
9. "The cheque is in the mail."
10. "I can't pay till pay day."
11. "The car is in the workshop" (for car loan collectors)

**Excuse 1:** **"I never got a bill."**

I'm sure this is one of the most frequent payment excuses in the world. When responding, you first need to decide if this is an excuse or an objection. If the customer is calling me, it's probably an objection. If I'm calling and I have left numerous unreturned messages, then I view it as an excuse.

New collectors will volunteer to fax the customer a bill. I avoid doing this if it's an outbound call. It takes time printing bills and faxing, especially if the debtor has no intention of paying. However, if the customer insists, then I will fax.

Response steps:

Step 1:    Verify address: *"Mr. / Ms Customer, sorry to hear about that, can you verify your address with me?"*

Step 2:    **If the address is correct:** *"Mr. / Ms. Customer, that's the address we've been sending the bills. You may want to check with your postman, however, the bill is now $_____ and needs to be paid today to prevent* (**negative action**) *from happening."*

If the address is incorrect, then I will offer to fax the bills and give the customer more time.

## Tips for "I never got a bill":

a) ALWAYS have the customer provide their address first Otherwise, you're giving the customer more time to think while you're reading back the address. Don't be surprised after you finish reading the address that the customer makes a slight change to your address to show it's incorrect and then request for more time. And don't be surprised if s/he doesn't have access to a fax, either.

b) If they complain it's unfair to demand payment when they have never received a bill, then look at the account history. If you have verified the address to be good and there are many left messages on the account, then consider "naming the game." Advise them the account is XX days overdue, and the number of messages you have left for them. However, if this is a long-time customer with a generally good payment record, then consider giving the person the benefit of the doubt

## Excuse 2:    *"I have no money."*

When customers say, "I have no money" they're withholding the full truth. They need to complete their sentence. They should be saying, "I have no money **for you.**"

When customers use this excuse we're usually talking on an active phone line, so they must have money for the phone. They likely have money for food, water and clothes. They might even have money for the karaoke bar, their car, and their friends. But they don't have money for you.

The "No Money" excuse involves no creativity from the debtor's part.
Response: *"I'm sorry; however the payment needs to be made today in order to prevent (negative action)."*

---

### Tip for "I have no money" excuse:

If the customer is still unhappy with your response, then "name the game": *"Mr. / Ms. Customer, may I speak frankly with you? (permission given). please don't take this the wrong way, but we all have money. The phone line is still active, so you must be paying that bill. It's just a matter of priorities. You need to find the money to take care of this bill today to prevent (negative action) from happening. I'd like to work with you."*

---

### Excuse 3: "Someone else pays the bill."

I would love to meet this guy and shake his / her hand. I'm sure this someone owes a lot of people money because I come across him all over the world. The goal on this excuse is to make the customer face reality and take responsibility. I will contact the "someone" once, but after that, if the payment still doesn't arrive, then I will go after the customer.

Response: *"Mr. / Ms. Customer, someone isn't paying the bill. That's why I'm calling you. You signed up for this account and you need to take care of your account today to prevent (negative action)."*

---

### Tips for "Someone else pays the bill" excuse:

a) Use the words "you" and "your" frequently. You want the debtor to take responsibility for the account since they're trying to walk away from it.

b) If the customer is upset about the other party's lack of payment, I tell the customer I'm sorry the friend betrayed him/her, but the bill still needs to be paid. Otherwise, their "friend" will continue doing more damage to the customer's credit history. In Asia, I use the words, "negatively affect your good name and reputation."

## Excuse #4:   *"The computer is down."*

Corporate accounts use this excuse frequently when they experience cash flow difficulties. It's important to "name the game." Remember, their bill has been overdue for weeks or months, and the computer must have been operational at some time or they would be out of business. Your goal is to get to the root of the problem in order to help solve the unpaid bill.

Response: *"I'm sorry to hear about that, please ensure a payment goes out today or tomorrow when the computer comes up?"*

### Tips for "The computer is down" excuse:

a) If they can't ensure a payment after the computer is up, then you need to "name the game" :

*"Mr. / Ms. Accounts Payable, please take no offense when I say this, but when A/P departments tell me their computer is down and they can't ensure a payment for a seriously overdue bill, it nearly always means they're experiencing cash flow problems. I'd like to work with you, tell me what's going on?"*

## Excuse #5:   *"Cheque signatory is out of town / overseas."*

This is similar to Excuse #4. If the cheque signatory is away for a few days, then maybe you can wait for his/her return, but if it's longer, consider the following response.

Response: *"Oh, I'm sorry to hear that. Who's handling these matters while Mr. / Ms. X is out of town?"*

### Tips for "Cheque signatory is out of town/ overseas" excuse:

a. Act mildly shocked if they reply with, "No one." You could "name the game", "What! No one manages the organization while Mr. / Ms. X is out of town? Do all your creditors remain unpaid? How is payroll done?"

b. If this excuse is frequently used, call the cheque signatory when s/he is back in town. Explain the problem, use the accounts payable person's name, and ask what to do in the future if this situation reoccurs. If you want, give the A/P person a call and advise him / her what was decided. I hope you will never hear this excuse again.

## Excuse #6: "I don't need your goods / services."

This excuse is difficult to handle. It shows the customer is beginning to justify why s/he doesn't want to pay. Most of us believe we should pay for the things we buy on credit. It's the right thing to do; otherwise, no one would extend credit. People generally view themselves as honest, never as credit criminals or defaulters, but over time some people start to justify a future default.

To prevent customers from looking for excuses to default, it's important to start the collection process early. You want to prevent debtors from intentionally or unintentionally forgetting about your bills. Remember: "Old bills have short memories."

Response: *"Mr. / Ms. Customer, I'm sorry you feel that way. After we're done, I'll have our customer service department contact you immediately. Now, please pay $_____ today to prevent* (negative action) *from happening."*

### Tips for "I don't need your goods / services" excuse

a) If the customer still doesn't want to pay after your response, then appeal to their innate sense of honesty about themselves.

*"Mr. / Ms. Customer, I know you're an honest person. And I know you follow through with your obligations. When will I be receiving the payment of $_____"*

b) If they still refuse to pay, dig deeper into the problem and be prepared to resolve it.

*"Mr. / Ms. Customer, can I understand your concern about our goods/services?"*

c) At a minimum, the customer should pay the undisputed portion of the goods or services delivered. Give the customer your guarantee that you will rectify the issues and apologize for any inconvenience.

## Excuse #7:  "I'm busy, call back later."

This excuse requires a small "rabbit punch" to be effective. There's no need for a full, round-house, knockout punch. You just need to give a short, ORAL "rabbit punch" to get the customer's attention.

When customers say, "call back later," what are they really saying? They're saying, "My time is more valuable than yours."

If I'm doing mass market, high volume collections, I don't have time to call customers back, especially for small balance amounts. If I take the time to "hold hands" and follow-up with each of my small balance customers, I will be unable to help a greater number of other customers.

Here's a "rabbit punch" response (say it quickly after identifying yourself):

*"Mr. / Ms. Customer, I'm sorry for disturbing you, but I'm trying to prevent (negative action) from happening to your account. Please pay RM_____today."*

### Tips on "I'm busy, call back later" excuse:

After delivering the "rabbit punch", don't be surprised how many "busy" people will suddenly break out of their meetings to speak to you in hushed tones and agree to pay today or tomorrow. The "rabbit punch" shows that you're serious and that the bill needs their immediate attention.

If the customer still wants a call back, and the balance is small, I give the customer my phone number to call when s/he is free. From experience, when I call back, they're still busy, or in another meeting, or at lunch, or they have gone home. In collections, holding hands for too long is ineffective. You need to decide if it's worth the extra time.

## Excuse #8: "I don't care."

This excuse is similar to #6. It's a tough excuse to handle as the customer probably has decided to never make the payment. The customer has crossed a "mental Rubicon." Getting payment will be tough. The key is to listen. You have to understand <u>why</u>?

Response: *"Mr. / Ms. Customer, I'm sorry to hear that. I'd like to help. Can I please understand your concern on this account?"*

### Tips on "I don't care" excuse:

Get the customer to open up. Get to the root of the problem. If necessary solve it or have customer services follow-up with the customer. If this is truly an objection, then ask the customer for "one last chance" to rectify this concern. Be prepared to spend a lot of time on this account.

Show you understand the customer's concern, but also explain that by defaulting they're only making matters worse.

When the customer begins to open up say, "Thank you for sharing that with me."

## Excuse #9: "The cheque is in the mail."

This is a common excuse in North America where most customers pay their bills via cheque. For this excuse, after saying "thank you for the payment", ask when it was sent and for how much. If the amount sent is less than the total balance, ask for the remaining balance immediately. Give the customer a view of what will happen if the cheque doesn't arrive.

Response: *"Thank you for the payment, Mr / Ms Customer. When was it sent? How much? Great, that'll prevent your account from* (negative action)." [17]

In Asia, the "cheque in the mail" excuse is rarely used as most consumers pay by cash. Asian organizations have larger payment processing departments than those in the West. A U.S. telco that uses a lockbox system to process 90% or more of its payments has a staff of six, whereas an Asian telco has 35 staff processing payments from multiple channels.

---

17  I find it a waste of time asking for cheque numbers as customers can give fictitious ones.

## Excuse #10: "I can't pay till pay day"

"I know you pay at pay day, however, your account is overdue 'x' months. There hasn't been a payment at payday for 'x' months. What do you suggest to get your account back to current status?"

## Excuse #11: "The car is in the workshop."

"I am sorry to hear that. When did you have the car problems/accident. Again I'm sorry, but Mr/Ms Customer, this loan is overdue for much longer. Why isn't it being paid?"

### *Handling Objections*

Whereas excuses are deceptions, objections are usually legitimate. Objections also take a lot of effort to resolve. However, to ensure the "objection" isn't an excuse, and to ensure the time spent resolving it is well-spent, I say:

*"Mr. / Ms. Customer, if I solve this dispute you're having; you'll pay the remaining balance, correct?"*

If they refuse to even pay the undisputed portion, then treat it as an excuse and avoid wasting time solving an unsolvable problem. However, most objections are truly objections; and they need to be handled differently than excuses. They require active listening from the collector because as long as the customer is in an angry, irrational mindset, there's no way you will get paid.

Here are some common objections and some tips on handling them. All responses involve some digging into the problem to solve them. Please customize them to fit your industry and work environment.

### *Common Objections*

"I'm not paying because

1) the quality of your goods / service is lousy."
2) what was delivered was not agreed upon."
3) I never got what the salesperson told me I'd get."
4) of a (hard luck story).

## Objection #1: "I'm not paying because the quality of your goods / services is lousy."

This objection requires listening and investigation. You might want to involve your customer service department.

Response: *"I'm sorry to hear that Mr. / Ms. Customer. Please tell me more so I can help you?"*

### Tip for Objection #1:

a) By trying to help solve the concern, you're making it difficult for them to be angry with you. It's difficult withholding payment from someone who's trying to help. If required, have the person short-pay the bill by the amount s/he thinks is fair until a final decision has been made for the difference. Top collection trainer, Tim Paulsen, uses this script:

*"Mr. / Ms. Customer, I don't want you to pay what you think is wrong. I want you to pay what you think is right."*

## Objection #2: "I'm not paying because what was delivered was not agreed"

This shipping objection will require investigation. Verify what was shipped and what was or wasn't received. Order a "proof of delivery" if necessary. It's difficult to pursue collection on goods that weren't proven delivered. Ask the customer that if you send them a Proof of Delivery (P.O.D.), will they immediately remit payment?

Response: *"Mr. / Ms. Customer, I'm sorry to hear about that. Let's verify what was sent and supposed to be delivered."*

### Tip for Objection #2:

If they agree that a partial delivery was made, then request a partial payment.

## Objection #3: "I'm not paying because I never got what the salesperson told me I'd get."

These customers want something before they will pay you. You need to investigate. If the amount is insignificant, then grant it. It's much cheaper granting a small waiver than referring it to your supervisor or to sales for further review. It amazes me the time and money spent by some organizations, especially in Asia, to investigate and issue small credit waivers. You also lose something even more valuable: customers' goodwill. Instead, wouldn't the resources used investigating small disputes be better spent on collecting high balances accounts, selling more goods, and maintaining better customer service?

Another method of handling this type of objection is to set time limits on when a waiver is issued. If the customer is only now mentioning the dispute, six months after it happened, then it's probably an excuse.

Response to Objection #3: *"I'm sorry to hear about that Mr. / Ms. Customer, can you please tell me what you were supposed to get. I'd like to help you."*

### Tip for Objection #3:

a. If the amount requested is reasonable, don't quibble and waste time with the customer. Just give it, especially if the customer has been a good customer of several years.

b. Convince management of the cost-effectiveness of empowering collections staff with some discretionary credit waiver approval limits.

c. If the customer uses this excuse frequently, they're becoming "credit junkies." If you're dealing with a junkie, you need to "name the game:"

   *"Mr. / Ms. Customer, it seems that every time over the last ___ months we've been issuing credits to solve this problem, but it's not being solved. What's happening?"*

d. If you notice multiple customers complaining about a certain salesperson's promises, then report it to your supervisor or to the sales manager.

## Objection #4: "I'm not paying....+ (hard luck story).

For this objection, you need to determine if it's factual or an excuse. If it's an excuse, "name the game." If it's factual, show you're a human being. Express sorrow for their hard luck. At the same time, remind the customer you're trying to prevent the bill from getting bigger and causing even bigger problems.

Response: *"Mr./Ms. Customer, I'm sorry to hear about (repeat an overview of the hard luck story). Now, I'd like to help prevent (negative action) from happening on your account. Please make a payment of RM____ by (date)."*

**Tip for Objection #4:**

a) If the customer complains that you're heartless. Respond with:

*"Mr. | Ms Customer, I'm sorry you feel that way. I'm just trying to help prevent another problem from occurring. Please pay RM_____ by (date)."*

b) Be prepared to offer payment arrangements for true hard luck stories.

### *Handling Broken Promises*

If you suffer from a high percentage of broken promises, it could be due to setting weak Promises to Pay (PTPs). Some questions to ask yourself :

- Do you take the time to reconfirm your PTPs before ending your calls?
- Do you stress the negative action that will occur if the payment fails to arrive?
- Do you build rapport with the debtor in order to have your bill placed at the top of his or her bill pile?
- Do you call a day or two before the promised payment date?
- Do you use the expression, "Do I have your word on that?", for those customers who frequently break their promises or give weak PTPs?
- Do you confront the debtor when they have broken their promise to you? Or, do you ignore it? After confronting them and hearing their story, do you say, "Why didn't you call me to let me know?" You need to make the act of breaking promises an unpleasant experience. Extinguish it.

- On a positive note, do you give "thank you" call backs or SMSs to those customers who previously have broken promises countless times, but now have FINALLY kept their promise? Do you reward this positive behavior?

The rate of broken promises, from my experience, is higher in Asia than the West. This is due to the concept of "face." In East Asia, rarely do you have a debtor who says they can't pay. Instead, they use non-committal words like "try", "hopefully pay", "see what I can do", "might", "maybe", and "perhaps."

The collectors will use the same words when asking for payment, *"Mr. Customer, maybe you can pay the car loan account?"* When you ask the collector what was the result of the four minute collection call, many times they will say, "I don't know."

It's a challenge getting Asian collectors to set high expectations on their debtors. If the collectors don't have confidence in the debtor's ability to pay, what will the debtor think?

Another challenge is getting the Asian collector to reconfirm the arrangement at the end of the conversation so that both parties are clear what has been agreed. Will there or won't there be a payment? Sometimes, in order to maintain "face", Asian collectors mistakenly believe an unclear arrangement is better than a clear one. I disagree. I believe you can still maintain all parties' "face" while achieving a clear result from your conversation.

## *"Pot-O'-Gold" Stories*

Debtors give collectors all sorts of "Pot O' Gold" stories to delay payment. A "Pot O' Gold" story goes like this :

> *"If you can just give us two more weeks, we expect a big deal to come through that will allow us to pay you off completely."*

After two weeks, they ask for another two weeks. The debtors want you to take the same risk they're taking on the company. By giving so much time, while extending more goods or services, you're setting your firm up for a big default later. In your experience, how often has the "Pot O' Gold" story paid off?

What usually happens is the big deal doesn't materialize. Or, if it does materialize, the reality of it isn't as big as the dream. The customer then makes a partial payment until the next "big deal" comes in. Even if it's their lucky day and the "big deal" finally comes in, they're so over-extended that you still only get a partial payment.

When people try to collect money from friends or relatives, "Pot O' Gold" stories are often used.

**Tip:**

A word of warning with "Pot O' Gold" stories, be firm but show that you care. Debtors want to believe these stories. They're so heavily leveraged that if one of their major creditors doesn't give them more time, they will verbally and financially explode. They're under enormous stress to prevent their business from failing. Many of these customers are business owners. If you don't agree to extend them, they will become irate and demand to speak with senior management. Be ready to support your decision if senior management asks you.

## Listening: The Key to the Treasure Chest

In business, listening skills are the key to success, especially where negotiation is involved. Nobody understands the importance of listening better than collectors. A good listener :

☑ Overcomes objections faster

☑ Avoids upsetting customers

☑ Increases dollars collected

☑ Reduces time per call

☑ Maintains customer goodwill and "face"

Here are some quick tips on listening skills:

- Don't interrupt the customer. Allow them to speak, even if you disagree.

- Admit if you don't understand certain things mentioned by the customer. Ask clarifying questions.

- Listen and "look" for the message behind the words. Sometimes what the customer says and what they mean are two separate issues.

- Take notes. This shows the customer you care rather than constantly asking the customer to repeat things because you didn't take notes.

- Show understanding by repeating what the customer said.

- Don't allow upsetting words to distract you from calming the customer down, solving the concern, and collecting the money.

- Show respect at all times.

## *Diffusing Upset Customers: The A.U.S.E. Technique*

Dealing with upset, irrational, fire-breathing customers isn't fun for most people, but I love them. I enjoy the challenge of changing an upset customer into a rational, bill-paying one. It's almost magical. When people are upset, the last thing they want to do is pay your bill. In fact, they probably never want to do business with your organization ever again. Your job is to convert such customers into rational, cheque-writing, cash paying ones. It takes skill. Imagine if every customer were rational, polite, and nice. Our job would be so boring that any monkey could do it.

Upset customers have two needs:

1. They need to have a problem solved

2. They need to be listened to (this is usually more important)

Collectors are so busy trying to solve problems that they ignore what is sometimes more important, just the simple act of listening.

## *Story:*

Recently, my wife—Choon— complained about a restaurant I chose. She said the food was lousy. She's an accountant and a quite detailed person. Rather than listen to her detailed explanation of each of the food items' negative qualities, I interrupted her and I said, "OK, OK, we'll never eat here again."

Thinking the problem solved, I returned to my dinner. Unfortunately, by failing to address the underlying problem (listening to my wife); I had not truly solved the problem. In fact, the problem grew.

Choon became more upset and advised me that I never listen or ask her opinion whenever we eat out. It took my male brain time to fully understand, but I finally realized there were two problems to her original complaint.

In collections, it's a good idea to avoid arguing with upset debtors. Arguing costs you time, money and customer goodwill. The problem with arguments is they're easy to get into, but hard to get out of. Collectors who easily get "hooked" with upset customers collect less.

On the other hand, I have listened to inexperienced collectors handling belligerent, crying, screaming, profanity-spewing customers. During the customer's tirade the new collectors remain silent. They're shell-shocked. They're caught in the headlights like scared rabbits. They lack control. They don't know what to say, so they say the worst possible thing: they say nothing. The customers then begin yelling even louder,

*"Are you even listening?"* Followed quickly by, *"Get me your supervisor!"*

Whether the collector argues with the customer or says nothing, both techniques cause the customer to remain irrational. This is because the collector didn't practice the first of three steps in calming upset customers: **Acknowledge.**

My approach in turning irrational, upset customers into paying, rational customers is called: A.U.S.E. It stands for:

A:      Acknowledge

U:      Understand

S:      Solve

E:      Empathy

A.U.S.E. is one of THE most powerful tools I have created to help me collect more money. It calms upset customers by establishing rapport, and once that's done, you're already half-way to the money.

This visual diagram makes the concept easier to learn. It reminds me of an eye chart. It has three simple steps and uses a key word: "Sorry."

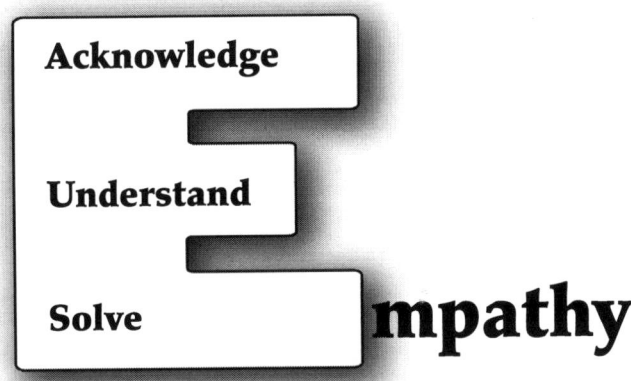

## Step 1: A = Acknowledge

Upset customers want to be acknowledged. They want you to show you're listening while they're shouting. When customers are upset they have a script inside their head that needs to come out. They require you to acknowledge them if you want the money.

Some collectors show acknowledgment by making sounds like, "Uh huh", "Yup", "Mmm." To me, these collectors sound more like farm animals. Instead, use words to sound more professional.

Some examples:

*"Oh my!"*

*"I see."*

*"Is that right?"*

*"I understand."*

*"I can't believe that happened to you."*

*"I would feel the same."*

*"Alamak!"*

*"Yakah."*

At the Acknowledgement stage don't interrupt to ask their account number, name, or to offer a solution. Just let them vent and acknowledge them. Once they're done venting, quickly move to the next step.

## Step 2: U = Understand

After venting the customer will still explode if you don't handle this next stage properly. This is where you show the customer you understood his/her concern. You show understanding by repeating or paraphrasing it from their viewpoint. You may also have to probe to completely understand complicated problems.

*"Mr. / Ms. Customer, let me make see if I understand you, (repeat the concern), correct?"*

After saying this simple statement, you will often hear a sigh of relief. The customer might even say, *"You're the first person there that ever took the time to understand me."* Now, I can smell the money.

There's possibly no other time where a person listens as closely to what you say as when you repeat back what you think they said. Repeating customers' words is a great tool to diffuse their anger and build rapport. And, once rapport is established, you have just increased your chances of getting paid.

By showing understanding, you calm customers. You give them confidence in you since you took the time to understand them. Once you understand the "real" problem, you can offer an appropriate and permanent solution.

Acknowledging and understanding a customer's complaint are a great "one, two" combination that sets you up for the next step. If you

140

take the time to do these two steps, many customers will apologize for their outbursts. Acknowledging and understanding the problem are the most difficult parts of A.U.S.E. Once the problems have been properly defined, finding a solution is relatively easy.

The solution is the third step...

## Step 3: S = Solve

Assure the customer that you will solve their problem. Show them that you will own the problem. The reason the customer is upset could be due to other people in your organization letting his / her problem go unresolved. Unresolved problems fester. The Solution stage works best when collectors are empowered to make hard and fast solutions. A phrase that I use at this stage is *"I guarantee..."*

Now, what do you do after solving their concern?

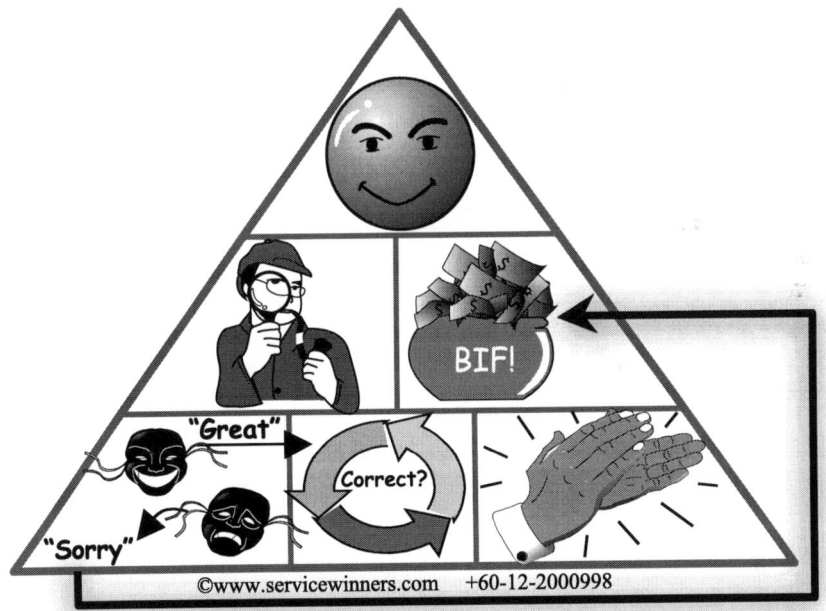

You ask for the Balance in Full (BIF)! Return to the Collection Pyramid.

What do you do if a customer has another problem?
You restart the A.U.S.E. model.

1. Acknowledge what the customer says.

2. Understand the concern.

3. Solve it.

Now, let's look at "E".

## E = Empathy

The A.U.S.E. model fails without Empathy. Empathy is the oil in this dispute resolution engine. It shows you care, hence, your tone is vital if you want to sound credible. My favorite word to show empathy is "**sorry**." Don't overuse it, but you need to use it at least once when diffusing angry customers. If you don't use it, you sound uncaring and it will lead to a supervisor's call. And guess what one word your customer will require your supervisor to say over and over? Upset customers demand their "sorrys" and if you don't give them, your supervisor must.

Usually the best time to say "sorry" is at the acknowledgment stage. Using "sorry" early throws water on the fire before it gets out of control.

### A.U.S.E. Tips:

- Don't jump to the solution stage. Human beings need to be recognized and listened to. They want you to acknowledge and understand what they have gone through before they want a solution. Collectors who jump straight to the solution stage sound like cold-hearted robots.

- Don't skip the solution stage. I have heard collectors acknowledge the problem, even show understanding and empathy, then ask, "So, when will you be making the payment?" The customers explode in anger. By skipping the solution stage, it makes the collector sound like a "money-face" and customers don't pay "money-faces."

- You can't solve all problems, especially if the customer is having personal problems. However, sometimes just the act of listening solves part of the problem and that will be enough for some customers to pay.

## Words to Use and Avoid

We have looked at how to handle customers' excuses and objections. We have also looked at diffusing upset customers using A.U.S. E. Now, let's look at some key words to use and avoid in dealing with customers.

## "You" and "Your"

Use "you" and "your" to build rapport and ownership in your debtors. E.g. "*Mr. / Ms. Customer, thank **you** for paying **your** bill.*"

E.g. *"Mr. / Ms. Customer, the third party isn't paying your bill. You'll need to make a payment today to prevent your account from being written-off."*

## *"Will" vs "Can"*

"Will" is stronger than "Can".

*"Mr. / Ms. Customer, I'm calling today to confirm the payment of RM____ will be paid today at our office."*

"Can" alerts customers you are willing to settle for less, at a later time. "Can" alerts customers of options. After using "can", customers react with, "Can I pay less?" Or, "Can I pay next week instead of today?"

By using "can", you are telling customers that you lack control. In fact, you are passing control to the customer. Instead of encouraging positive payment behavior, you are encouraging negative behavior.

## *"Today" or "Tomorrow" vs "Now", "ASAP", "Soon"*

"Today" and "tomorrow" are definite. Other words like "ASAP" and "Now" mean different things based on your personality and culture. In Asia, "now" has a completely different meaning than that in the West.

When you don't ask for payment today, you're telling the debtor you will accept it later. Why wait? The longer you wait the more risk you're incurring. A lot of unexpected events will befall debtors between "today" and "soon" such as: heart attacks, bankruptcies, divorces, lay offs, suicides, broken hearts, drugs, Friday nights, arrests, robberies and countless other circumstances.

## *"We / Our" vs "WE / OUR"*

Use lowercase "We / Our" to show the debtor that together we will work to get this bill current. It builds rapport. *"We agreed that you will pay RM____ and I would stop the legal action."*

Uppercase "WE / OUR" is impersonal.

*"Mr. / Ms. Customer, **OUR** terms are 30 days, your account is now 90 days, **WE**'ll commence legal action if **OUR** terms aren't followed. **WE** require you to pay RM_____ today to prevent this legal action."*

When collectors talk in uppercase, they show they don't care. As a result, the debtors don't care either. "WE / OUR" usage triggers arguments. It's easy to get into a nasty argument with a monolithic organization and its loyal robot. It's easy to withhold payment from such types. However, it's tough to argue with professionals who are trying to help and who use lowercase "we / our."

My Alaskan friend, Charlie Klever, broke me of my "WE / OUR" habit by saying each time he heard me use those words:

"Who's 'WE'? Do you have a mouse in your pocket?"

## Concern vs Problem

For early stage delinquent accounts, I try to use the word "concern" instead of "problem." "Problem" has a negative connotation and people find "concerns" easier to solve.

However, for late stage accounts, I use the word "problem" to stress the seriousness of their non-payment. This may be the last collection call I make on the account, and I want the customer to understand the ramifications of their non-payment.

## Names vs. No Names

At birth, we entered the world wet, cold and naked. We owned nothing to our name except our name. After the gift of life, it's the second gift we received. We value our names. How do you like it when people mispronounce your name? Names are a great tool in calming customers down. Using names builds rapport and the more rapport we build, the greater the chance we have of getting paid. Make sure the customer also knows your name. Avoid using generic titles like "Sir" or "Madame" as they build formality instead of rapport.

## More Words to Use:

☑ *"Sorry."*
This is a great under-utilized word that I wish was used more often. The Elton John song: *Sorry Seems to Be the Hardest Word* is especially true in Asia.

☑ *"Do I have your word on that?"*
This phrase works well on weak PTP's or customers who continually break their promises. I have yet to meet a customer, honest or dishonest, who deep down didn't consider himself or herself an honest person.

☑ *"I appreciate you sharing that with me, however......."*
Use this phrase when customers tell you the truth, even if it's to tell you they have no intention of paying. Telling the truth is a positive behavior that needs to be reinforced.

☑ *"Great", "Fantastic", "Thank you", "Super."*
EVERY time you receive a Promise to Pay (PTP), give positive reinforcement, even if the PTP or payment is insufficient. In such cases, you say:

- *"Great, however........"*
- *"Thank you, however......"*
- *"I appreciate that you want to pay the bill, however......"*

## Yale's Words

A Yale University study[18] discovered the 12 most persuasive words in the English language. Perhaps, some of these words will help in your negotiations? They're ranked here by importance (power).

| | | | |
|---|---|---|---|
| 1) You | 2) Money | 3) Save | 4) New |
| 5) Results | 6) Easy | 7) Health | 8) Safety |
| 9) Love | 10) Discovery | 11) Proven | 12) Guarantee |

Imagine a customer has offered us a partial payment of RM400, but we would like to use some of the "Yale Words" to persuade him to pay the total balance of RM600.

Customer: *I'll pay you RM400 today. That's the best I can do.*

Collector : *Mr / Ms. Customer, thank you for the payment. However, for only an additional RM200, I guarantee you'll save money in additional late charges. It's easy, all you need to do is give me your credit card number and your account will return to a healthy, current status.*

Do you talk like this? Should't you? Using the "Yale Words" makes us sound like sales people, which in fact, we are. Get creative and use some of these powerful words on your debtors. Sell the benefits of paying.

## More Words to Avoid:

☑ *"As I told you."*
Nobody likes to be told. It also implies that the customer wasn't listening. Get ready for an upset customer if you use this phrase.

☑ *"Henceforth", "as per", "remit", "forthwith", "duly", "aforementioned", "furthermore."*
It seems only lawyers and bill collectors still use these words. Lose them. We're trying to build rapport and increase communication. Avoid sounding like a law book or a time traveler from the 19th century.

---

18  Yale University, "Life Notes" , October 1983, referred by <http://www.dallas.net/~scotpeck/saleswebpage/twelve.htm> (6 June 2003), National Association of Underwriters.

☑ *"Maybe", "hopefully", "try", "cuba", "boleh", "if you can", "is it possible?".*
All these words express doubts. If you doubt the customer will pay, so will s/he. Instead, set higher expectations for both your debtor and yourself.

## Know Your Hot Button(s)

We have been discussing techniques to keep customers in a rational mindset solve their concerns and collect their money. But what about keeping our cool? Our primary role as collectors is to help people, and by helping people we build rapport. And by building rapport we increase our chances of getting paid. Establishing rapport requires that we build bridges with our customers. However, some collectors take more joy in burning bridges than building them. I have heard collectors say, after an especially heated bridge burn-down argument, "Well, I really taught that guy a lesson."

The collectors gloat and think they have won the argument. When I see gloating over this type of "victory", I ask, "Did you get the payment?"

Never have I heard them say, "Yes."

To reduce the risk of losing your cool, it's important to know your own "hot buttons." Collectors are hired to help customers get their accounts current, not to lecture or wrestle with them.

What are you hot buttons?

Your hot button is something that gets you upset. As collectors, we get called a lot of nasty names. It's part of the job. In most cases, customers say these statements out of frustration and we take no offense, but once in a while we become susceptible to a derogatory statement. The secret is in knowing our own hot buttons.

Your hot buttons are for you to examine deep inside yourself. In general terms, I have found two hot buttons for collectors, and the buttons depend on your gender. Men's hot button flashes when customers question their intelligence by using words like, "stupid", "idiot" and many others. Women's hot button flashes when customers use profanity, especially the "B" word. You know, "b i _ _ _" (I'm not even going to write if for fear of upsetting someone).

Although the buttons are different, the reactions are similar. Faces turn red and an oral slugfest begins. It gets nasty. The call ends when the phone is slammed down. The collector swivels the chair and begins to share the stressful encounter with prying colleagues. In the process, time is lost as now a team of people is engrossed in hearing a long story. After the story is finished, the storyteller is relieved of the stress because now the stress has been passed to ten other people. The ten stressed-out colleagues then start making stressed-out calls and pass their stress to customers. The cycle continues.

Know your hot button(s). If a customer continually pushes it, and you think you're going to lose your cool, then "name the game." Just say: *"Mr. / Ms. Customer, I'm trying to help you, but if you continue using such language, I won't be able to help you."*

## Tip:

Some customers are experts in fishing for your hot button. They might do this by asking you personal questions, especially when they want to take control of the conversation. Don't reveal personal details about yourself. Once debtors know a bit about you, they will use it against you. They will start casting out potential hot buttons like accusing you of being:

- A lousy collector, wife, husband, parent
- Ugly / stupid
- Uneducated
- A bad person
- Low class
- Lazy
- Unethical
- Plus many others

Don't take the bait. Be a fisherman, not a fish.

By understanding your hot buttons, you will be a more effective collector. As human beings, we all have hot buttons. We need the courage to examine them deep within ourselves.

I have swallowed my pride many times with customers. I try to let customers win every silly argument they want to win if it means I have a better chance of getting paid. I prefer collecting payments than winning silly arguments.

Constantly arguing with customers gets people fired. If your supervisor gets too many customer complaints about you, there could be a cost / benefit analysis done to see the value you add to the department. Supervisory calls and letters take time from busy peoples' lives. You're paid to help customers and collect money, not to argue and "teach" people lessons in life.

## *Summary*

- Overdue debtors are priceless. We need them more than they need us.

- By understanding the real reason a debtor can't pay, you increase your chances of finding a solution and getting a solid Promise to Pay (PTP). The key word to use is "why?"

- Have your responses to customers' excuses handy.

- Use A.U.S.E.: Acknowledge, Understand, Solve, Empathy. It calms upset customers, collects more money, and generates less supervisor calls.

- Key words to use with customers: "Will", "Today", "Tomorrow", "We", "Our", "Concern", "Sorry", "Do I have your word on that?", "Great," "Fantastic", "Super", "Thank you."

- Key words to avoid with customers: "Can", "Now", "ASAP", "Soon", "WE", "OUR", "Problem", "As I told you....", "Henceforth", "Remit", "Duly" (and other such legalese words).

- Focus on staying calm and helping your customers pay their bills. Don't focus on teaching customers' lessons and winning silly arguments.

# Don't Be a Slow Poke

# 10

*The Importance of Speed*

---

*There are no speed limits on the road to excellence.* – David W. Johnson

## After reading this chapter, you will be able to:

- Understand how to become a "Super Collector"
- Read and write basic "Collectionese"
- Learn the masters' short-cuts
- Recognize the importance of good administration support

## *Are You a "Super Collector"?*

How do you describe a "Super Collector"?

☑ Faster than an auto-dialer

☑ More powerful than the sales department

☑ Able to leap tall payment excuses in a single response

Super Collectors are the people who consistently blast through their department's collection targets while working as a respected team player. Super Collectors take angry customers, calm them down, collect the money, leave them with a positive experience, and then quickly move to the next account. Speed is a crucial component in their success.

Our job is to help as many customers as possible and in the process collect as much money as possible. Many collectors are "good." They have the skills, the attitude, and the brains to do the job, but they lack speed. They're good collectors, just not *Super Collectors*.

My father is a good tennis player. He studies the game constantly. He has played it his whole life, but if you placed him on center court against the world's top players, he would lose. This is because he lacks world-class speed (though for someone in his seventies, he's fast).

The collections environment is fast and competitive. We make outbound calls in between handling inbound ones. At the same time, we handle administrative work to clean up legitimate billing disputes or sales errors, we send emails. Our goal is to end the month with more wins than losses.

Our debtors are tough. Some are professional debtors with countless other creditors calling them. If those other creditors are as professional and as helpful as you, then you face some pretty strong competition for the debtors' limited funds. The only difference between you and the other professional collectors is who gets to the debtor – and his/her money - first.

If there's a recipe to becoming a Super Collector, it's this: C.A.S.H. + Speed. From Chapter 5, we learnt that C.A.S.H. stands for: Control, Attitude, Skills, and Human Touch.

This chapter concerns itself with speed. It will provide you with tips to increase your speed to contact more customers each day and, subsequently, collect more money.

## Can You Type?

In secondary school we took classes in geometry, algebra, biology, history, English grammar, chemistry, and other subjects. How often do we use any of that knowledge?

Me, too.

Of all my secondary high school courses, the two courses which I use nearly everyday to function in society are: Singles' Survival and Typing.

Singles' Survival was just Home Economics with a fancy title to attract boys. The class taught me how to cook. It also exposed me to girls. My typing class also taught me a skill I use daily, and it exposed me to even more girls. Without those two courses and the multiple skills they taught me, I would have become a different man.

Can you type? I mean really type. The "hunt and peck" method doesn't count. Can you type without looking at the keyboard? No?, then you're not a *Super Collector*. While you're looking at the keyboard searching for keys, *Super Collectors'* eyes' are on the screen. They're searching the system to read the account's notes, look for related accounts, and search for any other data to pull a Promise to Pay (PTP) out of a reluctant customer.

Fighter planes are designed to minimize the time the pilots need to keep their eyes in the cockpit. To be a *Super Collector,* you need to get your head out of the keyboard and into the screen.

Typing is easy to learn. It's just memorizing less than 30 keystrokes and matching them to your fingers. It takes repetition, but if you devote yourself to the task, you will master it fairly quickly. It will take you a week or two to learn, but you will enjoy a lifetime of increased productivity.

If today you type 20 words per minute by the two-finger, "hunt and peck" method, imagine your new speed if you added eight more fingers.

I recommend managers award any staff who is currently typing less than 45 words-per-minute with a one-time bonus if they boost their typing speed to 45 wpm or above. Some companies pay their employees if they quit smoking. Let's pay people to type faster.

Before hiring new recruits, give them a typing test. Make it part of the interview process. Use typing software for administering the tests, or just give the applicants a paragraph to type in Microsoft Word. Sit them at a PC and ask them to type for two minutes. Then go to the MS Word menu bar and select "Tools ", then "Word Count." Incredibly easy. Don't worry about misspelling as long as you still understand the message.

If your collection team is filled with slow typers, it WILL affect your department's productivity. Reducing bad debts and DSO is done by constantly tweaking your systems and processes. Ensuring the people in your department type quickly is one such tweak. How much longer can you carry your slow typers?

You're probably thinking, "You gotta be kidding. I don't have time to learn to type.

I ask you. Does two-finger typing save you so much time? Two-finger typing is preventing you from becoming a *Super Collector*. I don't care what your stats show. If you type faster, you will wrap up more accounts, allowing you to make more calls and surpass your current stats.

Keep your fingers sharp. Learn proper typing. Then take a cooking class.

## Typing Programs

CNET.com's download section has many kinds of typing software available for download for under USD25 (a few are free). Like learning any new skill, at first, you will work slower, but give yourself time to get accustomed to the proper way of typing and your speed will quickly increase.

If you want to spend USD30 to learn typing while having fun doing it, check out Sega's game "Typing of the Dead." You will find it on the Internet. Gamers need to type certain letters and words in order to kill zombies. It's a bit violent and young children shouldn't watch your learning sessions, but the zombies have probably taught more males how to type than thousands of secondary school typing teachers have over the years.

If the "Hunt and Peckers" still refuse to learn this skill, then there's "Voiced Keyboard" software that is readily available over the Internet. It allows you to hear the spoken word while you type. Perhaps it will save you time from constantly looking up at your screen to check if you have typed the words correctly. It costs less than USD20.

## *Can You Read and Write Collectionese?*

My Malaysian wife speaks Cantonese (among a few other Chinese dialects). I'm envious of her language ability, but I console myself with the fact that I read and write Collectionese. If your team reads and writes Collectionese, it will save time.

Standardize the Collectionese used in your department to avoid multiple dialects. Here are some examples:

| | | |
|---|---|---|
| **PTP** | = | Promise To Pay |
| **LMTC** | = | Left Message To Call |
| **S/W** | = | Spoke With |
| **Cust** | = | Customer |
| **NA** | = | No Answer |
| **Disco** | = | Disconnected line |
| **CBR** | = | Can Be Reached number of the customer |
| **VM** | = | Voice Mail |
| **Disp** | = | Dispute |
| **CTO** | = | Call To Office |
| **I/C** | = | Inbound Call |
| **O/C** | = | Outbound Call |
| **TT** | = | Talked To |
| **Re** | = | Regarding |
| **Serv** | = | Service |
| **L-T** | = | Long-Time or long term |

Translate the following:

"O/C. Cust ptp $300 2-day via cheque. Also, had disp re poor serv. Wants $40 cr. Advzd will giv as L-T cust. Csteve."[19]

I recommend all notes be signed by the person who wrote them. Many software systems leave the user's ID details at the end of the remark. But who is BCG00045? In addition to the name, there should be a letter representing the department. Csteve would be Steve in Collections, Sbernice would be Bernice in Sales.

---

19   Translation: "Outbound call. Customer promised to pay $300 today by cheque. He also had a dispute regarding poor service. He wants a $40 credit. I advised him I'll give it to him as he's a long-term customer. Steve in the collections department."

**Tip:**
By having proper signature sign offs, you save time resolving who said what to the customer.

## *Do You Know the Masters' Short-cuts?*

In the Olympics 100 meter race, the difference between first-place and second-place finishers is slight. The same holds true for *Super Collectors* and average collectors. Super Collectors work smart and hard. They know what to do, legally and honestly, to squeeze out a few extra PTPs in the work day.

To new collectors, Super Collectors seem like magicians or even "masters." Each month they leave the average performers scratching their heads and wondering, "How did she do it again?" The Super Collectors seem to be able to do more in the normal workday than the rest.

Here are some secrets revealed to increase your speed and become a "Super Collector."

## *1. Minimize (or eliminate) Account Review Time*

If you're primarily collecting early stage, consumer accounts, you're wasting time doing in-depth pre-call reviews. I know this goes against what most collection books and trainers tell you. I may burn in collector hell, but I advise collectors against spending time reviewing accounts.

**Tip:**
Reduce review time by reviewing while the phone is ringing and while you're delivering your opening script.

According to research done by ACA International, the average collector makes 20 call attempts an hour, reaches six debtors and gets two PTPs.[20] Why waste time reviewing account details when you're lucky to only reach six customers an hour?

In my experience, 50% of a collector's time is spent tracking customers' or leaving messages. Think about it. How many times have you

20 *"2002 Compensation & Collection Agency Operations Study"*, <http://www.collector.com/?cid=5431>, ( 12 May 2005), ACA International.

taken the time to review an account, prepare what you're going to say, take a deep breathe, manually dial the number, then get a no answer, disconnected number or voice mail? What a waste of time!

Instead, sort your accounts according to customer group, amount, aging or risk. If the accounts are sorted properly, the collectors will already know what to say to the batch of debtors with those characteristics. Avoid giving collectors a mixture of customer groups as it slows them down. Once they're done with one group of customers, give them a different group.

## 2. Work Hard: Secret to Success

Often, poorly performing collectors are unsuccessful because of poor focus. Instead of focusing on the accounts with the highest balance and the highest probability of payment, they focus on other things. The focus could be friends, personal calls, winning arguments with customers, day-dreaming, avoiding asking for Balance in Full, calling in sick on Mondays, or wasting time complaining about work.

Super Collectors appear different from the rest, but they aren't. They just work harder, every day. They are, in a word, professionals. Woody Allen said, "80% of success in life is showing up", but I want to increase success by adding two more components:

| | |
|---|---|
| Showing Up | 80% |
| On Time | 10% |
| Prepared | 10% |
| | 100% |

Now let's boost it to Super Collector success rates by adding the final component:

| | |
|---|---|
| Daily | 10% |
| Grand Total = | **110%** |

## The Secret to Success

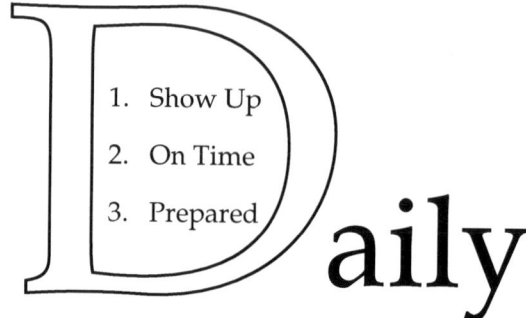

1. Show Up
2. On Time
3. Prepared

Daily

### 3. Finish Your Paperwork

Set aside time each day to resolve those disputes that you promised your customers you would solve. Resolving disputes gives you and your organization credibility in the customers' eyes. It also helps ensure the customer doesn't leave your organization for a competitor. Finally, it makes for a more pleasant work environment when team members work their accounts thoroughly.

> **Tip:**
> The best time to do administration work is when the "fish aren't biting." Late in the afternoon is usually better than doing admin work during the prime morning calling hours when it's easier to reach customers.

### 4. Do What You Do Best

You are paid to do what you do best, and I hope that is to help customers stay current and avoid negative actions. Unfortunately, some collectors lose sight of that fact and try to help in areas they are unqualified to help. And the assistance they do give is lousy. Let's admit it; we're novices in product knowledge or technical fault assistance. We're unqualified to give any other type of assistance than bill payment information. If we do, then we're no better than "quacks."

#### Story: Helping Too Much

When my brother was seven years old, my parents gave him a baby alligator. He was so excited. Mom wanted to first wash the aquarium that had been gathering dust for years, but Joe had to help her now. Mom reluctantly agreed. She passed the aquarium from her hands to his. The aquarium had a thick layer of sand at the bottom. "Joe", she said, "be careful, it's heavy."

The next sound I heard was "splat". Joe had accidentally dropped the aquarium on his new alligator's head. He had helped too much.

Stay focused. Do what you do best and you will help more customers while collecting more money.

### 5. Minimize "Hand-holding"

As a collector, I often felt that many customers used me more as an alarm clock than anything else. I would simply remind them to do something that they knew they needed to do. I enabled them to shift the responsibility of paying their bills on time from them to me.

Our ultimate goal is for debtors to embrace a new payment behavior that includes taking responsibility for paying their own accounts on time each month, without being told.

Hand-holding examples are :

- Calling back "busy" customers an hour later when they say they can't discuss the payment now, then when you call them back they're busy again.

- Following up on ALL promises to pay the day before the expected payment date. For some customers this might be the first time their account has been overdue, and they will likely take offense to your checking up on them.

- Resending or faxing bills each month to the same customers.

These examples seem minor, but they will consume large amounts of your time.

> **Tip:**
>
> Following up on lengthy payment arrangements takes time. It's "hand-holding." If debtors require lengthy payment arrangements, then require post-dated cheques. It shows if the debtor is serious about the payment plan. If not, you could be wasting your valuable time.

## 6. Speak Slowly and Clearly at the Opening

Collectors are under time pressures, and many of them talk like machine guns. Their tongues throw out all kinds of words, names, companies, balances, and dates at unsuspecting debtors in the first few seconds of the phone call. The debtors then throw back all kinds of questions trying to understand who's speaking and what's this call is all about. It's all takes time.

Instead, allow the debtor to catch his/her "mental breath" before speaking so quickly. Start your collection calls slow, then speed up. This reduces the time you spend having to repeat yourself.

> **Tip:**
>
> Speak slowly and clearly when leaving messages on voicemail systems or answering machines. It's senseless speaking so fast that your message confuses the customer. They won't return such calls.

If you didn't care about the message, they won't care to return it. Instead, leave a quality message and enjoy higher call back success.

**Tip:**
Use scripts. They make you sound more professional and confident while saving you time.

### Akrish's Tips

Here are three additional speed tips from Steve Akrish with Verizon Wireless. These tips have helped me squeeze out a few extra Promises to Pay (PTPs) each day.

## 1. Change "Left Message to Call" to "Promise to Pay"

Next time you call a customer (individual or company), and the person tells you the customer is away, don't leave a message. Instead, ask, "I'm sorry, who are you?" If that person is the spouse or a fellow accounts payable representative at the company, then say,

> "Maybe you can help me? Could you ensure (payer's name) sends out a payment of $_____ today if s/he hasn't already done so?"

If the person says, "OK," then you have just created a PTP and saved yourself and the customer call back time.

**Tip:**
For consumer accounts, be extremely careful about revealing information to third parties. In some countries such action is illegal. It's best to check with your legal team before using this time-saving technique.

## 2. Change "Can you hold?" into "Promises to Pay" (PTP)

The next time you ask a fairly good customer for payment and they say, "Can you hold while I go check?", try saying:

> *"That's OK, (payer's name), you've been a good customer for some time now. I'll note the account that a payment of \$_____ has been sent. If for some reason it hasn't been sent, can you ensure it's paid today?"*

I recommend this technique vs. saying, *"OK, I can hold"*, and then end up hearing a medley of disco hits from the 1970's.

## 3. Add More "Promises to Pay" (PTP)

This is for collectors who don't have an automated collection system, or if they do, it lacks related account details. Next time, after receiving a PTP try asking:

> *"Mr. / Ms. (customer), for your convenience are there any other accounts you have that I can help you with?"*

Be careful if you have an account ownership system in place. You don't want to take PTPs from another collector. At the same time, it doesn't make sense having multiple collectors calling the same debtor.

## 4. Corporate Collection's Speed Tips

To be a speedy corporate collector, you have different challenges. Here are some tips to save you time and increase "dollars collected."

Get the Person-In-Charge's (PIC's) contact name and number. Valuable time is wasted hunting for the right A/P contact in large companies. Ensure your credit application forms detail the A/P contact's name, direct number, and where to send the bills.

Buy a write-fax system where you can fax, or better yet, email bills to you're a/ contact as you speak.

Include monthly or quarterly "Statements of Account" to keep you A/P contact up-to-date on all open and closed invoices.

Be empowered to contra-off credits and debits with your corporate client. Ask you A/P client to kindly advise how to post any money they send you.

Make regular site visits to your largest accounts. This will increase your knowledge of their payable process. You also build relationships that ensure your bills get paid first.

## Unsung Heroes: Administration Support

It's impossible to end a chapter about speed without discussing the importance of the back-office people. These people are especially important in high volume work environments.

The admin people help the collectors spend more time on the phone collecting and less time off the phone doing admin work. Collectors solve relatively easy disputes quickly, but the more complicated disputes need to be handed off to a collection support team. Having a small, cheerful, competent admin team greatly improves a department's efficiency

Admin support teams often go unnoticed. They rarely participate in bonus schemes. Regularly recognize their contribution because without them, you wouldn't be hitting your goals.

Recognition doesn't need to be in monetary terms. Lunches, cards, certificates of achievement, a day off, flowers, movie tickets and many other relatively low cost rewards make a big impact. Make it visual. Announce it to the department. Have the admin team receive their prizes during your departmental meetings. People work for money, but they stay for recognition.

## Summary

- The formula for becoming a Super Collector is: C.A.S.H. + Speed.

- Speed is an integral part of collections. It weaves itself throughout the whole collection process.

- Slow typing will affect you and your team's overall success.

- Ensure you and your colleagues know how to read and write standard Collectionese.

- Some more ideas to collect faster:

  1. Minimize or eliminate review time

  2. Work hard (versus "hardly work")

  3. Complete your paperwork promptly

  4. Spend your time doing what you do best: helping customers get current to avoid future negative actions

  5. Reduce "hand-holding" customers' accounts

6. Speak slowly and clearly at the opening of the collection call

7. Change "Left Messages to Call" to "Promises to Pay"

8. Change "Can You Hold?"s to "Promises to Pay"

9. Add more "Promises to Pay" by looking
   for related accounts

# Getting to ¥€$:

*Negotiation Techniques*

---

*Business is the art of extracting money from another man's pocket without resorting to violence.* – Max Amsterdam

**After reading this chapter, you will be able to:**

- Understand the four basic steps in the negotiation process
- Gain tips on negotiating with customers
- Recognize the value of accepting most settlements

## Negotiating is a Part of Life

We negotiate every day; whether we eat dinner at home or at a restaurant; whether we watch a romance or a comedy; whether we take a vacation to the mountains or the sea, whether we ask our boss for a raise or more annual leave. In most cases, we evaluate the advantages and disadvantages of each choice and then make a joint decision. All parties share their reservations and feelings during the negotiation.

To make the best decision possible, we understand it's better to make our agreements jointly. It's no fun going on holiday if only one person enjoys it. Respect is given to all. Give and take is practiced throughout. The best outcome is one where both parties feel as if they have "won." When people believe they have "won"; there's a greater chance the deal will be adhered. On the other hand, no one likes owning a lousy deal.

Negotiating with customers is different in collections and in customer service. Customer service people like to exceed a customer's needs and fill a want. Whereas, collection people try to change debtors' wants into needs. A debtor may want to pay RM100 per month on a RM100,000 loan, but s/he will need to pay RM1,000 per month to stop litigation. In negotiating we need to be creative in selling the benefits of paying.

## *Negotiation Steps*

Negotiation experts make negotiating overly complicated. They provide lists of 8, 10, 12 or more negotiation steps. They take all the fun out of it. Instead, let's shorten the process to four stages:
Preparation, Opening, Bargaining, Closing

### 1.0:   Preparation

This is the stage where we need to know what we want. And I hope your position is Balance In Full (BIF) today! Although BIF today is our opening position, we are realistic to know that we might have to settle for less. We also need to know our minimum required payment. Once we have our floor and ceiling positions, we know our range.

Besides understanding what you want, study what you suspect the customer will want. Look at the account's history. Get an idea about the customer which will help you later during the negotiation phase. If possible, talk to people who know the customer. In negotiations, the party who normally wins more is the party who's better prepared.

Finally, decide beforehand what you will do if you cannot come to an agreement with the other party. Knowing your worse case outcome is important to determine if your initial negotiation goal is realistic.

### 2.0:   Opening

This stage consists of two parts:

1. Establishing rapport

2. Probing

### Establishing rapport

Negotiations usually start with introductions commonly called the "meets and greets." It can be a one sentence identification statement, or it can be face to face chit chat. With debtors, I'm careful to appear overly friendly since friends usually get paid last. Instead, I portray myself as a collection professional. When I'm visiting seriously delinquent customers, if I'm offered food or drink, I politely decline- it sets the tone that I'm here on a serious matter.[21]

---

21  In Asia, this behavior could be construed as rude. Asians expect small talk and exchanging pleasantries before negotiations start. If you are negotiating with an overdue customer, my advice is to reduce the amount of time spent at this stage that would normally be spent if the customer wasn't overdue. This subtle sign shows that you are still polite, but at the same time serious about the account's overdue status.

Although I'm not overly friendly, I'm also not a cold, heartless, money robot. People do business with people they like. They also pay people they like. I want to appear as an interested party, willing to listen, and willing to help as long as the outcome is fair to both parties.

More deals fall apart due to people problems than any other. I have seen customers and collectors who throw away perfectly fair arrangements just to spite the other party. My wife and I do it all the time. People sometimes prefer to lose so that the other party also loses than for both to win. Don't let this happen in your negotiations. Instead, establish polite rapport at the onset. Without rapport established, you are unable to probe.

| Rapport-building words | | Rapport-breaking words | Comments |
|---|---|---|---|
| Names | | Sir/Madam/ Encik/Cik | We all love to hear our names. Use them. It's hard for customers to be angry at collectors when names are used. You will come across as a person and not as a company robot. |
| We / Our | | WE / OUR | Lowercase "We / Our" builds rapport. Uppercase does not. E.g. "According to OUR policy, WE reserve the right to....." |

| More rapport-building words | | Comments |
|---|---|---|
| Thank you | | How often do collectors say this after getting a PTP or a payment? Do collectors ever call back customers after the account is fully paid to say thank you? Should they? |
| Help | | Wonderful word that helps diffuse arguments and collect money. It's hard to argue with someone trying to help you. |
| Sorry | | If you can't say "sorry" with an empathetic tone, then stay away from this word. An alternative is "I understand". |

| Appreciate | | Nice word to use when a customer is honest with you, even if you don't like to hear what s/he has to say, "I appreciate your honesty, however, ...." |
|---|---|---|
| Great/Fantastic/ Super/Bagus/ Thank you/ Shiok/etc. | | Use a positive word after getting a payment or a PTP. I use this even if a customer gives me a PTP for RM1, except my tone doesn't sound "great." E.g. "Great, Mr. / Ms. Customer, however, that amount won't stop your account from being sent for legal action..." |

| More rapport-breaking words | | Comments |
|---|---|---|
| No | | Nobody likes to hear the word "no". It's a show-stopper. |
| Legalese | | Nobody likes lawyers, so why sound like one? |
| I don't know | | Nobody likes talking to someone who doesn't know anything. Such people just waste other peoples' time. |

## Probing

In negotiations, it's more important listening than answering. Probing with open-ended questions is a great way to discover a debtor's needs and problems. The question, "Why?" is especially useful. Usually collectors are too busy asking "when?" and "how much?", and they miss the most important question in their haste to collect.

Adults generally don't like being taught. Their opinions and minds have already been decided. However, by listening more than talking, you stand a better chance of changing their initial position and paying you a little bit more. Negotiating bills isn't about controlling the conversation, it's about controlling the outcome and that outcome is to get paid.

The more we listen, the more information we gather and the greater chances of winning more. "Knowledge is power."

Some good, open-ended probing questions include:

- "Why is your account overdue?"

- "What do you suggest to return your account to current status again?"

- "I notice you usually pay at the end of each month, however, the account is five months overdue. How did we get into this payment pattern? How do you propose getting out of it?"

- "How would getting your account back to current status help you?"

Withhold judgment on their responses to avoid acting like a judge. The debtor may be overdue because s/he spent the money on a vacation, and you are probably thinking, "A vacation! Are you serious! Isn't this bill more important?" BUT never verbalize it, unless you want to see your chances of getting paid reduce to nil. Instead, appreciate them for their honesty.

## 3.0: Bargaining

This stage is where you state your initial negotiation position: BIF today. Start high and work down. At this stage you will give and receive concessions.

Rule #1 in bargaining: **Never give without getting.** For example, if the customer wants more time, ask for more money. If they want extended payment arrangements, ask for post-dated cheques.

Let's assume the customer owes RM700 in the following aging buckets:

| | |
|---|---|
| Current | RM250 |
| 31-60 days | RM150 |
| 61-90 days | RM100 |
| 91 days + | RM200 |
| Total | RM700 |

Your opening position is RM700 today, so act surprised and disappointed if the customer can't make full payment. Politely ask, "Why?" As creditors, we have the right to know why we're not getting our money. If you suspect the debtor's response, dig and pry further to get to the real reason.

The more we understand about our debtors' financial condition, the better chance we have of helping them (and us). We also learn what they fear most from defaulting – like a negative credit rating- and we can use that tool to induce payment. By understanding the "why", you strengthen your negotiating position and make it easier to offer valuable solutions.

Now, how do you respond to a customer who asks, "What's the minimum I can pay?"

What I often hear, to my disbelief, is "RM200." I call such collectors "bottom-feeders." They collect the easiest and lowest amount. They also end up near the bottom in most collection rankings because they fold their poker hand too easily.

Bottom-feeders avoid tough situations. The next time a customer asks, "What's the minimum I can pay?" ask for BIF, if that doesn't work ask for RM450. If s/he still can't pay after I have offered two amounts, then I "tai chi". Now it's their turn to propose an amount. I say, "Mr / Ms. Customer, what's the maximum you will be able to pay?"

I hate the word "minimum."

## 4.0: Closing

At this stage we are ready to summarize and document the **agreement**. Our end goal in every customer negotiation should be to get an agreement. Even if the agreement is to talk again in a few days. Not all our actions will result in PTPs or payments, but most should end in some kind of agreement.

A word of warning on closing, don't go here until ALL issues are settled earlier. You want to avoid the customer nibbling on your "final" agreement. How often have we had difficult negotiations that we finally conclude with what we thought was an agreement only to have the debtor take a little "nibble" that's we later discover was a huge bite?

Let's say you have just negotiated an agreement with the debtor to pay RM500 every 15th of the month, then as he sits with his pen in hand over the promissory note he says, "Mr/Ms. Collector, this month I'm a bit tight. I won't be a problem if I pay on the 30th, right?"

If the nibble is more like a bite, you can counter with some responses:

- "That will need approval from higher authority." (You will find that some debtors will say, "never mind.")

- "Would you like to restart our negotiations over this agreement?"

### *Putting the Steps Into Practice*

Let's look at a possible collections call regarding overdue telephone bills. For this scenario we will use the earlier aging schedule totaling RM700.

#### (OPENING + BARGAINING STAGE)

**Customer:**  Good morning. This is Bob Chan.

**Collector :**  Good morning, Mr. Chan. This is Steve with ABC Telephone Company. I'm calling to confirm the balance of RM700 will be paid today for the telephone account.

**Customer:**  No, I'm sorry. I can't.

Collector : Mr. Chan, may I know why you're unable to pay the balance today?

Customer: (customer gives the reason why he can't pay the full RM700)

Collector : Thank you for sharing that with me, and I'd like to work with you. However, to prevent late charges and a service disconnection, a payment needs to be made today.

Customer: What's the minimum I can pay?

Collector : RM450 to prevent late charges and a service disconnection.

Customer: I can only pay RM100 today.

Collector : Thank you for the offer, however, please pay RM300 to clear up the two oldest bills.

Customer: I think I can pay RM150.

Collector : Thank you for the new offer. However, for me to help prevent an immediate service disconnection I need RM200 to cover the oldest bill.

Customer: OK, I'll find the money somewhere.

Collector : Great. You know Mr. Chan, for only an extra RM100, you'll be able to clean up the two oldest bills, prevent late fees, and make your account look a whole lot better. (Collectors can nibble, too!)

Customer: Thanks, but RM200 is all I can do now.

Collector : OK, thank you. When will the RM500 be paid?

Customer: In a week's time.

Collector : Great. Will you be mailing a cheque or visiting our sales office with the RM200 payment?

Customer: I'll visit.

### (CLOSING STAGE)

Collector : Great. Mr. Chan, I'll note your account that you'll be paying RM200 today at our sales office and another RM500 to the sales office in a week's time, correct?

Customer: Yes.

Collector :  Thank you, Mr. Chan. I look forward to today's payment to prevent a service disconnection. In the future, if you have any difficulty in making timely payments, please call me immediately so I can work with you.

Customer:  OK, good bye.

Collector :  Thank you. Good-bye.

**Comments:**

It was a tough call. The customer wanted to pay the bare minimum, and thankfully the collector didn't jump straight to his bottom offer. Instead, he started high and worked down. I especially like the phrase:

*"For only an extra (amount$), you can make the account look a whole lot better."*

It's a nice technique to nibble a little extra money from customers while clearing another aging bucket. You will be surprised how many customers will pay a little extra to satisfy you. I also nibble if another bill cycle or due date is about to run. E.g.

*"Mr. / Ms. Customer, thanks for the payment, however in just a few more days another bill cycle / due date is going to run and the account will be another month past due. Why not add an extra month's payment to this balance to make better progress on getting your account back to current status?"*

**If you don't ask, you don't get.**

## Negotiations Tips

Here are some quick tips to use when negotiating with customers.

• **Control the location**

If meeting the customer, it's best if they meet you at your office where you feel comfortable, they feel uncomfortable, and you have all the necessary information nearby. If the meeting at their location, avoid meeting in their office behind a desk facing one another. They can become difficult. Instead, meet at a round table, or sit next to one another, or meet in the company break room, cafeteria, restaurant across the street, or even a bar stool. From experience, it's always more difficult negotiating from behind a desk or rectangular table facing one another. You want your debtor to view you as a partner, not as an opponent.

> **Tip:**
>
> Meeting rooms in collection departments are often sterile, unfriendly places. White walls, rectangular tables that occupy most of the room, and creaky chairs. Yet it's in these environments we have to negotiate big deals. Why not improve the room a bit? Use soft colors for the walls, hang some picture of people making deals, use comfortable chairs, heck– even put in a coffee machine. Negotiating deals with debtors is tough enough, try to have the environment work with you.
>
> Dental clinics play soft music and use soft color tones. They paste pictures of deserted islands on the ceilings that you look at right before they start drilling. It works.

- **Don't get cried into a bad deal**

Tears won't solve their problems, only payments will. If a customer uses tears, read the account history to see if this technique is used often. If so, you need to show the customer that this technique won't work on you, but don't be surprised if the debtor changes tactics from crying to becoming your friend, to becoming your enemy, or to becoming upset or angry until s/he finds the best way to handle you.

- **Don't jump at customers' first offers**

Try for more! The first partial offer is usually never the best. The debtors also know your BIF offer isn't your final offer, otherwise they would be current.

- **Be ready for excuses or objections**

If you handle these quickly and confidently your chances of successfully achieving your negotiation goals increase.

- **Never say "no" to money**

If a customer offers you money, accept it. However, beware of accepting money if customers make it a condition of full settlement.

I accept token "good faith" payments at all stages of the collection process, but I inform the customer that although the "good faith" payment is appreciated, it won't stop the collection process. If they want to avoid future negative collection actions, they will need to increase the amount.

- **Use your collection tools**

If the customer refuses to pay, help the customer understand the negative repercussions of that decision as well as highlight the positive benefits of paying. Let the customer know what s/he gets for paying. E.g. no disconnection, service fees, late charges, etc. Sell the benefits of paying.

Collectors sometimes feel intimidated using their tools. They will say things like, "If you don't pay, we will send your account for legal action." Instead, speak with more authority and customers will respect you more. Instead of "WE" use the word "I."

- **Don't be bullied into revealing your minimum amount**

The customer is the one who is long overdue. S/he needs to understand you're there to help. It's in their best interest to pay you as much as they can in order to prevent future calls and other negative collection actions. Put the pressure on the customer to try to negotiate down instead of you trying to negotiate up.

- **Don't be afraid to walk away from a bad deal**

Some collectors negotiate so competitively and passionately that they consider any negotiation breakdown as a personal loss. Remember, there are worse outcomes than a negotiation break-down, and one of them is agreeing to a lousy deal.

## *Negotiating with Hardcore Debtors*

Some days we negotiate with people who are downright mean, nasty, and stubborn. How do you tackle such people? First of all, don't think negative thoughts about them. They add color to our lives. Imagine how boring our job would be if all our customers were nice and agreeable?

Before we understand how to tackle them, let's understand why they are hardcore in the first place. Customers are hardcore for many reasons. They are hardcore because:

1. You or your organization are hardcore or you are perceived as hardcore. If customers feel they are being attacked, rightly or wrongly, they will counter-attack. Your job is to demonstrate you're trying to help, not hurt them.

2. Stress. Financial problems and bill collectors are some of the most stressful things that human beings can experience. Put yourself in their shoes and be grateful you don't have their problems.

3. They must win, and you must lose. They are competitive and hate the thought of losing in negotiations.

4. It works. They receive what they want when they act hardcore. They have become bullies.

5. They don't care. This is the hardest type of customer to tackle. If I face a debtor who honestly does not care about the debt and the consequences they will face, then there is little I can do other than immediately refer the account for write-off and legal action.

Now, let's analyze some hardcore customers attack and counter-attack strategies.

| Customer's Attack Strategy | | Counter-strategy |
|---|---|---|
| Push their positions. E.g. "My way or the highway" | | Welcome and listen to all positions. Even the unreasonable ones. The best way to diffuse this power play isn't by attacking it head-on, but by welcoming it. As a result, you surprise the debtor and avoid a head-on collision. The Japanese martial art of Judo uses the same technique. |
| | | Listen to what s/he has to say, no matter how unfair it may be. Then use the word "fair." Customers who argue from an unfair position will have difficulty countering a fair proposal from you. Try saying, "Mr. / Ms. Customer, I understand your position, however, I'm trying to come to an agreement that is fair for both sides." |
| Attack your positions, interests, or ideas. | | Again, welcome any attacks. Often they attack your ideas because they do not fully understand them. |
| Attack you personally or your organization. | | There are a few counter-strategies you can use here: |
| | | 1. Let them vent. As long as people are irrational and upset they won't be able to negotiate. They need to cool down first. |
| | | 2. Silence. Often you will find that customers apologize if they are met with stony silence. |
| | | 3. "Name the Game". Be direct and politely advise him/her that such behavior won't get them what they want. E.g. *"Mr / Ms. Customer, I'm trying to help you, but this kind of language won't solve this problem."* |

Note: The word "help" is a powerful word. It's hard being unreasonable to collectors who are trying to help them.

## Saving Face When We Trip Up

Negotiations in our business takes place in a fast-paced environment. It reminds me of sports or war. In both, the opponent capitalizes on the mistakes of the other. So, how can we reduce the chances of making mistakes?

1. Ensure your facts are true. Never bluff facts. Professionals just don't do it. Do what you say you will do. If you believe in bluffing, you're risking your credibility.

2. Take your time when negotiating. Think, don't react. If required, tell the customer you need a day to consider his/her proposal.

3. Keep cool. Don't lose your temper. Understand that if the debtor is angry, s/he isn't angry at you but at the problem.

4. Rehearse before an important negotiation. Practice makes perfect.

OK, I know it's easier said then done. So what happens if you unfortunately make a mistake? How do you recover?

**Two steps:**

1. Apologize immediately, but without a fuss.

2. Return to the negotiation by asking a question.

## Settlements

In negotiations, settlement offers often arise. A settlement means that both the customer and the creditor will lose a bit to gain a bit. The customer has lost his / her account and also must part with some money. You have lost a customer and will receive less than the full balance.

In accepting settlements, our biggest enemy is often our ego. We hate to lose, especially if the debtor has been one of our problem accounts. Still, we need to take our egos out of the negotiation process and decide what's best for the organization.

If you're unable to be impartial, ask a colleague what s/he would do. When referring to another, make sure you don't prejudice your colleague's mind about the debtor – just give the facts.

In general, settlements are better than referring the accounts to external collection agencies or for lengthy, costly, and generally ineffective legal actions. Even if you're successful in your legal action, the court can approve an impractical payment schedule lasting several years. Rejecting a settlement can push a customer into bankruptcy. In bankruptcy cases, normally, you will receive less than the initial settlement offer.

It's a good idea to get settlement offers and agreements in writing and signed by the debtor. The document should allow you to pursue legal action or recommence legal action if the settlement agreement is broken.

In Asia, many of the settlements come at the last stages of the legal process, sometimes even minutes before the court hearing. Asian debtors, generally, are unafraid of the legal or credit bureau systems.

**Tip:**

For more effective settlements, try to involve the debtor's feelings. Instead of offering a settlement and saying, "What do you think about that?" Offer and say, "So, how do you feel about that?" It's a small change, but sometimes that's all it takes to get a stronger commitment from the debtor.

### Handling Customers with Settled (or written off) Accounts Reapplying for Credit

What do you do if a written off account now wants to reapply for credit and do business with your firm?

In business, strange things happen. Occasionally written-off customers return. If this happens, consider requiring them to:

- Pay off the written-off amount first

- Pay a larger deposit on the new account

- Get a guarantor

- Receive a lower than normal credit line (if any)

- Sign up for auto-payment via a credit card

- Pay on "CASH ONLY" terms for the first 6-12 months

It's important that your credit system alerts you to written-off accounts reapplying for credit. Companies with poor I.T. systems don't know when such defaulters reapply for credit. As a result, they find that their new written off accounts had previous accounts written off from earlier years.

## *Summary*

- The art of negotiation is easy. We do it every day. Negotiating is part of human nature. Avoid making it complicated.

- The four negotiation steps suggested in this chapter are:

  1. Preparation (know what you want, what you will do if you can't agree, and what you expect them to want)

  2. Opening (set a professional, polite tone to establish rapport–then probe)

  3. Bargaining (give and take concessions)

  4. Closing (summarize and document the agreement)

- Some negotiation tips:

  ☑ Control the location

  ☑ Don't get cried or intimidated into a bad deal

  ☑ Don't jump at debtors' first offers

  ☑ Be ready to handle any excuse or objection

  ☑ Never say "no" to money

  ☑ Use your collection tools

  ☑ Don't be bullied into revealing your minimum offer ("floor")

  ☑ Don't be afraid from walking away from a bad deal

- Settlement offers are difficult to accept, but taking a debtor to court is usually worse.

- Ensure your credit system knows when debtors with written-off accounts re-apply for credit. You don't want to put them back in the "chicken coop" without stringent credit controls in place.

# Face to Face
# Without Losing Face

## 12

*Conducting Site Visits and Repossessions*

*What we learn only through the ears makes less impression upon our minds than what is presented to the trustworthy eye.* – Horace

## After reading this chapter, you will be able to:

- Understand the value of relationships and "face" in Asian culture

- Realize the value site visits offer to you and your customers

- Learn techniques when conducting site visits

- Gain tips when conducting a repossession

## Touching Customers

Organizations touch their customers in many ways:

- Their billing departments send bills

- Their marketing departments send emails, letters, or SMSs regarding upcoming promotions and offers

- Their advertising departments run snazzy ads in the media

- Their telemarketers make friendly calls trying to sell more

- Their sales people have smiles on their faces whenever they greet customers

- Their customer service people are pleasantly ready to handle customers' queries

All of these contact points are essentially positive, but collection contacts are completely different because they are essentially negative.

As collectors, we touch our customers primarily by calls, site visits and by the various actions in our collector's tool chest like collection letters, SMSs, credit holds, collection agencies, and legal action. In this chapter, we will cover how we touch customers via site visits and repossessions.

Site visits, although costly and time-consuming, are perhaps the best way to collect money. It's hard giving a payment excuse to a collector who's standing on your doorstep. Site visits provide a direct view of a customer's willingness to pay. Receiving a face-to-face Promise To Pay (PTP) and responding with, "Thank you, Mr. / Ms. Customer, do I have your word on that?" is a lot stronger than a PTP received over the phone. Site visits collect a lot of money, if you have the time.

## Value of Relationships

In Asia, where relationship building is paramount, site visits are a required tool to collect payment. This is especially true of the Chinese business community as they value *guanxi* (relationship) as their primary tool in doing business. Written contracts play a much smaller role. In the West, a contract signifies the end of the negotiation phase and the start of the business relationship. In Asia, the negotiation phase doesn't ever end. A contract is merely a piece of paper and in Asia, paper is just that. All is negotiable, even after the contact is signed.

In Asia, if your signed contract states the payment terms at 30 days, many customers will take that as your preferred payment terms instead of your real payment terms. Like bargaining, the contract terms are considered your starting position. The customer will constantly test whether your 30 days is 30 days, or if your 30 is really 90 days. You will need to constantly monitor your accounts and sometimes use drastic actions to enforce your 30-day terms.

Even time is flexible. If you call for a meeting at 9:00 a.m., don't be surprised if it doesn't start until 9:15 a.m. In Malaysia, they call it "rubber time."

If you have strong guanxi with your customer and do what you say if prompt payment isn't made, then you will have a better chance of getting your bill paid before others.

## Value of "Face" in Asia

A site visit, if properly done, is a positive experience for both the debtor and the collector. For Asians, "face" is important. At all costs you don't want the other party to lose face. The Malay culture uses the term "malu" meaning embarrassed. The concept of face is so high that it's difficult to hear Asians use the word "no" in order to prevent offending you.

The few times you do hear a "no", it's usually said with a smile. The smile implies the person wants to say "yes", but can't. In Malaysia, many

English-speaking Malaysians feel so uncomfortable using the word "no" that they replace it with the word "cannot."

**Collector :** Mr. Razali, I'm calling today to confirm the balance of RM400 will be paid today.

**Customer:** Oh, cannot, lah.

**Collector :** Tomorrow, then.

**Customer:** Still cannot, lah.

If the debtor proposes smaller or later than expected payment arrangements, the collectors will express "no" in a similar fashion. "*Mr Razali, sorry lah, cannot.*"

## Site Visits

It's important to understand the power of relationships and "face" before going out on site visits. Site visits can be announced or unannounced. I usually make announced visits to customers to collect money or financial information, and unannounced visits to check on the existence and condition of an asset (or a customer).

One of our site visits resulted in a law suit. The debtor was an adult who lived with his parents in an exclusive bungalow neighborhood in Kuala Lumpur. The field collector, from an external debt collection agency, was seen by the neighbors asking for the customer. The debtor's father, who possessed a honorific title, was ashamed that a bill collector was seen visiting his house. As a result, he launched a law suit demanding RM1.0m for this loss of face.

## Site Visit Story

On one of my first site visits, I was sent to a remote Alaskan island to visit a customer and perform a commodity check on a forklift he had financed through us. The customer had been a prompt paymaster. Upon arrival, he picked us up at the small airport. He was so happy that some finance guys from the big city had taken the time to visit him that he showed us off around the small town.

Once at his office, we interviewed him about his operations. All seemed well. However, towards the end of our interview, when we asked if we could see the forklift, his demeanor suddenly changed. He became uncomfortable. He smiled, shuffled his feet and said, "Sure, it's out behind the shop."

We walked behind the shop, but all I could see was vacant lot. "I'm sorry", I said, "I can't see it."

He laughed and said, "That's because you're standing on it."

He saw the confused look on my face and clarified, "We had a fire a few months back. The shop burnt down and the thing melted. I buried it."

The sales person who accompanied me on this site visit said, "Not a problem, Bob, just stay current with the payments."

Although I was still new on the job, my credit side became a bit nervous. I called my boss for advice. He demanded that we call the loan due immediately. The customer hadn't informed us of the fire, nor had he maintained insurance on the unit. We instructed the customer to write a cheque immediately for $15,000 to pay off the loan. The customer complained, but paid.

## Benefits of Site Visits

Site visits give you a view of a customer that financial statements, credit checks and sales people can't provide. You see if the office is orderly, the people are busy, the systems are automated, the work environment is professional, management is respected, management has a plan, or even if management shows up.

You interview the management to see if they're knowledgeable about their business, the industry and the debts they owe you. Do they know when your bills are due? Do they understand your bills?

You interview the Accounts Payable people to understand what you can do to help them pay you faster. You ask if they have any complaints about your service, your company or the billing processes.

As you walk around the premises, you sense if the organization wants you there. If the organization obstructs or hides information now, imagine what they will do when they're seriously overdue?

Site visits allow you and the customer to say things more directly than over the phone. If the customer tells you something that you sense isn't right, in a face to face communication it's easier to say, "Mr./Ms. Customer, please help me out. Tell me straight. Why aren't the payments being made on time?"

Site visits are a positive experience for both parties. Creditors who try to understand their debtors' operations and problems build rapport. This rapport leads to getting your bills paid before other creditors'.

I consult to firms to improve their cash flow. I find a large part of their problem is because the client isn't visiting their large corporate and government accounts to fully understand their accounts payable process.

Conduct site visits on your largest current accounts. This reduces the chance of a surprise default in the future. It also shows that you give attention to even your prompt paymasters. Instruct them to call you immediately if they ever run into financial constraints.

Visiting your largest current clients keeps your auditors happy. They will see that you are proactively managing all the company's receivables.

If you work in a mass market industry, site visits are impractical. However, you should at least consider visiting your largest corporate, government and dealer accounts.

Managing A/R is like car maintenance. If you do preventive maintenance now, like site visits, you will save yourself stress, grief and surprises later.

**Tip:**

If your field collectors have cell phones, you may want to use "Friend Finder" services offered by cellular phone service providers. This service allows you to know at all times where your "friend" is located. It locates the closest base station that your "friend's" cell phone is accessing. Hey, I bet some of us are tempted to ask some of our debtors to also sign up for the service.

## Repossessions

Most people think repossessing equipment, such as cars or bulldozers, is a difficult and dangerous profession. And it can be, but in my repo experience, I have found neither. A majority of the equipment I repossessed was from people who didn't accept prior offers of help. They didn't return my calls. They hid during site visits. They didn't want to negotiate payment plans. They swore when I called. It's easy repossessing from such people. Those rare customers who do keep in contact, who do accept help, and who do treat you with respect are the most difficult accounts to repossess.

Before repossessing, check with your legal adviser to ensure that you have followed the law by giving the debtor the necessary advanced warnings that are required, plus any other arising matters.

By the time it's repo time, most customers know the game is over. As a creditor, it's important to know when they have given up. Often, debtors will mentally give up months before you repo. They tell others about giving up, but rarely do they tell their creditors. Instead, some will try to use your goods and services to generate some quick income to pay their staff or other creditors before closing the doors.

If you maintain close contact with your debtors through calls and site visits, you reduce the chances of conducting an involuntary repo. If you have managed your A/R portfolio well, don't be surprised if debtors voluntarily deliver the goods to your premises in order to reduce their repo fees.

For those customers who refuse to pay, often the simple act of driving a customer's bulldozer up the low-boy trailer shows that you're serious and many will pay you on-the-spot. Some try to make last-minute payment arrangements, but usually the time to accept these has passed.

Nowadays, with the trend towards outsourcing and the potential risks that repossessions cause, many creditors are outsourcing their repossession activities to licensed third parties.

## Repo Tips:

- Never go alone on a repo. Bring along help.

- Check with your insurance company that you're covered in a repo accident.

- If you're physically threatened, stop the repo and contact your home office or police. Likewise, if a debtor forbids you from entering the home, stop the repo immediately.

- If you repo moveable objects, take the most expensive items first.

- Bring a camera to take pictures of the item(s) before and after you move them. This protects you from debtors' claims that the items were damaged in transit.

- Repo professionally. Ensure the debtor is always treated with respect- even if you are not.

- Ensure you repossess in a legal manner.

- If you're unable to locate the equipment, offer rewards. Include photos and descriptions of the equipment.

- If you need trucks to haul away your goods, have several haulers ready to pick up the equipment quickly. If possible, use haulers who owe you money and offset their charges against any overdue payments. A side benefit of using them is they see what happens if they don't pay.

- If safe to do so, take the time to inspect whatever you're driving away. An American repo expert, Charlie Klever, learned this the hard way after repossessing a semi-truck only to later discover a woman asleep in the back!

**Tip:**

As a collector in the construction equipment financing business, I felt frustrated when debtors would say:

*"Hey, I can't pay, and if you don't like it, you can come over here and pick up your damn equipment."*

The customers knew the last thing I wanted was to go through the inconvenience and costs of repossessing equipment. At the same time, I didn't enjoy losing control of my collection calls to such debtors. My boss, Kirby Pain, gave me excellent advice.

He advised that the next time a debtor used that excuse to respond with:

*"Mr. / Ms. Customer, I'm sorry you feel that way. I'll be over tomorrow with the low-boy trailer. What time is convenient for you?"*

I have used that phrase several times and I have never had to repo a unit. Instead, the customer's tone completely changes and I'm back in control. Customers will say things like, "Oh, Mr. Coyle, I'm sorry I was a bit harsh there, I think I can come up with a payment by ......"

Even if you have a customer who "calls your bluff", you still win because now you know he's given up. It's much better knowing now than weeks or months later when you would be repossessing the equipment anyway.

## Skip Tracing Asian Style

Of course, before making a site visit, you first need to know where the customer lives. In the West, collectors have extensive databases at their fingertips to locate customers. In Asia, these databases are mostly non-existent. We skip trace the old fashioned method by using the phone book, reviewing account history details, and gleaning the original credit application for information.

Even getting a possible address is problematic as often when we arrive at the debtor's "new" location it is already old.

Here are some tips that Asian field collectors use to locate debtors:

- Talk to the local postman, police, and dry goods shop owner. These people have a key pulse of the neighborhood, especially if you are collecting in a village.

- Talk to the village headman.

- Check water or electricity meter.
- Talk with the cooking gas and newspaper deliverymen.
- Talk with the local laundry. Often they make deliveries.
- For Muslim debtors, inquire at the neighborhood surau (small prayer hall). When inquiring, it helps if you too are a Muslim.

## Summary

☑ Site visits are time-consuming and costly, but they have their benefits. They help us to :

- Receive firmer PTPs than those received over-the-phone
- See if the goods and even the customers actually exist
- See if the goods are properly maintained
- Evaluate the management expertise and office efficiency
- Speak frankly with our customers about problems both parties are having
- Meet our Accounts Payable contacts to ensure our bills are paid promptly
- Establish rapport by learning about our customers' industries, processes and problems
- Reduce the risk of future surprises by advising customers to call us direct about any future delays in payment

☑ Consider site visits for your largest current customers to avoid future delinquency problems later. Such visits give you a "pulse" on your organization's overall receivable portfolio.

☑ Repossessions or the possibility of repossession are necessary parts of collections. They're often less difficult than they seem. Some repo tips :

- The key to effective repossession is cutting your losses early. Know when the customer has given up as soon as you can.
- Beware of payment arrangements offered during the actual repossession unless the offers are in cash or certified funds. Make sure the payments cover a significant portion of the debt.

- Don't repossess alone, especially if it's an involuntary repossession order. **Exercise caution** and leave if the debtor makes any threats to you or your repo partner.

☑ Skip tracing Asian style is different than in the West. It takes more footwork and less systems work.

# Stress is Part of the Job

## 13

*Handling Stress in a Stressful Job*

---

*There must be quite a few things that a hot bath will not cure, but I don't know many of them.* – Sylvia Plath

*S-T-R-E-S-S is the most recognized foreign word in Japan.* – Associated Press

## After reading this chapter, you will be able to:

- Understand the importance of stress
- Practice a few stress reduction techniques

## Stress Is a Part of Life

**Stress is good!**

If the human race wasn't stressed, we would all be extinct by now. Stress keeps our minds sharp.

Life is like a highway. When someone is right behind us, on our heels, and ready to overtake, we stay focused. If you have ever driven on Highway 2 in eastern Washington state, you will know what I mean. The road is straight as a preacher and cuts through fields and fields of corn and wheat. It's one of the most boring drives you will ever experience. The highway is predictable; the drivers polite. You feel drowsy driving it even in the early morning.

So, why do people drive more competitively on congested city roads fighting for inches than they do on spacious rural highways? Maybe it's because there's less of a race on the uncontested roads.

In South East Asia you will find some of the most easy-going people in the world, but once they're behind a wheel their easy-going demeanor does a 180° turn. They're "Asian Tigers."

In collections we're fortunate. In many other fields, performance is based on qualitative factors like age, beauty, office politics, and education. In collections, the qualitative factors are weaker than the quantitative ones. A great looking, office politician, who consistently collects under target month after month risks termination. Who needs a good looking collector who can't collect?

An adequate amount of stress should be placed on all of our shoulders in order to perform, and a lot of stress placed on the shoulders of non-performers. A performance-based work culture applies to collectors just as it does to our debtors. Poor performing collectors need to understand that the benefits of performing outweigh the benefits of poorly performing. Just as our customers' stress levels increase if they stop paying their bills on time.

Jack Welsh, the former CEO of General Electric, had his 10% rule. Each year the poorest performing 10% of each department were fired.

Professional sports teams practice the same managerial style, if you don't produce, you're gone. Firing the poorest performing 10% isn't an option for all companies, but all of us need to address poor performance.

Exactly how to manage poor performers (and good performers) is discussed in Chapter 18.

## Collections is Stressful

As collectors, we're monitored by many factors:

- Dollars collected

- PTPs

- Bad debt rates

- Customer satisfaction ratings

- Aging and DSO levels

- Profits

In addition, our work environment is often noisy and cramped, and staff turnover is high. Those who collect in a call center environment are monitored by additional factors like :

- Total abandoned calls

- Percent of calls answered within 15 seconds

- Average talk time

- Number of inbound / outbound calls

- Call quality

- Adherence

Although stress is good, excessive levels of it leads to distress. When people reach a state of distress, they feel as if they're losing control. If such a feeling continues too long, people eventually give up. As distress builds, productivity drops and errors increase.

Surviving in today's business environment is difficult. Nowadays, companies face global competition. If costs rise too high, whole departments are outsourced. Employees need to do more in less time than in the past while constantly learning new skills to prevent job loss. A collector today is doing the work of several collectors in the past. The question shouldn't be: "Are we stressed?" Instead, the question should be: "Are we distressed?"

## Stress and Collection Departments

When I visit collection departments with low levels of stress, I notice they lack a buzz. Busy collection departments have a buzz that other departments don't have. Have you even seen people in accounting or marketing run to get coffee and then return quickly to their desks?

Call center collection departments have the loudest "buzz." Ideally, collectors should be jumping on incoming calls as quickly as possible since that's where the "easy money" is. There should be little if any "hold" time for customers when calling a collections department. It's fast-paced because besides pouncing on inbound calls, collectors also make outbound calls. The work environment is hectic.

Stress is a vital component of our jobs. We politely and legally add a little stress to our customers' lives in order to help them avoid greater stress later. As collectors, we sell the benefits of paying (less stress) vs. the negative actions that occur from defaulting:

> "Mr. / Ms. Customer, I'm calling to help prevent your car from being repossessed."

Money problems are one of life's biggest causes of stress. By helping customers handle debt, we help reduce their stress levels. Less stress gives people more time to devote to more enjoyable activities. Collectors help people.

## Stress Reduction Tips

Every day we receive stressful customer calls, and once in a while a particular customer "hooks" us and give us excessive stress. What's the first thing many of us do after receiving such a call?

We swivel our chairs around and tell others sitting near us about the call. Does it sound familiar? Instead of sharing the stress with others, take a quick break. Walk down the hall, breathe, laugh, smile. Stress is contagious, so don't pass it on!

If you experience a stressful call, consider sharing it with your supervisor away from the work area. This is better than keeping it inside and coming out on your next call. After you share it with him/her, don't walk away from the listener, ensure you didn't pass your stress along.

I find supervisors are better than colleagues to share stressful customer experiences since their job is different. They listen calmly, then return to work.

Here are some ideas to ensure your stress doesn't hit distress levels.

## 1. Open Communication (to speak and to listen)

If the person next to you taps her fingernails on her desktop all day long and it drives you crazy, speak up. Otherwise, you will go home a mess, pass the stress on to your loved ones, or your dearest pet.

Promoting an environment of open communication isn't only about talking, but also of listening. It extends throughout the whole department and includes the giving and receiving of feedback at all levels.

To promote better communication in my collection department we implemented daily "morning chats." Each day we arrive 15 minutes early and it's off-set by receiving an extra 15 minutes at lunchtime. During the morning chats, the supervisors and their teams share new policies, goals or other subjects. The teams also practice new responses to various customers' objections. The collectors voice their concerns or ideas about the department. These simple chats – and the increased lunchtime - helped decrease the stress levels in our work environment.

If you find five days of morning chats excessive, then use one of the time-slots for a 15 minute morning exercise routine, or watch an instructional video, or have someone make a presentation to the whole department. It's an efficient way to start the day.

When employees feel they have no control over their future, stress levels rise. Management needs to share the department's goals and the steps to achieve them. The lower level staff's ideas and suggestions must be taken into consideration when setting new departmental goals. Not all their suggestions will be implemented, but at least they have been heard and sometimes that's enough to boost peoples' morale.

I know of no better workplace stress remedy than open communication. Humans fear what they don't know, and fear causes stress. By voicing these concerns and understanding them, fear is reduced.

Of course, creating a work environment with open communication is easier said than done. Sometimes we're not open because we don't want to hurt another person's feelings, but it eventually comes out later and hurts even more. Sometimes we're closed because our work environment doesn't promote it. Sometimes we don't promote open communication because we view meetings as a waste of time, but I would rather spend time in meetings than spending more time combating low morale and quashing rumors.

## 2. Breathe

*"Sometimes the most important thing in a whole day is the rest we take between two deep breaths."* - Etty Hillesum

When stress hits us, we tend to feel it first in our chest, heart and lungs. We have difficulty breathing, our heart beats faster, we get hot, we turn red and some people hyperventilate.

When you feel stress coming, try stretching out your arms and taking a few deep breaths. If you need to tip the head back, do it. If you need to get off the phones, do it. Concentrate on breathing. Focus on yourself and you will have less chance of passing the stress on to others. Just breathe.

## 3. Smile

Smiling is a great stress reliever for yourself and for others watching you. It's contagious. Smiling shows you possess a sense of humor. It also reflects confidence: "smiling in the face of danger." Smiling is easy, free, and highly contagious.

In collections, we need to realize that we can't "win" ever call. Some customers will get the better of us. By understanding that concept, you will begin to feel less stress. Instead, the next time you "lose" a call, consider that the customer just gave you a free lesson. Smile about it. Get over it. Learn from it.

## 4. Move

Moving is a simple action to reduce stress. Next time you feel stress building and tightness of breath; just stand up, stretch and take a brief walk. Moving increases blood circulation to the brain which helps change that stressful feeling.

## 5. Quit

Collections is a stressful job. If you're unsuccessful in reducing your stress levels and hate your job, then it's better to find a more suitable job. Not all people are cut-out to be collectors. Think about your health, your family, and your customers.

## *Summary*

- Stress is a fact of life. It challenges us. Life would be boring without it. How could we ever get up each morning to "hit the road" if we weren't challenged?

- Beware of excessive stress (distress) as it impacts productivity and peoples' health. We can't eliminate stress, but we can control how we deal with it.

- Stress is a tool we use to collect more money. We give a little stress to our customers now to help them avoid more stress later.

- The following are some quick stress reduction tips:

  ☑ Communicate

  ☑ Breathe

  ☑ Smile

  ☑ Move

# A Few Words to New Collectors

# 14

*Or, Advice from an Old Guy*

---

*The purpose of life is not to be happy- but to matter, to be productive, to be useful, to have it make some difference that you have lived at all.* – Leo Rosten

## After reading this chapter, you will be able to:

- Understand the importance of the collection profession
- Analyze the future job outlook in the collections profession
- Learn tips to be successful in the profession
- Understand "Coyle's Collector Commandments"

## Nature of the Job

Bill collectors, recovery officers, account adjusters, financial services representatives, associates, credit analysts (or whichever title you use) are vital for the survival of your company. Although, at times, it may seem otherwise.

As collectors, we add a dose of reality to companies. We tell the customer service people that not all customers are good or always right. We tell sales people that although they work hard to get the sales, they need to work harder to get quality customers. Our position exposes us to more departments within an organization than any other job. Our actions are felt throughout the organization.

We also give doses of reality to our customers. It may be unpleasant for them, but it's the truth. Think of yourself as a dentist. Unlike most doctors who you visit to receive immediate pain relief, a dentist works backwards. You must first go through pain before you get any relief. Sometimes the pain involves just a filling; while other times it's a root canal. It's by experiencing some pain now that you avoid a whole lot of pain later. Collectors work on the same principle. Customers may not like paying, but by paying something now, they avoid a whole lot of worse actions later.

## *Future of the Job*

When a new collector asks me, "What's my future in this job?" I try to be as frank as possible. At some companies, collectors find it difficult to transfer to other departments due to people's misconceptions that we're cold and mean and odd. One person may say, "Kris wants to apply for our entry-level marketing position?" While another says, "No way, she's from collections; they hate customers down there."

On the other hand, for those wanting to stay in collections, it's an interesting career. It's enjoyable to plan collection strategies, run and analyze champion challenges, implement technical solutions to increase productivity, lead employees, see quantitative results from your efforts, calm upset customers and negotiate settlements.

Ensure that you keep your greatest investment – your brain - in shining condition. Continually develop yourself by attending training, going back to school, or getting qualifications from credit or collection organizations. In Asia, the value of qualifications is even higher. All these efforts will help you in your career. The more knowledge, skills and qualifications you receive, the greater career flexibility you will enjoy. The fact that you're even reading this book means you're already a step ahead of most people in this field.

The future of our jobs is bright both in the U.S. and Asia. According to the U.S. Bureau of Labor Statistics, there are approximately 413,000 collectors and their outlook for job growth is expected to "**grow faster than the average**", which is defined as a growth rate of between 21-35%. The reason for this growth is due to the rise in consumer debt levels.[22]

Consumer debt worldwide is exploding, especially with younger debtors. In the U.S., Nellie Mae[23], a student loan organization, finds the average graduating college student has $19,000 in student loans as compared to $11,000 five years earlier; while holding $3,300 in credit card debt. Eventually these young debtors will become middle-aged and senior debtors.

The U.S. Federal Reserve has reported that American consumer debt has hit the $2 trillion mark at the end of 2003. Cardweb.com Inc. reports that the average U.S. credit card debt per household has grown from $2,966 in 1990 to $9,205 in 2003.[24]

---

22   Bureau of Labor Statistics, *"Occupational Outlook Handbook, 2004-05 Edition: Bill and Account Collectors"*, <http://www.bls.gov/oco/oco1005.htm> (12 May 2005), U.S. Department of Labor. Note: The job outlook for credit authorizers, checkers, and clerks is expected to decline, but the outlook for loan counselors and officers is expected to **"grow about as fast as the average."**

23   Margaret Webb Pressler, "Young and in Debt", 2003, <http://www.msnbc.com/ news/1002396.asp?vts=120720032029> (2 November 2003), displayed in MSNBC News for The Washington Post.

24   CardWeb.com, Inc., *"Table of Average U.S. Credit Card Debt Per Household"*, <http://www.cardweb.com> (11 May 2005).

In Asia, the future for collections looks just as bright with the increasing acceptance of credit cards. *Asia Times Online* reports that South Korea has the highest credit card penetration rates in the region, while credit card receivables have doubled in Thailand, Taiwan, Malaysia, India, Singapore and Hong Kong over the past five years.[25]

Malaysia's Bank Negara records total outstanding credit card debt at April 2003 to be RM1.19 billion, compared to RM347.9m in 1999.[26]

When I first arrived in Malaysia in 1995, credit cards were a rarity, but nowadays you find credit card sign-up booths in supermarkets, malls, subway stations and employee cafeterias. Any person with a minimum yearly income of RM18,000 qualifies. As at December 2005, there were 7.9m credit cards issued, or one for every two working Malaysians, an increase of 21% over December 2004.[27] With the increase in consumer credit, Malaysia has experienced a 32% increase in bankruptcies from 2002-2004. This has happened despite the government raising the minimum bankruptcy debt requirement by 200%.[28]

There will be plenty of job for collectors in Asia. China alone has US$137b in bad loans.[29]

## Job Difficulty

Is debt collections a tough job?

Yes, but it gets easier.

My first day as a bill collector was a day that I still remember. I hated calling people for money. Asking people for money is hard. I felt like I was begging. I was brought up to believe that people know they need to pay for the things they buy. They don't need reminding. Unfortunately, that's untrue.

The reality is that asking for your organization's money isn't begging, and some people do need constant reminding in order to honor their obligations.

I was a new collector, but I used an old collection technique: the "iron-fist". That technique got a lot of people upset, including myself upset. My customers were upset because I was going after their money and didn't care a damn about them. I hated my job. I was about to be fired. I had to make a change.

25  John Mulcahy, "Asia's Hello Kitty consumers lap up credit", 10 September 2003, <http://www. atimes/Asian_Economy/EI10Dk01.html> (8 December 2003), Asia Times Online.
26  P.Y. Chin, *"Dangers of consumer debt bubble bursting"*, New Sunday Times, 20 June 2004,  15.
27  Vasantha Gamesan, *"Warning on credit card expenditure"*, New Strait Times, 8 February 2006, quoting Bank Negara Malaysia statistics.
28  Anis Ibrahim, *"More going bust"*,  New Strait Times, 11 April 2005.
29  Bloomberg, *"Bad loans cast pall over China bank's US$10b IPO"*, New Strait Times, 17 May 2006

The change I made was to understand that I wasn't calling to collect money. I was calling to **help** customers avoid negative actions. Once I made this mental shift, the calls became easier. The money started rolling in and I enjoyed my job. Customers were actually grateful that I had called. I went from near the bottom of the collector standings to near the top. I was soon promoted.

Once you're able to confidently ask people for money, collecting from easy debtors isn't challenging. You actually look forward to the upset, screaming customers who absolutely refuse to pay. You plan your strategy while listening to them. You calm them down, you help them, and then you ask for the money. You negotiate with customers. You try to get the best deal, confirm it, and thank the customer. The "best deal" isn't only best for you; but it's also best for the customer.

## Throwing Down a Challenge

**To all new collectors**: After reading this book, I challenge you to outperform the "old-timers" in your department. Take the ideas that work for you, customize them, and use them.

Be mindful that whenever you make a change from your current process, you will experience a short-term period of degradation in your performance. This period is called "The Valley of Despair." Don't despair! You're just implementing something new. Give yourself time to feel comfortable with the change. Be patient. Psychologists say it takes 21 days of daily activity before something new becomes a habit. Just like going on a diet or working out at the gym, positive results aren't immediately seen.

In my experience, after receiving training, new collectors often outperform the "old-timers." Some "old-timers" are complacent and fearful of change. As a newcomer, you have the chance to teach them a few tricks.

## Coyle's Collector Commandments

You're now ready to receive Coyle's Collector Commandments. These five commandments drive the way I do collections. They are my collections belief system. Collectors, like sales people, need a positive attitude to be successful. I arrive to work believing in these five principles to help me collect more money.

### Commandment 1:   Everyone has money

"I have no money" is probably the world's number one payment excuse. However, I don't believe it. When a person uses this excuse they aren't telling you the whole truth. They just need to complete the sentence, "I have no money **for you**." Collectors need to believe that everyone has money; it's just a matter of priorities. You need to convince the debtor that your bill takes precedence over their other payable priorities. You need to sell the benefits of paying.

### Commandment 2: Don't play games with customers

Customers play all kind of games to avoid payment. They will use excuses like "no money", "no time", "too busy", "never got a bill", "yeah, yeah, I'll pay, now can we hang up?", and countless others. If you sense a customer is playing a game with you, you need to 'Name the Game'. Debtors are experts at game playing, not me. If I'm going to counter their expertise, I need to let them know I'm not playing. I do this by politely asking if I can speak frankly with them. My goal is to 'Name the Game.' I want my negotiations with the debtor to be based on truth and facts, not games.

### Commandment 3: It's not about the money, it's about the customer

I focus on the customer. We all put ourselves at the center of the universe. If I show the customer I care about them and that I'm trying to help prevent negative actions from occuring, I'm able to collect more money. I want to be seen as a partner, not as an enemy.

### Commandment 4: Collections is about habits

Whenever customers do something positive, I reward them. When they do the reverse, I try to punish. Getting people to pay involves getting into people's heads. If I can get them to see me as a partner, and they like me, and they're aware of the consequences of not paying, then I have a better chance of getting paid.

### Commandment 5: Set high expectations (BIF Today!)

I come to work expecting that I'll help a lot of customers and collect a lot of money. I aim high by asking customers to pay maximum payments, not minimum ones. I negotiate downwards, not upwards. I find if I set higher expectations, I collect more. I may not get BIF each time, but I often get the next best amount.

I can't promise following these commandments will lead you to the Promised Land, but they will help you collect **more money in less time** while retaining more customers' goodwill.

## *Summary*

- Collections is a valuable profession.
- The job outlook in the field is brighter than most other jobs.
- Follow Coyle's Collector Commandments:
  1. Everyone has money
  2. Don't play games with customers
  3. It's not about the money, it's about the customer
  4. Collections is about habits
  5. Set high expectations (BIF Today!)

Part V:
# Fostering Alliances and Strategic Partnership

# Avoiding Self-Inflicted Pain

**15**

*Working WITH Key Groups within Your Organization*

*It is easier to find men who will volunteer to die, than to find those who are willing to endure pain with patience.* – Julius Caesar

**After reading this chapter, you will be able to:**

- Realize the obstacles we face within organizations
- Avoid internal obstacles to collect more money

## *"With friends like these, who needs enemies?"*

We face many external obstacles in our quest for increased collections. Some of these include: the economy, customers' excuses and objections, new government regulations, credit criminals, power failures, world-wide competition, corruption, and unforeseen bad luck. With such a difficult work environment out there, why would we ever want to create internal obstacles?

This chapter discusses ways to reduce the number of internal obstacles that prevent you from achieving your collection goals. Internal obstacles are those which you have some power or influence to affect.

Now, let's look at a few internal obstacles that negatively affect our results.

### *1. Poor Product or Service Quality*

Selling inferior goods or services is one sure-fire way of increasing your bad debts. Nobody wants to pay full-value for something worth half-value. So guess where most of these disputes land?

As collectors, it's difficult improving your company's product quality, but we can certainly give feedback. In fact, our feedback is more valuable than most departments. We have **direct** contact with customers **every** day. Our feedback should be a primary driver in the design of good products and services. We speak with authority.

## 2. Poor After-sales Service (customer service)

Providing poor after-sales service will negatively affect the aging of your account receivables. If customers are unable to solve their concerns, then the aging will be affected as customers will make partial payments or no payments. Poor service is due to various reasons such as:

- Staff are measured solely on quantitative factors like total number of calls, average speed on each call, or total number of customer transactions they process. Instead of customer satisfaction levels.

- Poorly designed 1-800 number routing system. When customers call to pay or make payment arrangements, their calls get lost in the IVR. Customers feel frustrated because they can't speak with a human. When will more collection departments start acting like sales departments? How long do you have to hold after dialing a 1-800 sales hotline number? Make it easy for customers to contact and pay you.

- Lack of empowerment for the front-line staff. They understand the customers' problems, but aren't empowered to solve them quickly.

## 3. Inadequate I.T. Systems and Support

If your IT systems are inadequate, then your accounts' aging will deteriorate. A collections department needs good IT support. The collectors' workplace, especially in a call center work environment, needs to be automated. Phone lines must work, PABX / ACD function properly, collection calls be recorded, servers up and running, billing systems that rarely crash, accurate reports timely generated, automated collection treatments, and payment files from your organization's multiple payment channels uploaded correctly and quickly into the system.

An effective I.T. department helps ensure the smooth running of the collection department's systems. They also assist collection managers in planning for future system enhancements to boost the department's productivity while reducing the company's overall bad debt level.

Many collection managers rely on the I.T. department to provide them with fast and accurate reports. These reports track the company's accounts receivable portfolio and allow collection managers to evaluate whether the current collection treatments are effective. If change is needed, then have the I.T. department assist in running "Champion Challenges" on a small sample of accounts.

Other than the sales department, the I.T. department is the collection department's most important partner in hitting its bad debt targets.

## 4. The Bills

Generating bills quickly and accurately is a big factor in our success or failure. Organizations that bill customers based on usage like telcos, credit cards, utilities, department stores, suppliers, and hospitals will spend significant amounts on their billing systems and processes. A poor billing process will negatively affect an organization's bad debt levels and increase DSO.

The billing process needs to look at the following key areas :

4a. Bill generation and mailing

4b. Bill format

4c. Returned bills

### 4a. Bill Generation and Mailing

It seems that whenever there are serious billing delays or errors, it's the collection and customer service departments' whose phone lines ring with upset and confused customers. However, the department which caused this pain faces few repercussions. Instead, they usually blame "the system". Billing errors cost collectors valuable time as they now have to handle billing questions instead of locating and calling defaulting debtors.

### 4b. Bill Format

Marketing, collections, customer service and the I.T. departments need to ensure the bill is easy to understand. A complicated bill serves no one. The collections toll-free number should be displayed, but it shouldn't be displayed too prominently as it may encourage people to run past due, or it could encourage current customers to call collections whenever they have a billing question. Perhaps, place the number on the reverse side?

If the bill's format is even slightly confusing, some customers will use that as an excuse to pay slowly. The bills should clearly state the overdue balance, current balance, total balance due, and due date. Avoid the following confusing bill:

*Example 1: Confusing bill summary*

En. Abdul Latif bin Abdullah
No. 54, Jln Tunku
46150 Petaling Jaya
Selangor DE, Malaysia

Bill Date: June 1, 200_

| Overdue balance | Current balance | Total balance | Due by |
|---|---|---|---|
| RM200.00 | RM200.00 | RM400.00 | July 1 |

En. Abdul will interpret the overdue balance as due by July 1 when it's due now. Instead consider something like the next example.

*Example 2: Clearer bill summary:*

En. Abdul Latif bin Abdullah
No. 54, Jln Tunku
46150 Petaling Jaya
Selangor DE, Malaysia

Bill Date: June 1, 200_

| Overdue balance | Current balance | Total balance |
|---|---|---|
| RM200.00 | RM200.00 | RM400.00 |
| **Due NOW!** | **Due by July 1** | |

## 4c. Returned Bills

In many companies, returned bills sit in piles, gathering dust, in a corner of the office. The pile becomes a hill or worse a mountain. Instead, put on your hiking boots and conquer "Returned Bill Mountain." Often another department is responsible for processing returned bills, but in effect they don't process them as they believe they have more important functions to perform. Take ownership of it yourself.

Consider returned bills as alerts for "first payment defaults" and other potential defaulters. Customers who don't inform you when they're moving are high risk. Use your staff, or temporary staff, to process these bills. One method is to divide the mountain up amongst the total staff in the department.

People and businesses don't move at a moment's notice. They plan it months in advance. If your firm is one of their most important creditors, and they didn't alert you of the move, consider the account high risk.

## 5. Poorly Trained Collection Staff

Poorly trained staff are an internal obstacle that prevents us from hitting our targets. Although most collectors are "worth their weight in gold", they're generally paid low salaries. As a result, many organizations view spending money training them as low priority. This is unfortunate since collectors handle an organization's two most valuable assets: its accounts receivable and customers.

A poorly trained collection staff **WILL** adversely affect a company's bottom line. They cause customers to leave. They cause lawsuits to be filed. Poorly trained collectors do extensive damage.

Spending money on training and development opportunities each year reaps rewards in motivating them to collect more, faster and still keep your customers. You will likely see staff turnover also reduce.

### ServiceWinners International Sdn. Bhd.

We provide collections training and consultancy services to our clients. This book gives you an idea of our customer-centric (CRM) collection philosophy. Our programs are designed to help organizations reduce bad debts, Days Sales Outstanding (DSO) levels, increase profits and customer satisfaction levels. Our programs are designed for collectors, supervisors and managers. We tailor each course to your unique environment. Our goal is to impart practical training solutions to our clients.

ServiceWinners is based in Malaysia and covers the Asia-Pacific region, including the Indian sub-continent. We occasionally run in-house programs in North America. For more information, please contact us at:

Telephone : +60 12-2000-998
E-Mail : info@servicewinners.com
Web Site : www.servicewinners.com

## 6. Lack of Senior Management Support

Is your senior management an obstacle? As credit or collection professionals, whenever we have a good year it's nice to take the credit and say it was due to our expertise. But was it? What do we say when we have a bad year?

In both cases, we're hiding the full truth. There's an old saying, "Success has many parents, failure is an orphan."

Whether we have a good year or bad year is partially due to our performance and our team's, but it's also heavily contingent upon senior management's support. As a collection manager, if you see the aging portfolio deteriorating and you recommend tightening up the company's collection treatments, but senior management withholds support, then you can't be totally faulted for missing the organization's bad debt targets.

If senior management wants to capture more market share with aggressive promotions, relaxed credit requirements, and loose collection treatments, then expect bad debts to increase. If this year, senior management supports your desire to tighten your collection treatments, then expect it to decrease.

The same applies to sales managers. They can't claim all the glory for a banner year. Any sales increases are dependent on quality products, combined with great advertising, fast and creative credit approvals, professional customer service, and a high percentage of accounts kept in a current- active - buying status.

## 7. Yourself

Take a good look at **yourself.** Are you your own worst enemy?

Do people find you difficult to work with? Do people complain about you to your boss or to your H.R.? Are you a major player in your organization? Do your peers and superiors in other departments know you? Do you network throughout your organization? Self-analysis is notoriously inaccurate as we're all in love with ourselves. Why else does it feel uncomfortable seeing pictures or hearing audios of ourselves? We say incredulously, "Do I really sound like that?"

We all have egos that we try to protect. Husbands, try telling your wife that she snores. Women hate to believe they do. Wives, ask your husband for his underwear size. If you look in any department store, the smallest size starts at medium. How many men would be confident enough to ask the young sales clerk for a pair of smalls?

As collections professionals, it's a good idea to ask your supervisor and peers for an analysis of your working style. Don't ask subordinates as they will feel too intimidated. Feedback is painful but it's definitely valuable. The Chinese call it "medicine for the ears."

Here are two more questions to ask yourself:

### 1. Are you too nice or too timid?

Do you "surrender" to sales and marketing on the big issues? Do you highlight to senior management the need to maintain reasonable credit risk levels? Are you assertive enough? Is your niceness causing bad debts to increase?

### 2. Are you creative?

Do you consider multiple solutions to improving a process or solving a problem? Do you solicit input from others to create better quality solutions? If you lack creativity, do you have creative members on your team to address this gap?

In Asia, creative thinking is problematic. Asians are brought up in a family environment that is secure and authority-based. It's common for unmarried adults, in their 30's or 40's, to live with their parents. Or, after marriage, the children will buy the home next door to their parents'. You will sometimes find a stretch of homes all occupied by relatives.

This dependence on elders and family is transferred to the workplace where the supervisor is viewed as a "parent", always right and at all times his/her decisions are to be respected. The work environment is one in which obedience, compliance, and harmony are encouraged-- sometimes at the expense of creative thought. Soliciting others' ideas and opinions can lead to conflict, and conflict is discouraged in Asia. Creativity is messy.

The Asian school system, although secure, is pressure-filled. It focuses on memorization and passing multiple choice tests. Essay tests are rarely used. Schools that use "show and tell", run public speaking classes, require group research, and teachers asking students' opinions to encourage critical thinking are rare this side of the world.

Although Asian countries like Singapore routinely achieve some of the world's highest student test scores, in the business world most of the concepts are from the West. The combination of authority-based households, school systems, and work organizations stifle creative thinking skills. It also plays havoc on some Asians' self-confidence to stand up to make a simple presentation on a new collection strategy they have just created.

Asian credit people need to evaluate their own creativity level in solving their organization's accounts receivable problems. If your organization's credit or collections policy doesn't make sense, question it! Asian bad debt level is higher than it should be, and the creativity needed to address this problem is sorely needed.[30]

**Tip:**

When I first joined the collection department in one organization, my boss had me buy 50 cheesecakes whenever our department hit our "Super Bonus". We would pass out the cakes to the internal departments who helped us achieve our target. Key groups to receive the cakes included sales support, customer service, finance, IT, and the branches. Although costly, the cakes increased our exposure throughout the company and helped us hit more targets.

---

30  An excellent book written by a Singaporean on the Asian creativity gap and how to address it is: *"Why Asians are Less Creative than Westerners"*, by Ng Aik Kwang- PhD, Published by Prentice Hall (2001). The book is also useful for Westerners to gain a better understanding of their Asian counterparts.

## *Summary*

- We face enough external obstacles in our quest to collect money. Why create internal ones?

- Beware the following internal obstacles that prevent your department from hitting its goals:

  ☑ Poor quality product or service

  ☑ Poor after-sales service

  ☑ Inadequate I.T. systems to support your department

  ☑ Ineffective billing process:

  ☑ Slow generation and mailing of bills

  ☑ Inaccurate bills

  ☑ Bill format is confusing

  ☑ No handling of returned bills

  ☑ Poorly trained collection staff

  ☑ Lack of senior management support

  ☑ Poor credit and collection controls

  ☑ Take the time to examine yourself. Are you part of your organization's bad debt problem or solution?

# Avoiding Friendly Fire

## 16

*Working WITH the Sales People*

*The most important trip you may take in life is meeting people halfway.*
– Henry Boye

### After reading this chapter, you will be able to:

- Recognize the importance of the sales department in your organization

- Study ways to make the sales department your ally

- Learn tips to encourage communication with the sales department

## The Importance of Sales

It's true when sales people say, "It all starts with a sale."
Sales people are critical for any organization's survival, and it takes a particular kind of person to excel in sales.

Sales people suffer from stereotypes as much as we do. Many people think that the best sales people are loud, talkative, and boisterous. However, the best sales people are often the quiet, diligent, and organized ones who partner with their customers to provide them with the needed goods or services. They don't oversell. They act as account managers and follow up on their customers' needs. They represent their customers' interests to their organization. They are strategic partners.

Our role as collectors isn't as high a profile as sales, but it's just as important. The initial sale starts the sales process, but it's the collection department that completes it. Collections is part of the sales process.

The sales and collection relationship is, by its nature, full of checks and balances. Hopefully, these checks and balances result in the overall strengthening of the organization. However, if an adversarial situation develops, the organization suffers.

I have seen sales departments make credit decisions out in the field in order to get more commissions. These sales people were more concerned with commissions rather than building a relationship with the customer, or protecting their employer from a future bad debt. Such sales people often don't return existing customers' calls because they're too busy selling to make time for account management.

Eventually the customer gets upset and stops paying. Now the collection department is involved to resolve the dispute and re-build the relationship. Often the problem is fixed by the credit guys acting as inside sales support guys. In the meantime, both groups mistrust each other.

So how can sales and credit work together for the common good?

## *Partnering with Sales*

Frequent and open communication is the key to building good working relationships. Credit and collection people need to get out of their departments and meet the sales people in the field.

Getting out of the department adds another benefit: It promotes your department. Too often, credit and collection departments are seen as an organization's black hole where no one ever comes out. It's up to you to raise the profile of the department; you are, after all, guarding the company's "crown jewels."

Avoid taking a combative stance with the sales department as senior management will usually side with sales in any internal battles. If you have fostered a combative relationship with sales over the years, maybe even relished baiting them, don't be surprised if you find yourself out of a job soon.

Like it or not, the sales people are a major determinant on whether you hit your bad debt targets. If they become your ally, they will help you achieve your goals, and you will help them hit theirs. Zig Zigler, the king of sales, says it best, "You will get all you want in life if you help enough other people get what they want."

## *Tips on Improving Communication with the Sales Department*

Some companies have sales people calling the credit people, "credit geeks", and the credit people responding with, "sales jerks." This type of rough communication is due to a lack of communication. If the heads of credit and sales communicate well, it usually filters down to the lower levels.

Here are some ideas to improve credit and sales relations within your organization:

## 1. Joint Site Visits

Going on site visits with sales people gives both parties a view of each other's job functions. The credit people observe the problems the sales people face in the field such as trying to get the required financial documents from customers for credit approvals. The sales people observe what the credit people search for when meeting customers and asking for payments. Having sales people observe repossessions gives them an understanding of what happens when a deal goes sour. Regular site visits may be the most important tool you can use to improve your department's relations with sales.

Often the sales / credit conflict is due to a lack of understanding on both parties. We are quick to judge each other, although we haven't "walked in the shoes of another". Site visits are an excellent way to do some walking.

Site visits allow you to observe the sales peoples' mistakes. Do they ask for updated financial statements? Do they ask for the accounts payable contact? Do they correctly explain the payment terms and conditions? Site visits allow you to see the problems as they're being created versus dealing with them months later when the customer is upset.

Site visits allow the sales people to see you in a new light. The visits will give you a human face. If you're not going on regular site visits now, chances are your sales people see you as the company pit-bull, Guido, or even deal- breaker.

## 2. Pairing Collectors with Sales Reps

Consider structuring your collection team to ensure sales people only deal with one collector for all their accounts. By pairing sales people with a single point of contact in collections, they will begin to form a stronger working relationship. The sales person knows whom to contact if the customer has a credit or collections complaint. The collector keeps their sales person informed on key accounts that face negative actions. At the same time, the collector runs aging and DSO reports per sales person.

## 3. Sales Support

Most sales departments have an inside sales support team. This team acts as a liaison between sales and credit (or collections). Often, sales support interacts more with the collection department than the sales people who are in the field selling.

Sales support teams are important, without them, existing customers' complaints will be neglected if the sales people are rewarded more for booking new business, than for servicing existing accounts. If this sounds like your organization, and a sales support team doesn't exist, then I bet it does exist it's just called the "collection department."

## 4. Meetings

Sales and collection people need to meet regularly to discuss action plans on key accounts. Often customer disputes are over quality issues or promises made by sales people that could easily be resolved with frequent meetings.

Collection people should attend the annual sales conventions that most sales departments throw. They should present a quick overview of the health of the company's receivables.

However, if your presentation skills are lousy avoid this. Instead, supply the sales folks with a monthly credit/sales newsletter.

If possible, bring a neutral third party to the sales meetings such as an attorney or your company's chief financial officer to present. Sales people will often listen to their point of view on the effects of a sale gone sour versus the credit manager's point of view. Just make sure the guest has good presentation skills or your sales people will dislike you even more for wasting their time.

Whenever new credit or sales procedures are launched, key sales and credit people should proactively meet to strategize how best to implement the changes.

## 5. Bearing Good and Bad Tidings

Just as we get annoyed when sales people make special promises and arrangements with customers without first contacting us, they too get annoyed when we fail to communicate negative activities on their key accounts.

Sales people should be contacted before the following negative situations happen to their accounts:

- Sending particularly forceful collection letters
- Involuntary reduction in customers' credit lines
- Credit holds
- Suspension or disconnection of service
- Repossession
- Commencement of legal activities
- Related accounts affected due to non-payment of an overdue account

Involving sales in the collection process helps reduce delinquency as key corporate accounts represent a large chunk of a company's receivables problem.

On the flip side, whenever they make a big sale, congratulate them on their efforts. Ask them how your department can better support them. Afterwards, feel free to tell them how they can better support you.

If the big sale was to a dubious customer, avoid saying something negative about the customer at first. The salesperson will just defend the customer even more. Instead, congratulate them on the sale, then say, "Well done! Now, let's plan how we're going to collect from them."

## 6. Rewards, Recognition and Sales Commissions

Sales people and collectors' job functions are similar. Both jobs are quantitatively measured. Both jobs are competitive. Both sales and credit people enjoy rewards and recognition programs to reflect this competitiveness.

So, create joint incentive programs or monthly challenges that foster greater sales and lower bad debts?

The contests could measure:

- Best aging by sales person or sales team, plus collector or collection team

- Best DSO by sales person or sales team, plus collector or collection team

- Lowest first payment defaults by sales person or sales team, plus collector or collection team

- Lowest bad debt per sales person or sales team, plus collector or collection team

- Highest sales approved by a credit team within a low bad debt range

- Fastest credit approval team within a low bad debt range.

Offer monetary rewards or visual awards like trophies, VIP parking spots, training courses, or lunch with the collection and sales manager.

Ensuring your organization has the right sales commission structure is one sure-fire method to keep sales and credit working together. If your organization pays commissions upon the sale being made, then the sales person needs to be in charge of collecting it if the account goes bad. The sales person shouldn't be allowed to "have his cake and eat it, too."

If your organization practices commission charge-backs, then it's only fair that the credit department provide each sales person with charge-back alerts to avoid any surprises. You want to avoid hitting someone's wallet without telling them so.

The ideal commission structure is one where the sales person gets the commission upon payment. This structure focuses both the credit and sales people on the sales process from start to finish. If possible, the commission payout should be based on a sliding scale method.

*For example:*

100% commission payout if customer pays according to terms

90% commission payout if customer pays within 31-60 days

80% commission payout if customer pays within 61-90 days

## *Summary*

- The sales people are vital to any organization's survival. Collection people need to understand their importance.

- Sales and collection people have similar job functions. We both persuade people to part with their cash and in the process handle their excuses and objections.

- Tips on improving your working relationship with sales:

    1. Conduct joint site visits to learn from each other

    2. Pair collectors with sales people

    3. The sales people need a sales support team to assist them in their account management work

    4. Meet frequently

    5. Keep the sales people informed of any upcoming negative actions on their accounts

    6. Consider implementing joint reward and recognition programs

# Bringing out the Hired Guns

## 17

*Selecting and Managing Collection Agencies and Law Firms*

*People have been known to achieve more as a result of working with others than against them.* – Dr. Allan Fromme

*Many hands make light work.* – John Heywood

## After reading this chapter, you will be able to:

- Understand the importance of collection agencies and law firms
- Learn how to select a collection agency or law firm
- Receive tips on managing and monitoring agencies and law firms
- Learn how to terminate the services of an agency

## Importance of Collection Agencies and Law Firms

What impression do the words "agents" and "lawyers" give you?

I hope you said something like, "Strategic partners dedicated to helping me succeed."

Collection agencies and law firms are your external business partners. They spend money and resources to handle your "dead" or "near dead" accounts to allow you to focus on the "living." Conversely, companies that don't use these partners find themselves devoting resources to accounts at the bottom of their aging buckets. These companies are "bottom-heavy" because they're neglecting mildly overdue accounts to concentrate resources on older accounts with the least chance of paying. This collection strategy isn't designed to win; it's designed to lose but not too badly.

Why do some companies devote so much time and money on the accounts with the lowest probability of paying? Perhaps they were instructed by sales or senior management to be easy on customers until they hit 90 days? Then, at day 91, this massive, lumbering "collections machine" awakens from hibernation to contact these accounts. But, by then, the debtors' bills are so large that they either stop paying, or ask for lengthy payment arrangements that need more resources to track. Another strategy is to attack early and if some of the accounts still remain unpaid, then quickly hand them over to the "hired guns": collection agencies and law firms.

Agents and lawyers are a tool in your collection tool chest. In the West, they're a powerful tool that many debtors fear. By using these partners, you will be able to advise customers that you're trying to prevent their account from being referred to them. Just mentioning this fact (never as a threat) often shakes money out of the tree. If this still doesn't work to get payment, stop wasting your time and immediately refer the account to them.

Since agents and law firms touch your organization's two most valuable assets– money and customers– special care needs to be taken on how they're selected, supported, and managed. By assisting them in their work, they will help you reduce your organization's bad debt levels.

In Asia, the purpose of using agents is often misunderstood. Boe Gill, CEO of Buekhen International (www.beukhen.com) says that many Asian collection professionals miss the value of agents. They focus on the agents' commissions instead of the reduction in their operating expenses.

From personal experience I have tried to reduce agent expenses by collecting more of the older (90-120 day) accounts in-house. The net effect was I hurt myself. My in-house collectors lacked the resources the agencies had. In Asia, collection agencies have the resources to conduct site visits. They also have more unofficial skip-traces contacts than most businesses.

## Pre-selecting Collection Agencies and Law Firms

Before selecting any agents or lawyers, I highly recommend you and your management create a collection agency and law firm selection policy. The policy is an attempt to remove graft from the selection process. It will also help prevent a senior management member from instructing the collection manager to put an agent or law firm on the panel when you already have enough already. The policy should be signed and approved by senior management. Involve your procurement department and internal audit team as well.

## Selecting Collection Agencies and Law Firms

Take time selecting these external partners. If you choose the wrong partner, it will negatively affect your results and increase customer complaints.

Once they're selected, advise them that they're on a trial basis. Send them some files, see how they perform. If you're satisfied, consider signing a Service Level Agreement (SLA) with them.

**Tip:**

Err on the side of selecting too few instead of too many. By selecting only a few, you guarantee them a steady stream of accounts. Hence, the agents and lawyers will acquire the necessary resources to handle this steady stream. You will also need fewer resources to manage them. Finally, you will receive top service from them since you're one of their steady clients.

## *Collection Agencies*

Selecting collection agencies requires special care. These companies come and go overnight. It takes little capital to rent office space, buy a few chairs and install phone lines. Just about every collection manager I have met, including myself, has thought of starting their own agency at one time or another.

Selecting reputable agencies in Asia is problematic as there's less regulation and codes of conduct here. Many are reputable, but some are high class loan sharks. There's limited certification of Asian agencies, although Hong Kong and Taiwan do have an association of collection agencies.

Some points to consider when selecting an agency:

- How long have they been in business?

- Are they members of professional collection agency bodies like ACA International http://www.collector.com, or the Commercial Collection Agency Association http://ccaacollect. com? (some Asian agencies are members).

- Are the principals experienced?

- Can you contact their work references?

- How many staff do they have?

- Is the agency automated? Do they have an online debt management system? Do they have predictive dialers? Do they have a voice-recording system to measure call quality? Can they generate status reports on your files?

- Do they train their collectors? (Most Asian agencies lack formal training programs).

- Does their organizational chart make sense to you? Are they top-heavy?

- Do they have sufficient bonding or indemnity insurance?

- Have they been blacklisted by the Better Business Bureau?

- What's the agency's owner's collection philosophy and methodology (brutes or professionals)?

- Do they have adequate admin support?

- Is the Head of Admin competent?

- (For Asia) How many field collectors do they have? Are they located where your customers are located?

- Are their collection letters professional?

- Are the supervisors actively involved in the collectors' actions?

- Do commissions comprise a large portion of their collectors' salaries?

## Asian Collection Agency Profile: Dialers Call Centre Sdn. Bhd.

Dialers is a well-organized, Malaysian collection agency that I used as a collection manager at a large telecommunications company. I was impressed with their efficiency in handling large number of accounts that we sent each week. Dialers was consistently one of our top agencies in terms of recovery rates and the service they provided. They would also pass our surprise audit process. Blue-chip, listed Malaysian companies entrust Dialers to collect their accounts.

Dialers allocates teams of collectors for each client based on the number of accounts delivered. Besides telecollectors, they also have field collectors who visit the debtors' homes or places of employment. In Asia, skip-tracing is problematic due to a lack of available data-bases and good credit bureau information. Dialers has a network of search systems and contacts unavailable to most creditors.

Unlike many Asian collection agencies, Dialers is a modern agency. Their collectors attend regular training programs resulting in lower attrition rates in an industry that can average 100%. In addition, Dialers has designed its very own debt management software called, CMS (Collection Management System). The CMS system has several modules including an import module, a collector queue screen, a main debtor and activity screen, as well as an enhanced security module. All accounts sent by their clients are done via the Internet. The importing module allows Dialers to do bulk account transfers in a matter of minutes, allowing their collectors to immediately start contacting the debtors.

The company also uses a sophisticated voice recording system called Voicelink. This software records all inbound and outbound calls from its Kuala Lumpur offices. The recordings derived from the software are used not only for coaching, but also for monitoring and audit purposes.

The key principals are Vic Suppiah and Biruzz Singh. They can be contacted at +60 3 2692-0556 or at dialers@streamyx.com.
Website: www.dcc.malaysia.biz.

## Other Well-Known Asian Collection Agencies

To avoid steering you to only one agency, I'm highlighting some other well-established agencies throughout Asia-Pacific.

### Malaysia:

Beukhen International Sdn. Bhd is one of Malaysia's largest, and most well-known agencies. Contact Boe Gill at +60 3 2612 3000.
http//:www.beukhen.com

Basis (RMS) Services S/B. Malaysian client contact +60 3 2616 1647. Collections@basis.com.my. International clients contact Andrew Hwang andrew@basis.com.my. http://www.basis.com.my

TGS & Partners Sdn. Bhd. Contact Steven Tan at +60 3 4045 6088, or +60 12 2116882. Email: tgs@tgs.com.my

### Philippines:

Riscuity collects both offshore (U.S.) and Asian accounts.
http://www.riscuity.com

### Singapore:

Credit Management Consultancy pte ltd. This agency has a predictive dialer. Contact Dominic Lee at +65 6325 2033, http://www.cmc.com.sg

### Taiwan:

United Credit Services. Contact James Brown at http://www.ucredit.com.tw

## Law Firms

Selecting law firms is less complicated as they're usually more established. Using small legal firms is usually cheaper and they provide better service. Small firms often will provide free legal advice in order to get your business. However, a larger firm gives you access to a larger "Legal Brain" that can give you advice and contacts across multiple fields and industries.

Some selection criteria include:

- Length in business

- Experience of the principals

- Will my work be done by clerks or lawyers?

- Prices for standard services. Availability of volume discounts?

- Number of cases they can file per day in the courts

- Work references

- Is there adequate administration support?

- Do they specialize in commercial law and collections?

- Do they know the key collections court precedents when seeking judgments?

- How quickly will they return my calls if I need legal advice on a particular case or scenario?

- Do they charge for advice?

- Are they automated?

- What kind of status reports will they provide on your accounts? How often?

## *When to Use Collection Agencies and Law Firms?*

### Collection Agencies:

The earlier you refer the accounts, the better the chance the agents will have of collecting the debt, and the lower the commission rates you will pay.

I know of an American telco that refers accounts at day 90. In Asia, another telco first splits its customers into two classifications: "good" and "bad" paymasters. The "good" accounts are referred at day 90, the "bad" at day 75. The criteria for a "good" paymaster are:

- No bounced cheques or credit cards for the last six months

- No phone lines interrupted due to non-payment for the last six months

With a behavioral scoring system, you can refer accounts based on behavioral scores. For those customers with good scores, refer later. For those with poor scores, refer immediately and stop wasting your collectors' time.

If you lack a scoring system, then refer the following accounts earlier than normal accounts:

- First payment defaults
- Can't be reached debtors (skips)
- Accounts with multiple bounced cheques or credit card chargebacks
- Small balance accounts
- High balance new accounts (often they are fraud)

Sending accounts to collection agencies should be done frequently and automatically. Avoid sending agents many accounts all at once. Unplanned, large account deliveries are hard for agencies to process. Send regular, bite-sized chunks and the agencies will attain better recovery rates. They will commit the required resources if they expect to receive a steady stream of your accounts.

**Law Firms:**

Decide at what value you will refer to legal. Is it worthwhile pursuing small balance accounts if the legal expenses are greater than the overall debt?

Take note that once you refer an account for legal action that you have essentially terminated the business relationship with the customer. In addition, legal expenses are high and the success rates are generally low- especially for non-secured creditors. However, referring nothing at all is a worse message to send to the market.

**Tip:**

It's easier working with collection agencies that also do legal actions. Since the agencies are already working the accounts, they know which accounts stand the best chance of paying once legal action is commenced. The legal charges are normally borne by the collection agency, but their commission may increase if they're successful in collecting payment once legal action has commenced. Although legal in the U.S., some Asian countries prohibit collection agencies and legal firms from combining these two functions.

One company in the U.S. has an interesting eight stage referral process. However, if at any time during the process the agency decides to commence legal action, the referral process ends and the account is "owned" by that agent. The agent's in-house legal department then takes over and guides the account through the legal process. Once legal action starts, a higher commission rate is paid for any monies recovered.

## Monitoring Collection Agencies' Performance

Once the agencies have been selected, you will need to put in place processes to ask these questions:

- How do I evaluate their performance?
- How do I reward them?

### Collection Agencies' Remuneration

Agencies work off an aging scheme, the older the debt, the higher the commission they require for any monies they collect. It's usually easier paying all agencies a flat commission based on the age of the accounts and the amount they collect.

Although flat commissions are easier to monitor, a tiered commission structure is more effective. It works on the simple principle that the higher the recovery rates, the higher the commission rate. So, instead of paying a flat 20% for all monies recovered for accounts aged 90-150 days, you pay the following:

| If an agency achieves a recovery rate of: | You pay this % of the recovered amount: |
| --- | --- |
| Greater than 35% | 22% |
| 30-34% | 20% |
| Less than 29% | 18% |

To maximize the benefits of a tiered commission scheme, tie the file allocation to the commission scheme. For example, if you have four agents and 100 accounts, allocate the accounts based on the agents' recovery rates. The agent with the top recovery rate gets 35 accounts, second place 30, third place 20, and fourth place 15. Why send an equal number of accounts (and value) to average performing agencies when you could be sending more accounts to your more efficient agencies?

### Account Sorting

Ensure the sorting system is impartial, automated, and fast. Collection agencies, especially in Asia, complain that some clients give "juicer" accounts to certain agents in return for kick-backs. Other agents complain they need to pay kick-backs to get on a client's panel.

If your organization uses a manual process in allocating accounts, you WILL experience internal fraud!

Here are some signs to look for that **could** indicate fraud in your department. Alert yourself when:

Collection agencies frequently:

- Deliver food and gifts to the office

- Take your people to lunch and after work events

- Stop calling the collection manager and instead deal only with the person who sends them accounts

- Some agencies don't get paid on time, while others do

- You see collection agents at your lower level staffs' weddings and baby showers bearing expensive gifts

- The employee who oversees the agents has been in that job for many years. S/he also refuses to accept a transfer to another collection team

In addition, ensure the accounts are sent to the agents immediately after your organization's collection actions have stopped. Avoid having the accounts linger in your system or desk before sending them out. Ideally, you will be online with your agencies.

**Tip:**

If you refer accounts early, second referrals are still "juicy." Second referrals are those unpaid accounts that the first agency was unable to collect. Use second referrals as an incentive for your agents to become top performers. Consider giving second referrals only to your best performing first referral agencies.

Use second referrals as a testing ground for new agencies. Give them second referrals only for a period of six months, and then evaluate their performance.

## Agency Support

Your agencies are your business partners. They require adequate support. Assign people and systems to manage and assist them. These people will ensure the agencies receive their accounts on time; the accounts are aborted on time, and commissions paid on time.

Ensure the accounts that you refer contain as much debtor information as possible such as name, address, contact numbers (ideally a couple of addresses and contact numbers). It also helps to include Social Security numbers or – for Asia – Identification Card numbers. If possible, include date and amount of last payment, and the most recent account history. Include any "returned bill" notes so the agency knows that the address on the account is questionable. The more debtor information you provide, the better chance the agencies will have of collecting the debts.

If you don't already have one, work with your agencies to implement a web-based tracking system. Such systems allow the agencies to view and add notes to their assigned accounts.

The system benefits are many:

- Agents see the accounts you refer them and view the latest contact information.

- Agents can update the accounts with the debtor's latest contact information. This will save time later if the account becomes a second referral. It also helps the legal firms serve the debtor the required court documents at the most recent address.

- Agents can check to see if the payment was made. This reduces the time taken by the agents calling your people to check for this information.

- Customer complaints are reduced. Customers complain that agents "harass" them, especially after they have paid the bill. This happens when the agents don't know that the customer has paid.

- You measure how fast and vigorous the agents are working the accounts assigned.

- The system automatically generates reports, calculates commissions, and allocates accounts.

Companies without such systems need to keep their agents updated by email, faxes or phone. Such manual and low tech systems are time-consuming as both parties need to constantly call each other to check on each other's account activities.

There are many I.T. vendors selling systems catering to this need. In many cases, the automation cost will be shared by both parties. It's a good idea to check with your organization's I.T. department for their security concerns, but most systems nowadays address this concern. The systems are designed to allow the agents to only view those accounts they have been assigned.

Agents are a vocal bunch. If I receive one complaint above all others it's this: "We're not treated as business partners." Why would you treat people who are trying to collect your organization's money - and make you look like a hero – any less than a full-time business partner?

> **Tip:**
>
> In managing, or mismanaging agents, I have learned the hard way that terminating a collection agency can result in a lawsuit. Consider taking the following two ideas:
>
> 1. Make sure your Service Level Agreement is created by your legal people
>
> 2. Make sure it allows you to easily terminate the business relationship. The easiest termination clause is one in which you don't need to give a reason.
>
> E.g. *"We hereby terminate your services according to clause 2.36 of the Service Level Agreement contract dated _____."*

However, before terminating any agent, be careful. Be sure this drastic action is required. Many agencies operate at low profit margins. They rent space and hire staff to handle your accounts. If you terminate them quickly, without warning, they will experience difficulties. Some alternatives to immediate termination include:

- Sending warning letters pointing out their deficiencies

- Temporarily reducing their number of accounts

- Temporarily cutting their first referral accounts

- Temporarily suspending them from receiving any accounts

If you still believe termination is justified, involve your legal advisors in the process. Make sure the reason is significant. E.g.:

- Poor recovery rates

- Repeatedly failing audits

- Using unprofessional or illegal collection techniques

- Bribing your staff or other unethical actions

## Monitoring Law Firms' Performance

Just like the agents, you will need to decide how to measure your legal firms' performance. With legal firms, the primary concern is speed, not recovery rates. How quickly do they process your accounts through the legal system? They will also need to keep you posted on the accounts' status either via reports – or better yet– an automated web-based system. It's easier to manage law firms than agents since the legal firms' role is limited to sending and filing documents. Rarely will they need to call a customer.

### Law Firm Remuneration

Negotiate fees based on the different services they offer. If you refer many accounts to them, request volume discounts. Some firms tack on additional "legal fees" to the debtor's balance. Again, check with your legal department if this is acceptable, if so, your collectors and agents can use it as a collection tool:

> *"Mr. / Ms. Customer, I'm trying to help prevent your account from being sent for legal action and save your money in additional legal fees."*
> (Ensure this statement is a fact).

Similar to the agents, consider allocating more accounts to the more efficient law firms.

### Law Firm Support

Like collection agencies, legal firms also deserve your wholehearted support. Generally, the amount of support they require is less. If an account goes to court, the legal firms will require copies of open bills, contracts, and any collection notes on the account. Again, consider using a web-based system to keep you and your legal firms updated on each step of the legal process.

## Auditing Collection Agencies and Law Firms

To ensure your collection agencies and law firms provide you and your debtors with good service, you will need to frequently audit their performance. You will need to know how to conduct audits on collection agencies and law firms.

## Collection Agency Audits

Agents should be audited a minimum of once a year. Ensure you send at least two auditors together. To avoid possible conflict of interests, send auditors who don't manage that particular agency.

Audits tell a lot about your agents. You see if their collection tactics are compliant with local laws. You see if the operation is professional and well-organized.

Don't announce your audits. Pop in at the start of the business day. Then consider evaluating some of these areas.

## Management's Ability:

- Is management present when the workday starts? No? Ask the staff what time management usually appears.

- Does management value my business?

- Do supervisors give feedback to the collectors on their activities?

- Does management take responsibility for any problem areas discovered in the audit? Or, do they blame lower-level staff?

## Collection Efficiency

If you lack a web-based tracking system, then present the agency with a list of 150-250 accounts and ask for a status report on the accounts. Look for:

- Date assigned and the date of the first collection activity

- Number of collection activities on the accounts

- Quality of activities. Are the agents working smart? E.g. If a high balance account has many CNAs (call no answers), then are the agents following it up with the next logical action such as a site visit?

## Collection Professionalism

Since agents touch customers, one of their measurements should be professionalism:

- Are the collectors professional and confident on the phone?

- Do the collectors harass and threaten customers resulting in legal violations?

- Are the collectors fast?

- Are there dedicated collectors assigned to handle my files or do they work multiple clients' files?

- What's the rate of employee turnover?

- Do the supervisors monitor the collectors' call quality?

## Administrative Support

- Is the Head of Admin knowledgeable?

- Are there enough administration staff?

- Are there enough field collectors?

- Are the collection letters legal and professional?

- Are the field collectors allowed to receive payments, including cash? If so, do they issue numbered receipts? Are there any missing receipts?

> **Tip:**
>
> Occasionally send your agents a few "dummy" accounts of varying value to measure their efficiency and professionalism. The dummy accounts could be aliases for people in your own department. You will get to experience first-hand what your overdue customers' already experience.

### Audit Report

When writing the audit report, link it to the agreed Service Level Agreement's key performance indicators. Be specific. Give account numbers for those files where a mistake was made. Perhaps, the field collector received the money, but it wasn't banked in within the agreed SLA. Perhaps, a high balance account had four CNAs (call no answers) without the collector ordering a site visit or a skip trace. Perhaps, an account was given to the agents on June 1, but the first activity was 15 days later.

In the audit report, detail what changes you want the agent to make before the next audit. The agent should write an explanation to the points raised with their plans to implement the changes.

Call for a meeting with the agency's managerial staff or owners to present the audit findings. Be willing to listen to their explanations to the concerns you raised. Give them a copy of the report and allow them to write anything they would like to add. Ask that they sign the audit report to show receipt and understanding; this protects you later if they contest a suspension or termination.

Just as you have collection treatments for your debtors, create agency treatments. The treatments are based on the performance of the agencies' recovery rates and audit ratings. The treatments trigger different actions based on their performance. For example, an agency with a "pass" audit rating requires another surprise audit in 6-12 months, while a "fail" rating could trigger a second audit in 30 days.

Agency treatments are triggered not only by their audit performance, but also by their recovery rates.

What action is triggered if:

- An agency's average recovery rate is significantly below the group's average recovery rate?

- Your best performing agency suddenly becomes your worst?

- You give a consistently poor performing agency a written warning, their recovery rates improve, but shortly thereafter the recovery rates slip again to below average?

And also, what action is triggered if:

- You catch an agency bribing your staff?
- You find agencies using illegal or improper collection techniques to collect your organization's debts?

"Triggers" could be:

- Warning letters
- Surprise audits
- Reduction in files sent to the agency
- Partial suspension (no first referrals)
- Complete suspension (no files sent to the agency)
- Complete termination of services

**Tip:**

When your legal department creates the SLA contract, include a clause that clearly states what the agency must do with your accounts upon termination. Some questions you need to answer:

- Does the terminated agency continue working the accounts until the batch expires?
- Does the agency immediately return all accounts?
- What happens to the accounts that have long-term payment arrangements?
- What happens to the agency's commissions if customers pay after the termination date?

I recommend you immediately take back all accounts assigned to terminated agents and pass them to another agency. In the meantime, include in their final commission cheque any amounts received within two weeks of the termination date. Finally, all long-term payment arrangements the agency negotiated, that were approved by you, will need to be monitored in-house and any rightful commissions paid to your ex-agent.

After terminating an agency, prepare for the fall-out. The agency will likely give you a personal visit to win-back the business. If this fails, your boss will likely be contacted, and then your boss' boss. Make sure all parties agree before any termination is done. The agency's poor performance has cost you dearly in lost collections. Is it worth retaining such partners?

In Asia, I have seen terminated agencies make all kinds of "offers" to take them back. The offers include cartons of cigarettes and bottles of liquor. Stay firm.

## Legal audits

Legal audits are similar to agent audits. Show up early, unannounced, and start digging to see how effectively they manage your accounts.

Legal audits are usually simpler. The key criteria is the timeliness of their administrative procedures. How quickly were the legal actions taken from the date the account was first assigned?

Track 100 or so accounts that have gone through the complete legal process to see how quickly they were processed at each stage. Set agreed Key Performance Indicators (KPIs) with your legal partners for each stage of the legal process. Law firms generally perform an administrative role, so spend time evaluating their admin strength. Is the head of admin competent? Do they have enough admin staff? Can they provide you with a status report of 100 accounts you assigned them within minutes from requesting it? Is their admin system automated?

### Law Firms' Audit Report

The law firms' audit report is usually less detailed than the agencies'. It will still list specific customer examples of where the KPI's were missed. The report should include recommendations to improve their processes. Similar to the agencies, allow them an opportunity to respond. Depending on the audit's "pass" or "fail" rating, there will be another unannounced audit scheduled to see if the problems the audit discovered reoccur.

**Tip:**

If you allow your legal firms to collect customer payments, ensure you audit this process in-depth, especially in Asia as cash payments are common.

## *Another Option: Debt Buyers*

North American creditors have an additional option if their collection agencies were unsuccessful in collecting the debt: Debt Buyers. These companies purchase written-off debts for pennies on the dollar. Some of the largest debt buyers are Asset Acceptance Capital Corp, Portfolio Recovery Associates, Asta Funding, and Encore Capital Group.

The debt buying business is booming in the U.S., and with it more opportunities for collectors. One example is Asset Acceptance Capital Corp. According to their 2004 annual statement, $67b worth of credit card debt was sold in the U.S that year, a ten-fold increase from ten years ago. Their own cash collections have rocketed from $44m in 2000 to $268m in 2004. Asset Acceptance had 60 employees in 1998 and 1,768 in 2004.

## *Summary*

- Collection agencies and legal firms help you concentrate your limited resources on those accounts with a higher probability of paying.

- Be cautious when terminating a collection agency.

- The earlier you refer accounts to collection agencies and legal firms, the higher the chances for recovery.

- Treat your collection agencies and legal firms as business partners. Provide them with support. The more you help them, the more they will help you.

- Audits are necessary to see if the agency or law firm is abiding by the Service Level Agreement.

- Just as there is a collection treatment for debtors, there should be a treatment for your external partners that activates immediately when an audit is failed or if their performance deteriorates.

Part VI:
# Leading Collection Professionals

# "I've Been Collecting Before You Were Even Born!"

*Leading a Collection Team*

---

*Remember the difference between a boss and a leader; a boss says 'Go!'– a leader says 'Let's go!'* – E.M. Kelly

## After reading this chapter, you will be able to:

- Understand the importance of building a performance-based work environment
- Design incentive programs for collectors based on multiple "qualifiers"
- Learn the four steps in giving effective recognition
- Realize the importance of open communication and "serious fun" in promoting a productive work environment
- Learn how to reduce employee turnover
- Use different interview techniques to choose the right people
- Learn how to manage poor performers using the "dental office" concept

## *Importance of Good Supervisors and Managers*

Having the proper policies and systems in place are important for the overall success of your team or department, but another equally important factor is effective leadership. Without effective leadership, the best laid plans won't be implemented effectively.

If you look at exit interviews conducted by Human Resources departments, one of the chief reasons employees leave is due to their supervisors and managers. Ineffective leaders cause companies a lot of damage. This chapter looks at what you can do, within your control, to lead a collections team or department.

Using effective people leadership skills builds a positive work environment, and a positive work environment gives you a better chance of hitting your targets. Leading people is never easy. A management book's title sums it up nicely, "Managing People Is Like Herding Cats."[31]

Do you like to be managed? Do you like to even manage yourself? Most of us don't, but we can be led, provided, we're inspired and involved. Uninspired and uninvolved employees say things like, *"Why should I listen to you? I've been collecting before you were even born!"*

My collections style is Customer Relationship Management (CRM) based. Its goal is to help debtors avoid negative actions by getting them to pay their bills. My style of leadership is Employee Relationship Management (ERM) based. Its goal is to help employees hit targets they once thought impossible. Helping people builds rapport which in turn increases your chance of getting what you need. "I scratch your back, ....."

## Importance of a Shared Departmental Vision

Creating a performance-based work environment is great, but if your people don't buy-in to the department's vision and goals, you will achieve limited success. A vision is the future picture of what the department is striving to become. The most effective visions are those that receive input from all levels of the department. They're sometimes called "visceral visions" since they're seen and felt.

Some supervisors view their employees as "hands". They're just concerned with the department's results. These managers should be called "man agers". They're not leaders. Instead, today's leaders must focus on their employees' heads, hearts, and hands.

## Getting Buy-in for Operational Processes

Leading collection teams by barking orders rarely succeeds in getting a team's buy-in. Nobody likes being told what to do. Be it employees, spouses, or children. Instead, identify the problem you face and solicit others' input on possible solutions. A leader's part is mostly to fine-tune their solutions. Avoid giving straight-away solutions to operational problems as they usually don't work, especially if you—like most supervisors—aren't 100% operational. The operational guys know the problems, and the solutions, better than you.

---

31    If interested, the book is *Managing People is like Herding Cats Warren Bennis on Leadership,* by Warren Bennis. Published by Executive Excellence (reissue 1997).

By encouraging people to suggest solutions, you get them to think. Plus, you will get a better solution, and, most importantly, you stand a greater chance of getting that solution implemented because you cared to get their input. The solution changes from a "your" solution to an "our" solution.

In Asia, supervisors who solicit input on solving problems are sometimes considered "dumb" supervisors. Some employees believe that the supervisor is supposed to have all the answers. The employees are merely supposed to do. However, this attitude will change with time once the staff see that their input is used and that overall efficiency is improved. I would prefer being considered dumb at first and smart later – than the reverse.

At one challenging consulting assignment in Malaysia, I was asked to improve the creative thinking skills of a credit department. During my investigation, I found that large credit decisions were made by the regional credit manager based in Singapore. The regional credit manager would ask the local credit manager to gather the necessary facts on the credit applicant. The local credit manager dutifully gathered the information and sent it. After a week or two a "yes" or "no" decision would come from the regional office.

The process didn't promote thinking or learning. It promoted doing. The regional credit manager acted like an all-knowing seer. He had all the answers and never asked for the local credit manager's own recommendation, nor did he share his decision-making process in deciding a "yes" or a "no".

## *Motivating Your Teams*

Fostering a performance-based work environment, with an element of "serious fun", combined with a participatory management style promotes a work environment where people can be motivated. Motivation is important in collections as it's difficult to motivate and sell debtors on the benefits of paying if we ourselves aren't motivated.

Here are some suggestions to promote a motivated work environment for your team :

- **Ask them what motivates them.** Too often supervisors complain that no matter what they do, their teams aren't motivated. They naively think that they could motivate staff without taking the time to understand what motivates them. As supervisors, we need to understand what motivates each staff member. It's surprising to find the number of supervisors who never ask their staff what motivates them. If they did, they would find out that not all collectors are motivated by incentives or bonuses.

By understanding what motivates your team members, you build rapport, and foster a better work environment.

- **Increase job satisfaction.** If you find that some of your team members are demotivated, ask them why. Our work is – at times – boring and stressful. We need to ask our demotivated staff for their input :

  *"What do you suggest we do to make your job more challenging?"*

- Share the big picture. People become demotivated if they don't see the fruits of their labor. Share the impacts they make to the department both individually and as a team. Ensure you recognize them for their positive impacts.

- Implement individual awards. Display the daily collection results per collector. This awakens their competitive spirit. It leads to an energized environment. On the report, consider shading or noting any collectors' names whose trend is below target.

- Implement team awards. A supervisor influences an employee only so far, the key to influencing them further is from their fellow co-workers. In battles, soldiers risk their lives not for their superiors, but for their fellow soldiers. The same holds true with staff. If a respected peer tells a poor performer to "buck up", there's a better chance of improvement than being told by a supervisor.

- Set high expectations for everyone in the department. We set high expectations for our debtors, we should also set high expectations for our staff. We fully expect they will perform a good job. If they provide anything less, we should be shocked.

  Think back to when you were a teenager and how your parents trusted you. What was the most hurtful word they could possibly say? For me, it was "disappointed."

  *"Steve, I'm disappointed in you."*

  A disappointed, calm boss makes more of a lasting impression than an angry, screaming one. Employees will try to show the disappointed bosses that they're valuable employees. They will give up on the irrational ones.

Fostering a highly motivated environment takes a holistic view of their working conditions I see it as such:

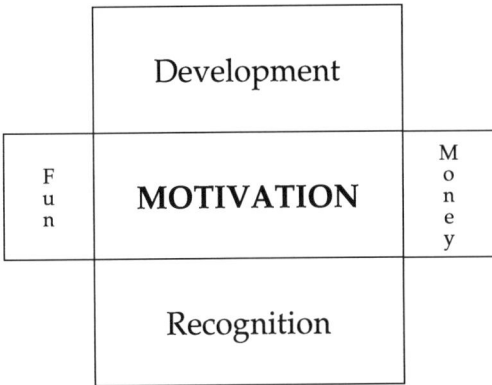

Exhibit 18.1

## Building a Performance-based Work Environment

There's a saying made famous by Deng Xiaoping that crystallizes the essence of a performance-based culture :

*"It doesn't matter what color a cat is as long as it catches mice."*

If we're purely performance-based managers, then performance-based measures should be the main criteria to evaluate performance. Non-essential factors like ethnicity, education, beauty, age, gender, and others must be eliminated.

Once staff are clear that the only departmental "favorites" you have are those who perform well, then many will try to live up to your performance standards. By being open with your staff on the importance you place on performance, they will understand how you think. How many times have you wished you could figure out how your boss thinks?

The next few sections will examine how to create and manage a performance-based collections department.

## Make It Visual

I'm a firm believer in making good or poor performance visual. The portion of our brain devoted to sight is the largest of all the senses. Human beings are visual creatures. We learn much through observation. Your team observes what happens to staff who perform well and who perform poorly. Whatever action or inaction you choose is observed.

As active leaders, we highlight behavior – positive or negative. We don't hide from or ignore certain behaviors. We constantly reward positive performance and extinguish negative performance. Here are some ways to publicly highlight good performance:

- Announce the top performers each month.
- Recognize the top performers at departmental meetings.
- Promote from within whenever possible.
- Give special projects to the top performers.
- Physically move people to new teams based on their performance.
- Allow top performers to handle supervisor calls.
- Publicly pass out money or prizes to the top performers.

## How to Recognize Good Performance

When highlighting good performance, do it right. Don't pat someone on the back and give confusing general compliments like, "Frank, nice job, keep up the good work." Poor Frank won't know what you're talking about. What "job?" "What did I do?" Instead, take the time to be specific and genuine when giving recognition. It will provide Frank with more information so that he will be able to repeat the good performance. It will also make a lasting impact.

A sincere compliment has a few key elements:

1) State the specific good performance

2) Explain what he or she did to achieve that performance

3) Explain the impacts of the performance

4) Express gratitude

**For example:**

1) *"Frank, you had a good month last month. You collected 20% more than your team's average."*

2) *"It took hard work and proper time-management skills to accomplish that."*

3) *"It helped us hit our monthly collection target."*

4) *"Thank you."*

Studies have shown that an oral congratulatory message from the boss – for most people – leads to higher levels of job satisfaction and motivation. Higher than even a written message or email. Recognition is a great, cheap way of encouraging top performance in your department. You should be recognizing good performance daily. Don't wait until the end of the month to recognize people. Do it after observing a good call, or a good day's results. People rarely tire of hearing sincere praise.

Poor performance is more difficult to highlight as people generally view themselves as "good" or "above average" performers. It's the same when you hear people talk about other peoples' driving. How many times have you heard someone complain about their own driving ability?

We all desperately want to maintain our self-esteem. It's part of being human. So, to reduce hurt feelings and increase the chance of extinguishing the negative behavior, give improvement feedback privately and early. Giving improvement feedback privately is especially important in Asia to maintain "face".

One method I have used to give improvement feedback is through a concept I call, "The Dental Office". It will be discussed later in this chapter.

## Creating Incentive Programs

### Monthly Incentives

Everyone in the department must understand what's expected of them both quantitatively and qualitatively. The collectors should know the monthly targets before the month starts. Each month, the manager or supervisor should set the monthly target using the number of work days that month, plus analyzing past collection figures. Once you calculate a minimum daily collection target, factor in a *small* "buffer" for lunch breaks, illnesses, time away attending training, holidays, vacations, and other scenarios.

*For example:*

This month has 20 working days. By looking at previous months, you find that the average collector who worked 20 days, collected RM50,000 a day. You have analyzed other factors that pull people away from their desks to arrive at a buffer of 10%. For this month, you will require the collectors to collect at least RM900,000. Any collector who collects less than RM900,000 will be considered missing the monthly target.

Now that you have collection targets, put in place a small bonus scheme where the collectors get additional money for exceeding the target. It could be something like this:

| Exceeding the target by: | Results in bonus payment of: |
|---|---|
| 10% | RM200 |
| 15% | RM300 |
| >20% | RM400 |

In addition to an individual bonus, a team bonus promotes team-work. It operates the same way. Let's say you have a team of 10 people.

The team target is RM900,000 x 10 people = RM9,000,000. To hit the 10% bonus, the team will need to collect RM990,000. If they collect that amount, then every team member who hit or exceeded their minimal target of RM900,000 receives a team bonus, too.

The teams will decide if every qualifying member receives the same team bonus amount, or if the amounts are scaled based on their individual performances within the team.

Each quarter run a special contest. This could be a contest to reward the top 5-10% of collectors who get the most credit card payments in a day or month. Or, a prize to the collector who collects the largest PTP each day, and so forth. The prizes could be in the form of cash, gift vouchers, electronic items or whatever the employees value. Adding a special incentive once in a while adds excitement.

Be careful setting "dollars collected" as the only determinant for achieving a bonus. By doing so, you could be building a culture of "money faces." To avoid this, add "qualifiers" to your incentive programs.

Here are some "qualifiers" to ensure collectors don't solely focus on the money:

### 1.  Percent of Promises to Pay (PTP) Kept.

This is calculated by taking the Total Number of PTPs Kept / Total Number of PTPs Created x 100.

This requirement encourages collectors to set strong PTPs and avoid putting PTPs on all accounts. It should be based on the number of kept PTPs, not their monetary value as a PTP with a large value will skew the results.

### 2.  Roll Dollars:

This is useful if your collectors manage account portfolios. Look at the value of the collector's portfolio at the beginning of the month and compare it to what it is at the end. Depending on the size of the decrease, you reward the performance.

### 3.  Aging and DSO:

Evaluate collectors by the total aging and DSO levels in their accounts. You will need separate reports per collector to do this. In the past, I have assigned individual corporate collectors by bill cycle to easily monitor their performance.

### 4.  Call Quality Ratings.

Create a call quality form which instructs the collector on what steps and scripts the collectors are expected to use. It helps ensure the collectors sound professional over the phone. If they don't follow the form, they get poor call quality ratings. Set a minimum score and listen to about 10 calls per collector twice a month. Take notes while listening and give the collector immediate feedback.

### 5. Number of Times Tardy Each Month

Perhaps allow one or two a month, then anything over that is counted against the person's statistics?

The above factors are weighted to create a final score to determine a collector's ranking within the department. "Dollars Collected" is the main determinant, or *driver*, and the secondary determinants are the "*qualifiers*." Once a collector hits the driver, the qualifiers are analyzed to see if they're also hit before paying any bonus.

Consider adjusting certain collectors' targets if they were away from the phones due to training or "special projects." Collectors shouldn't be negatively affected for taking the time to learn new skills or help the department.

Avoid adjusting their statistics for sick leave or vacation leave as this figure has already been calculated in the monthly target as a buffer. Instead, they need to also feel the pain of their absence. When they share the pain, people will plan their vacations more wisely.

**Tip:**

At one Asian company, collectors are paid quarterly bonuses. As a result, collectors manage their time closely since they could lose a large quarterly bonus. It has also helps reduce sick days and tardiness. It promotes self-management.

### 6. Incentives for Collection Call Centers

Besides having the previous five qualifiers, collectors working in a call center environment with a PABX (Public Automated Branch Exchange) and an ACD (Automatic Call Distributor) will be rated on additional criteria. Sometimes these criteria are more important than dollars collected, especially for the front-end team. Early stage delinquent accounts are usually collected with a "light touch". As a result, service level is important.

Service level is normally calculated as the percent of calls answered within 15 seconds. A "good" service level rule-of-thumb is usually 85%

or higher. Some teams, like the VIP team, will have different service levels targets of say 90%. That said, service level vary by industry.

In addition to service level, there's abandonment rate which is the percent of hang-ups before the 15 seconds expires. The abandonment target for many companies is <5%.

In order to meet your department's service level targets, supervisors need to consider the following individual measurements.

### 7. Average number of calls per day.

Set a minimum number of calls per day a collector must make or receive.

One American call center limits the number of inbound calls a collector receives. If the collector makes more than 20 outbound calls an hour, the collector is considered as "rushing" the customer. The system then blocks the incoming, more lucrative, customer calls until the collector's average talk time increases.

### 8. Average number of hours (or minutes) on "available" status

This KPI requires collectors to be on-the-phone for a certain number of minutes / hours each day. Allow time for breaks, lunch, "wrap-up time" after the call, and administrative work.

## Dangers of a Commission-based Salary Structure

Beware of incentives that focus heavily on commissions. I fully support bonuses for above average performance, but I have seen ill effects of collection environments where commissions are paramount. In some organizations, collectors receive a percentage of what they collect, even if they fail to hit their monthly target.

In commission-based work environments, I hear and see how customers are treated. They're treated like "money bags" instead of people. If collectors treat customers like "money bags", you're going to lose customers.

In commission-based work environments, when you ask for volunteers to work on special projects to improve the department's operations, you won't get any takers. Try getting them off the phones to attend training. They will calculate how much money they will lose before volunteering. By contrast, in other collection departments, being asked to work on a special project is considered an honor and a nice break from the phones.

In many collection agencies in Asia, collectors are paid mostly by commissions. Such work environments lead to poor customer service and unprofessional collection methods.

## *Yearly Performance Ratings*

Rating collectors and supervisors on their quantitative performance each month is easy, but how to rate them at year end?

Performance ratings are used to determine salary increments and promotions. These ratings shouldn't be based 100% on quantitative results. You don't want to encourage "slash and burn" collectors within your department. These collectors are the hard-working, results-orientated ones who do their job and damn anyone (or any customer) who gets in their way. The department's monthly bonus is based 100% on quantitative factors, but the yearly performance rating is a mixture of both quantitative and qualitative factors.

The qualitative factors are defined by the Human Resources department, who will likely call them "competencies." Here are some examples of qualitative factors used in some organizations to evaluate staff:

1. Adaptability (ability and willingness to accept change)

2. Self-development (willingness to learn new things)

3. I.T. savvy (ability to learn new I.T. systems or technologies)

4. Team work (ability to work with others)

5. Attitude

6. Initiative

7. Customer orientated (give top service to both internal and external customers)

8. Creative thinking

9. Risk taking and decision making

10. Integrity

11. Accuracy in work

12. Business savvy (ability to focus on cost, profits, and the big picture)

13. Knowledge sharing

14. Time management

15. Valuing diversity

16. Communication (ability to listen, speak, and give / receive effective feedback)

In North America, performance reviews are commonplace, but in Asia they aren't.

## Promoting Open Communication

Open communication is the oxygen a performance-based work environment needs to thrive. Feedback needs to be freely given to congratulate good performance and address poor performance. If we're truly a performance-based department, feedback should come from all groups and at all levels. Everyone should feel empowered to offer ideas and suggestions to improve their supervisor's performance, their colleague's, their own, their manager's, and even their department's.

Allowing people the opportunity to give input helps to change negative attitudes about their jobs, the organization, or even you. It also encourages creativity.

## Promoting Creative Thinking

Today's workplace requires collectors to be creative thinkers. Our debtors are incredibly creative when it comes to avoiding payment. If our brains are less creative than theirs, guess who's going to win less in our negotiations?

People think Charles Darwin said, "Survival of the fittest." He didn't. In fact, if that were true, there should be dinosaurs walking outside your house right now. What he did state was "survival of the most adaptable." As humans, our primary advantage over other species is the power of our brains. As collectors, if our brains are less adaptable than our debtors', we will lose. As a collection leader, do you encourage your people to use their brains? Do you solicit their advice, opinions, and ideas?

## Promoting Fun!

Collections is a stressful job, and part of our job is to give customers a little stress now to avoid more stress later. We're constantly measured on dollars collected, PTP kept rates, number of calls, service levels, recovery rates, bad debt percentages, aging, Days Sales Outstanding (DSO) levels, and other measurements. While all these measurements are going on, we're asked to do more, faster, with fewer resources.

Working in stressful jobs is difficult enough, but if the workplace isn't fun then it's sheer torture. Admit it. Who wants to work in a place that isn't fun? Life is too short to be spent working in a dull place. To avoid burnout and distress in our industry, our work environment motto should be: "Work hard, play hard."

Do you have fun at work?

Fun is an important component in managing people, especially in the collections field where employee turnover and low pay cause managers headaches. According to the U.S. Bureau of Labor Statistics, the average American, full-time worker earned $18.79 per hour, whereas the average full-time "bill and account collector" earned 24% less, or $14.29 per hour.[32]

Combining a stressful job, in a dull environment, at a below average salary is a recipe for high employee turnover.

Some employers have scrapped dress codes if their collectors never meet customers. You see collectors in the U.S. wearing hats and shorts at work. One Asian employer lightens up their work atmosphere with televisions hanging from the ceiling playing MTV – without the volume. I call it "MTV Lite". Other departments have regular fun activities. Consider ways to pump up the fun levels in your work environment. It's cheaper than hiring and training new staff. It's also a lot of fun.

### Some Fun Ideas

There are many fun ways to improve your work environment. Buy books or visit websites that are geared to this subject. I have included a few ideas here, but I suggest your collectors set up a "fun committee" themselves to organize the events.

Some quick ideas:

- Quarterly contests with small prizes. The contests are based on performance.

- Last Friday of the month dress-theme day. Let the collectors choose the theme. Award small prizes to the winners.

- Birthday or joining date anniversary cakes.

- Awards for best call, best new idea, biggest PTP, best dispute resolution, best response to an excuse or objection.

- Decorate the office with motivational posters to change the drabness of the work environment.

- Healthy "fun" competition between your department and another department. For example, have a competition between the customer service department and the collection department on which department has the best service level for a particular month.

- Yearly or bi-yearly staff outing or departmental dinner.

---

32   Bureau of Labor Statistics, *"National Compensation Survey: Occupational Wages in the United States"*, July 2003, < http://www.bls.gov/ncs/ocs/sp/ncbl0635.pdf> (12 May 2005), U.S. Department of Labor.

**Tip:**

Some words of warning on fun events. To speed things up, offer the "fun committee" a choice of three options, then have them decide and organize the event.

## *Reducing Employee Turnover*

Employees leave companies for many reasons such as: stress, dull work environment, boring jobs, lousy supervisors, low pay, poor communication, and other factors. According to a call center survey conducted by Cutting Edge Information, employee turnover in the U.S. financial services sector runs as high as 39%[33]. Imagine trying to hit your goals if you lose 39% of your trained staff each year?

Money is the reason why we work, but money isn't the "be all end all" factor for all employees. We take jobs for money, but we often stay in them for non-monetary reasons. Studies have shown that organizations that provide the following usually experience lower employee turnover rates:

1. Performance-based work environment

2. Respect and integrity

3. Interesting work

4. Good communication

5. Fun

6. Training (formal and on-the-job)

7. Career paths

Dr. Charles Gahala surveyed 358 credit practitioners and found they ranked "workshops and conferences to update credit skills" as their most important task to advance in their careers.[34] People expect to be developed, and if they're not, they will find another organization that will.

---

33  Cutting Edge Information, *Financial Services Call Centers Experience 39% Employee Turnover Rate*, Press Release, July 14, 2005. <http://www.biz.yahoo.com/prnews/050714.html?.v=16> (10 September 2005). Full report available at http://www.financialcallcenters.com.

34  Charles L. Gahala, Credit Management: *Principles and Practice*,(National Association of Credit Management, 1996), 9. Referring to his research: "Tasks of Business Credit Personnel, An Occasional Paper" , *Credit Research Foundation* (February 1985).

## *Career Progression Scheme*

A career progression scheme is a roadmap that shows people their future career path. The diagram starts at the bottom left and flows upward.

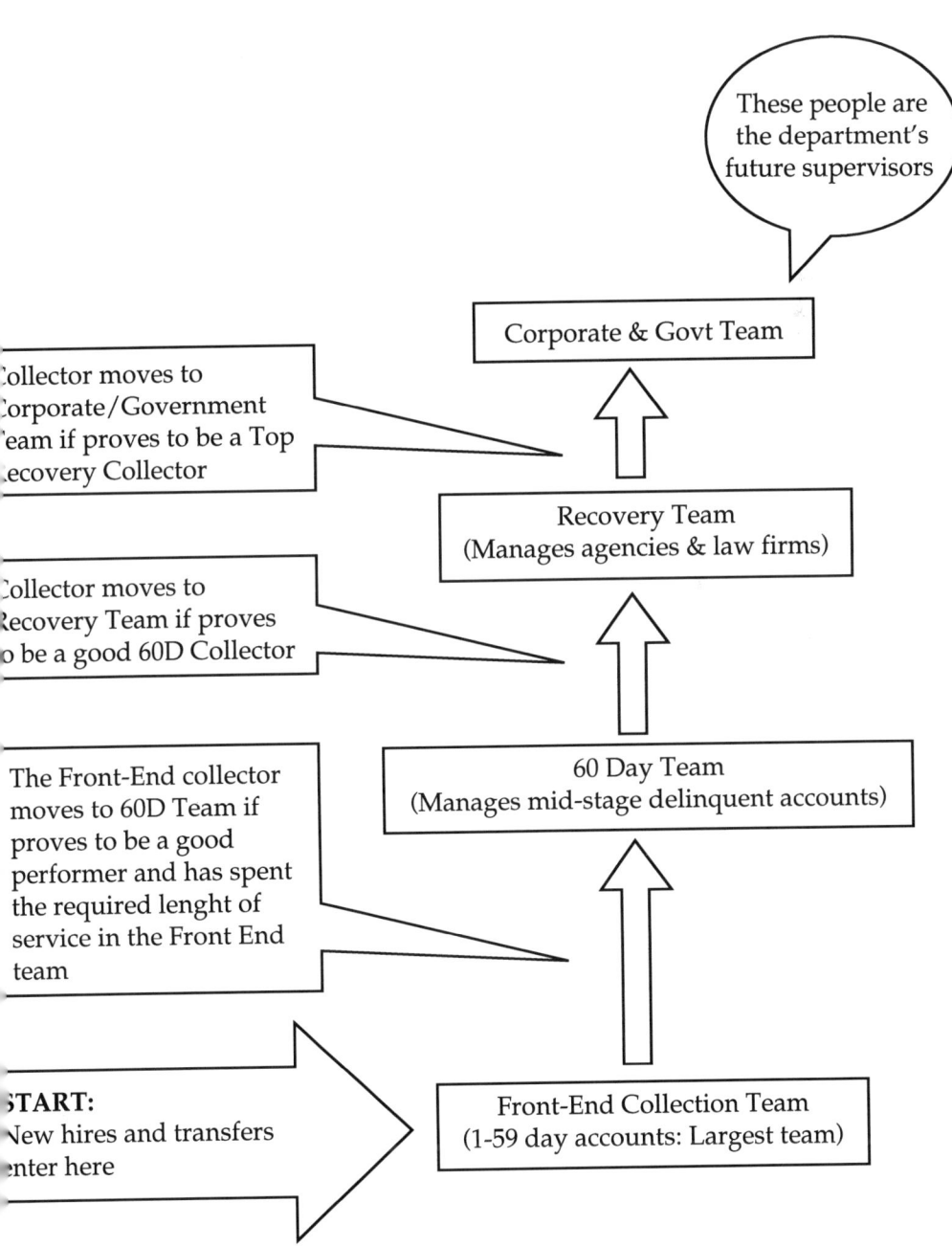

The scheme is visual. Each team member sits with his or her team. As a collector moves up or down the career ladder, according to his / her performance and length on the team, s/he must change desks to join the new team members. This scheme also applies to collection supervisors. You wouldn't want the less experienced supervisors handling Corporate or Recovery teams' accounts.

In the above career plan, the majority of collectors are in the Front-End team. A typical Front End collector is a:

- New employee
- Newly transferred employee
- Experienced employee who enjoys the Front-End
- Experienced employee with performance problems

After some time in the Front End team, the better collectors progress to the 60 Day, Recovery, and Corporate teams. Your corporate team consists of the department's top collectors. They're the department's "cream" and cream floats to the top.

## Making Them Stay On

Reducing turnover and getting people to stay is about establishing routines. People like routines. They like to know what's expected of them, where they have to do it, how they have to do it, and how they're evaluated when doing it. If you establish routines that are enjoyable, people think twice about leaving. The longer they're in a routine, the harder it is to leave. We are, after all, creatures of habit.

## Choosing Your Leadership Team

You and your supervisory teams' leadership skills are a vital component in the effective running of your department. Bad bosses cause severe damage. They cause top performers to leave and businesses to fail.

According to a study of 15,000 mostly white-collar workers by Bavendam Research Inc.,[34] they found "leadership" to be the third highest factor selected in regards to job satisfaction. They write:

> Employees are more satisfied when their managers are good leaders. This includes motivating employees to do a good job, striving for excellence or just taking action.

---

34  Bavendam Research Inc., "Special Repot:  Managing Job Satisfaction", 2000,
    <http://www.bavendam.com> Vol. 6, (4 June 2004).  Note:  Opportunity and stress where the
    top two job satisfaction factors respectively.

Their advice:

- "Make sure your managers are well trained. Leadership combines attitudes and behavior. It can be learned.

- People respond to managers that they can trust and who inspire them to achieve meaningful goals."

Bring a **mix of personalities** to your supervisory team. Some supervisors are hard, others soft, but all must be FAIR. The hard supervisors will push the collectors to attain targets they thought unachievable. The soft supervisors coach their people to become more effective. Avoid a department of all "hard" or all "soft" supervisors.

---

**Tip:**

Don't neglect team leads or lead collectors. They are an integral part of your leadership team. These top performers serve as coaches and role models. They can take supervisor calls, do call quality evaluations, coach poor performers, and train new staff. The impact they have in departments is huge. Supervisors coach poor performers on how to improve, but whether the actual behavior change takes place is another story. Team leaders on the other hand change collector behavior. People listen to top performers; they don't always listen to supervisors.

In basketball, I have heard countless players express gratitude for the advice Michael Jordan has given them. However, I have yet to hear as many kind words about their coaches or team owners.

---

## Choosing the "Right Stuff"

Most job interviews for collector positions take less than 30 minutes. The supervisor then makes a snap decision whether to hire. If the candidate is hired, s/he may stay in your department for the rest of their working lives. The supervisor's total decision-making process was less than 10 minutes, but the results of that decision last for years. Be careful in making hiring decisions. They have a way of coming back to haunt.

Think back to when you first met your spouse. How long did it take to choose him or her? Did you propose or accept the marriage proposal on the first date?

How long do you spend with your work colleagues right now? Don't be surprised if you spend more waking hours with your work-mates than with your soul-mate.

In America, 50% of marriages end in divorce. In your hiring decisions, what percent of new hires turn out to be top performers?

Why so low?

Starting today, consider spending at least 60 minutes interviewing new job candidates. Put them through a series of interviews that includes HR people, yourself, and their future supervisor. Have them interviewed by your team leaders, too.

Here are some additional tips to select the right people:

## 1) Role play

Give the applicant debtor situations you face in your work environment. See how the candidate responds. Your focus isn't whether the candidate got the role play correct or incorrect. You're looking to see if s/he went through a logical mental process:

- Did they ask the right questions?

- Did they try to help?

- Were they confident?

You're mostly looking for intelligent people with the right type of attitude. You can fill in the skills gaps with proper training later.

## 2) Ask unexpected questions (within the law)

Unexpected questions get candidates to reveal more about themselves than the commonly asked, rehearsed interview questions. Ask them questions about themselves. Pry as deeply as the law allows into their character and motivations. Their answers will give you a better idea if the candidate will work well in your department.

All too often, we focus on the technical skills when hiring new staff, but we later fire people based on their lack of people skills.

Consider asking these questions:

- What's your philosophy of collections?

- Do you like people who don't pay their bills on time?

If the candidate's mindset and job style is completely different from your organization's, then there could easily be problems in getting that person to adapt to the new work environment. This is especially so if that behavior has been learned over the years and the person has achieved some measure of success and recognition using it. Changing behavior is often met with resistance- either overt or covert.

## 3) Take the time to do a background check on the candidate

Call the work references and see how they performed at those organizations. I will choose to run "short-handed" temporarily any day over making poor hiring mistakes. Hopefully we credit check our customers, we should also carefully check our future employees.

## Managing Poor Performers: "The Dental Office"

Nobody likes visiting the dentist, but the longer we postpone it, the more serious the problem becomes. I use a concept called the "dental office" to deal with poor performance.

Each month collectors with performance problems – and their supervisor – meet in the "dental office." The dental office is the office of the collector's supervisor's supervisor. At this private meeting, the collector explains why s/he failed to hit the monthly target. The supervisor then shares the plan to get the staff back on target. Notes are taken. A plan is agreed. The collector is wished good luck and told what will happen next month if the target is still missed.

Staff that miss the monthly target for legitimate reasons like maternity leave, vacation, critical illness or other such reasons are exempted. Still, it's a good idea to pleasantly chat with them about the impact their absence caused the department.

The dental office's goal is to ensure that poor performance is tracked, discussed, and extinguished early. It's a preventative treatment. It's like a good collection treatment that politely but aggressively addresses any negative payment behavior early to prevent it from becoming worse later.

Visiting the dental office is never fun, but having a formal process in place is better than having an ad-hoc feedback system. Ad-hoc systems don't work because many people are lazy or too busy to give regular feedback. With ad-hoc systems, managers and supervisors put up with a poor performer for months, little communication is shared, then once the situation becomes unbearable, the poor performer receives either a harsh letter or a "talk down" to shape up. The employee becomes demotivated and performance drops further. Eventually the employee is transferred, asked to resign, or fired. Both parties blame the other for the situation since there was little communication.

The "dental office" concept provides for a formal feedback review each month. It gives the poor performers an early opportunity to improve their performance. It avoids unpleasant surprises at year-end review time. It forces supervisors to coach the staff with the staff's input.

## Transferring Poor Performers

What do you do if your collector (or supervisor) still doesn't improve after months of "dental office" visits?

Consider a job transfer.

Perhaps, the reason for his or her poor performance is due to poor job fit. Some people fail as collectors. Transfers are an excellent way to allow people to excel in something else. Transferring poor performers demonstrates – visually - what happens to people who don't perform. It adds stress to the poor performers and causes "borderline" performers to take notice if they fall below average.

A word of warning when transferring poor performers, be careful how you do it. You don't want to send the message that poor performance allows people to transfer and good performance causes people to be trapped in the department forever. It's essential you create two kinds of job transfers: High value and low value.

**High value transfers** are for people who consistently hit or exceed their targets. These transfers are to highly valued teams or departments to do valuable, interesting work. These transfers are either lateral or upward.

**Low value transfers** are for collectors who consistently miss their targets. These transfers are to work in less important teams, or to do monotonous jobs that most collectors try to avoid, or low value transfers to other departments.

Get to know the managers in those departments that your staff consider "low value". Why? Because you can swap each other's poor performers. I would much rather swap a person with a proven performance problem in my department, for a possible performance problem in your department. Just because your employee failed in your department doesn't mean s/he will fail in mine. In my experience, when I tell an incoming problematic employee that s/he will have a "fresh start" in my department, they usually perform. They're grateful I took a chance on them. Sometimes their new performance will even be exemplary.

**Tip:**

A word of warning when transferring employees to do monotonous tasks. Ensure the transfer is only temporary. The reason being some employees, if given their choice, will do that task for years. I say this from personal experience. You don't want the task to be seen as a reward. Poor and borderline performers may see the task as a way to still collect their salary without having to think much, or to still "cari makan" (earn a living as they say in Malaysia). Doing such tasks for long periods doesn't help your employees' brains or the running of your department.

## *Summary*

- Proper leadership skills are needed for the effective running of a collection department. Without the proper skills in place, supervisors and managers cause significant damage to their organizations in terms of lost employees, customers, and profits.

- Team leaders and lead collectors play a vital role within the department. Their quiet impact is often greater than a supervisor's.

- A shared vision helps motivate a department.

- An incentive program that's heavily based on commissions will lead collectors to treating customers as "money bags" instead of as "people."

- Recognize top performance correctly:

  1. State the good performance

  2. Explain what s/he did to achieve that level of performance

  3. Explain the impacts of that performance

  4. Express gratitude

- An open and fun work environment leads to higher motivation, more productivity and less stress.

- Create a career road-map for your people. It improves morale and reduces employee turnover.

- Take the time to carefully select your leadership team and collectors.

- Put in place a formal process where poor performance is regularly addressed. This helps people improve while reducing unpleasant future surprises.

Part VII:
# The Future of Collections

# What's Around this Corner and the Next?

## 19

*Technical Advances in the Collection Field*

*Do you realize if it weren't for Edison we'd be watching TV by candlelight?*
– Al Boliska

**After reading this chapter, you will be able to:**

- Evaluate possible low tech and higher tech solutions to improve your department's efficiency.

- Get a snapshot of future technologies in the collections field.

## Introduction

With debt levels rising globally, technical solutions are catching many peoples' attention. No longer is collection one of the few departments to still lack technical work solutions. Technology helps us hit our targets, but more important than technology is to first have the right people and processes in place. As a manager, I prefer having excellent people and processes combined with low tech systems, than having the best systems money can buy with the wrong people and processes in place.

Of course, the best solution is having great people, processes, and systems.

## The Meaning of "New"

I would like to qualify myself before going deeper into this chapter. The word "new" means new at the time I'm typing this. And "new" means new for collection departments. Some of these technologies aren't that new at all, but I find that collection departments are generally late adopters of technologies. Sales and customer service departments usually have more high-tech goodies. In Asia, collection departments are generally further behind in terms of systems and automation than in the West.

Note: For any great technical solutions I have missed, please go to my website and drop me a line: http://www.servicewinners.com

## *Low Tech Solutions*

### Headsets

According to an ACA survey of collection agencies, the number one technological improvement for collectors is headsets. Yet even today headsets are difficult to find in many collection call centers. Instead, you will find plenty of sore necks and demotivated collectors.

The short-term expense of purchasing headsets is small compared to the productivity increase. If headsets help each collector save enough time to squeeze out a couple extra "kept" PTPs each day, then their cost has already been paid.

### Fax Server

One of the most common customer excuses worldwide is, "I didn't get a bill."

Collectors then ask if the customer wants the bill to be faxed, and they usually do. The collector dutifully prints the bills, walks over to the printer, then to the fax, faxes, and then waits for the fax receipt slip. All of this takes time. Imagine the calls you could have made instead of taking the time to fax bills to customers who probably won't pay anyway.

A fax server allows you to fax bills via your PC and confirm with the customer if the fax was received.

It not only saves time, it also reduces customer complaints. How sure are we that the collectors actually fax the bills that the customers request? By making faxing easier for the collectors, you stand a higher chance that they actually do it.

### Automated Letter Generation

Your I.T. and billing departments should be able to send bulk collection letters automatically to overdue customers. Your collection software system should trigger an auto-letter for certain types of accounts. Then relay this information to the I.T. department. The I.T. department then sends out the letters, or at least, sends the data file to a print vendor to print and mail the letters to the affected customers.

If your system can't do this, there are vendors that do automated bulk printing and mailing of collection letters.

## *Higher Tech Solutions*

### Predictive dialers

Dialers are usually used for large collection teams of 10 or more collectors doing consumer collections. A dialer frees your collectors from having to manually dial the debtors' phone numbers. The dialer connects the collector with both the customer and the customer's account screen.

Dialers can :

- Detect a live human voice from a recorded one. Hence, collectors are connected to calls answered by humans. No more answering machines, no answers, busy signals, voicemail, or disconnected numbers.

- Leave pre-recorded auto-messages on answering machines or voicemail systems.

- Automatically set call backs for those accounts where the dialer encountered a busy signal or no answer.

- Do inbound only, outbound only, or "blended" (inbound and outbound) dialing.

- Eliminate account review time. For example, create a call campaign of 5,000 accounts, owing for three months, with balances of RM1,000-RM3,000, located on the east coast. You alert your collectors of the campaign so that they will know what approach to take on such a uniform customer profile.

- Provide "live" statistics showing the collectors' productivity and PTPs on the currently running campaign. You know exactly what your collectors are doing (or not doing) at all times.

- Run multiple calling campaigns.

- Run "blast" campaigns for low balance accounts that don't require direct collector contact, but do require a pre-recorded voice prompt to pay.

Dialers come in different types. There are hardware-based and software-based dialers. There are web-based and traditional. The best dialer for you will depend on your needs and the size of your team.

Here's a quick summary of the pros and cons of "hard" and "soft" dialers:

| Hard Dialers | Soft Dialers |
|---|---|
| Faster | Slower |
| More accurate in connecting to right parties | Less accurate |
| Difficult to link system to non-collection departments | Easier |
| More complex to run | Less complex |
| More difficult to add / drop extensions | Easier |
| More difficult to run remote call centers | Easier |
| Usually more expensive | Usually less expensive |

**When not to use a dialer**

Think twice about buying a dialer if you :

- Have poor customer contact information
- Have small collection teams
- Have poor I.T. support
- Collect mostly corporate accounts

That's a brief overview of dialers. They are powerful tools. Marianne Weedman, Director at Verizon Wireless, said their accounts receivable aging improved better with the dialer than with the implementation of a new debt management system.

**Tip:**

Whichever vendor you use, think twice about getting the latest version, especially if you are their first customer to get it. You don't want to end up becoming their test bed. There are hundreds of dialer vendors depending on your needs and budget, but some of most sophisticated ones are made by Concerto, Avaya, and Cisco.

## *Best-Time-To-Call Software*

These packages link to your dialer to determine the best time to call a particular customer. The software increases the effectiveness of your dialer. Your collectors now get to speak with more decision-makers instead leaving messages with friends, relatives, roommates, or work colleagues. Collectors will also like seeing an improvement in their PTP hit rates. One vendor is Austin Logistics.

## *Voice Messaging*

Michael Kinneman, head of credit and collections at T-Mobile, is using a voice messaging system. It's designed for customers who prefer to interact with a machine rather than a collector. It based on the logic that many people don't like receiving embarrassing collection calls. They would rather interact with a machine to get the information they need, namely: How much do I have to pay and when?

In voice messaging, the debtor answers the call and hears a recording advising the debtor who's calling and that there's an important message for the debtor to hear (a PIN can be used to hear it), the message then informs the debtor of the balance owing and the importance of making the payment. The debtor decides what to do next: hang up, press a key to discuss payment arrangements with a "live" person, or press another key to inform when payment will be made. The customer's response is automatically updated into the collection system.

Michael has found this system works well on both early stage accounts and later stage accounts. Vendors include Par 3, Premiere Global Services, and Soundbite Communications.

## Computer Telephony Interface (CTI)

CTI allows a collector receiving inbound calls to know who's calling. The system can be programmed to recognize either the cell phone or fixed line number that the customer uses. When that number dials your call center, the CTI system will also pull up the customer's account.

It saves a few seconds, but multiplied over many collection agents, the time savings is significant.

## Debt Management Systems

Most modern collection departments have software systems to track their receivables. In the West it's rare to find collectors still working off ledger cards. Competition, slimmer profit margins, and outsourcing make automation a necessity. Asia, however, is a different story. Many Asian collection departments are still paper-based or operating using old system versions.

Ideally a good collection system allows the collectors to focus on only one or two main screens. There should be enough information in these screens to handle 90% of the customers' calls. If collectors need more information, they can investigate within the system. Being successful in collections is as much about speed as skill.

I have found that the enterprise wide systems such as SAP do generate nice reports, but they lack functionality at a collector's level.

**Tip:**

If you're implementing a new system, avoid making it do too much in the first phase. A "perfect" debt management system usually takes years to create. For your initial system launch, save most of the customizations and "dreams" to later versions, scaling down will help get your system launched cheaper and faster.

**Tip:**

Debt management systems should be easy to use. If you over-complicate them, you face a greater risk of errors, system crashes, and files not being updated. Complicated systems do wonderful things, but if they're more unstable than simpler systems, they're not worth it.

Besides ease and simplicity, ensure your system has the following functionalities:

### 1) Queuing or worklist functions

The system should queue accounts into the collectors' daily worklist, either to each individual collector or as a team. The system should return accounts that have broken their PTP, unreturned messages, or other types of non-productive activities back into the collector's queue for follow-up. The queues should allow the manager to sort accounts by age, balance, behavioral score, location, customer type, account status, and multiple other factors. If staff strength is reduced due to resignations, sick leave, vacations or other reasons; the supervisor should be able to reassign those accounts within those worklists to other collection teams.

### 2) Reports

The system should be able to generate the required reports for the department. Such as the number of PTPs and other actions done on each account by each collector, team, and department. The number of PTPs kept (paid). It also needs to track the dollars collected by collector, team, and department. Aging reports by customer groups or other criteria should also be a feature.

### 3) Notes

The collector needs to be able to easily read past history and notes on the account. I prefer reading pages of text versus clicking on individual line items to read each note. Ideally, any notes made in the collections system should link to other systems within the organization. This allows other departments, like customer service, to see what collections is doing on the account and collections to see what they're doing.

### 4) Auto-collection

The system should be able to automatically send collection letters, SMS's, perform credit holds, and other negative actions. The negative actions should be done for both overdue accounts and for current accounts that have exceeded their credit line or bounced a cheque or credit card.

### 5) System Updates

The system should update within minutes- or at least nightly- all payments received by the company. This will stop collection calls and negative activities on customers who have just paid. It also needs to update quickly for bounced cheques and charged-back credit card payments.

### 6) Predictive dialer feature

The system should allow for easy integration with a dialer.

### 7) Credit and behavioral scoring feature

The system should allow for easy integration with scoring systems.

### 8) Web-based feature

Can the system link to the Internet for your external collection agencies and law firms to view their accounts? Or, will you have to buy a "bolt-on" system to allow this to happen? If you need to buy a bolt-on, will your system easily accept bolt-ons? The web feature will also allow field collectors and sales people to check if their accounts have paid.

### 9) Agency feature

Can the system automatically assign batches to the respective collection agencies and legal firms? Can it monitor their progress? If you use a sliding scale account allocation scheme, can the system allocate accounts unequally?

## Revenue Collections & Debt Management System Profile: Profitera's PowerCollect™

One debt management system to consider is *PowerCollect* from Profitera Corporation, a company with offices and business partners throughout Asia and the U.S. PowerCollect runs on multiple operating systems like Windows, Linux, Solaris, HP-UX, AIX, OS/400, etc. It can run on major database platforms including DB2, DB2/400, Oracle, MS-SQL Server, Sybase, Informix, MySQL, PostgresSQL, and others. PowerCollect uses Java and XML.

Its robustness allows it to handle millions of accounts handled by large numbers of collectors. PowerCollect is targeted to the enterprise market. Its customers are in the credit card, banking, leasing, auto loans, telco, utilities, and government (local, federal, social security, tax, etc.) sectors.

PowerCollect has in-built host system adaptors for CardLink, Sema-Cards, Silverlake Banking, AMDOCS Billing, CASS Billing, and others. This feature saves implementation time and cost.

It's a score-based system, not an aging-based one. PowerCollect's scoring engine generates behavior scorecards for every account. It takes a "sniper" approach which helps you allocate collection resources to only those accounts that need a collection action. It avoids targeting those "good" accounts that will likely "self-cure." As a result, you run less risk upsetting good customers. You avoid having collectors calling ALL over-due customers. Your teams end up working smarter.

Profitera leverages the advantages of doing development work in Asia, which is reflective in their competitive pricing against other debt management systems from Europe or the U.S.

### Key features

- Customer and account management. Collectors can view the customer's entire relationship. From a single screen, you can also see the account's associated accounts and products. The main information screen gives collectors an in-depth snapshot of the account's vital information. This helps reduce time spent screen-hopping.

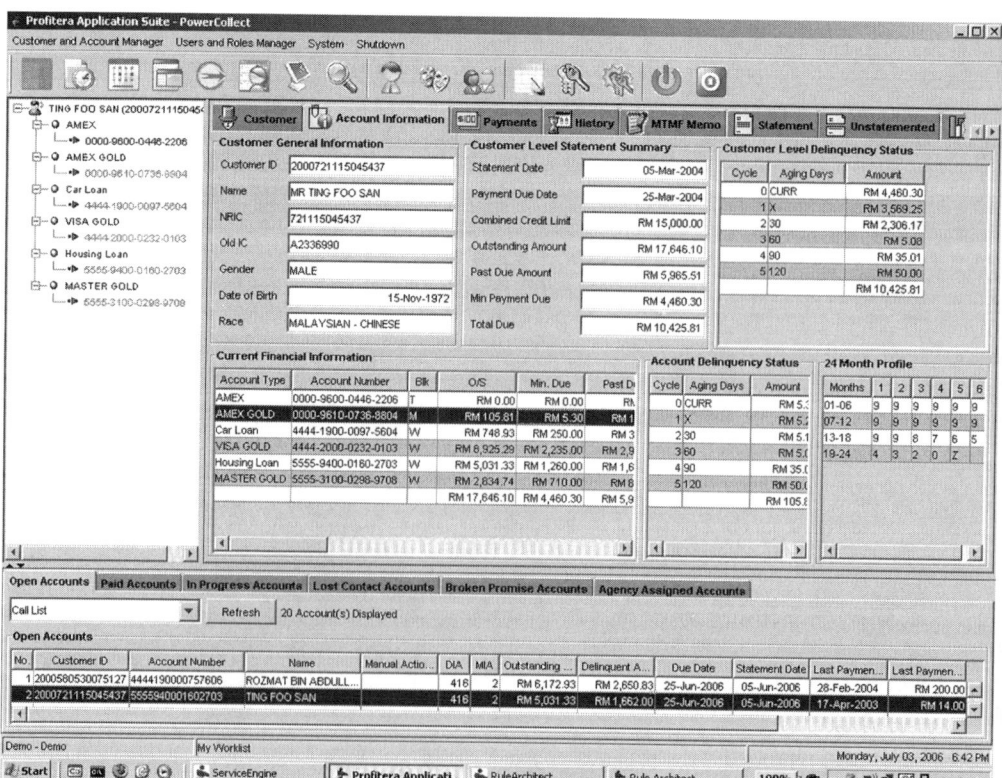

Exhibit 20.1  Customer and Account Information Main Screen

- Adaptive visual treatments manager. You can create automated collection treatments customized to a debtor's unique payment behavior or profile score. However, the auto-treatments can be quickly interrupted to perform a special intervention.

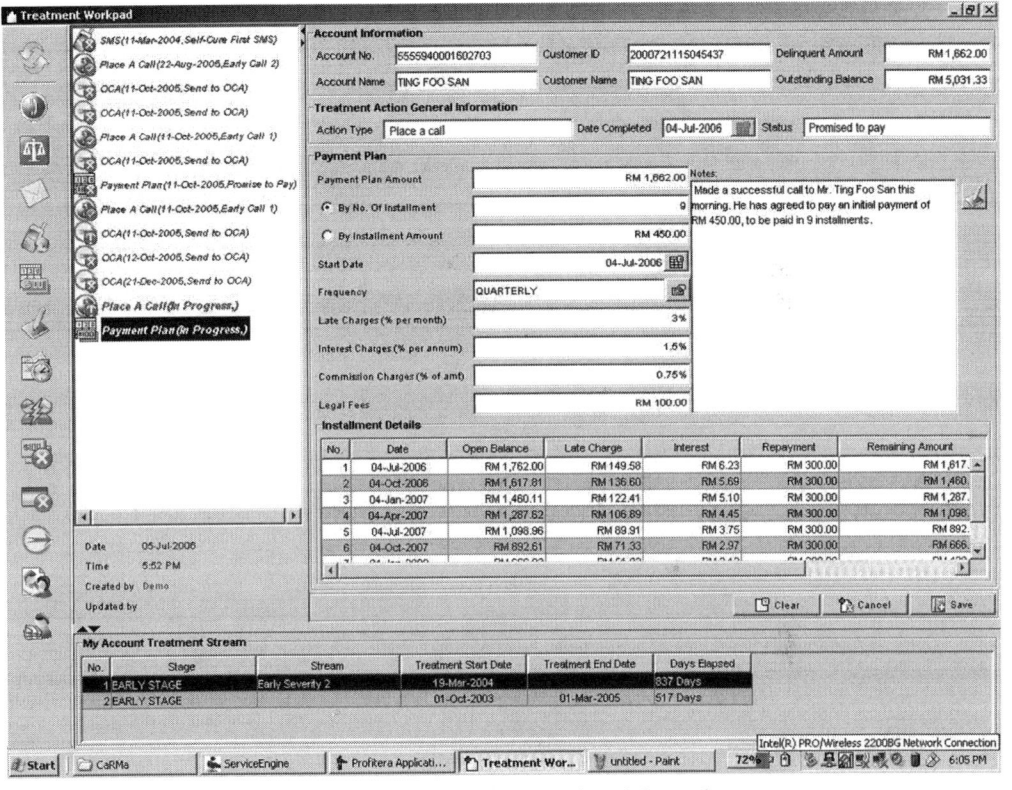

Exhibit 20.2  Treatment Workpad Console

- Daily re-aging engine. Each day the system can provide the current aging on all accounts. You no longer have to wait until the bill cycle or month end occurs at the host. This is particularly beneficial when the host systems stop computing aging for "charged-off" or "written-off" accounts.

- Payment processor. The system tracks payments and payment details of each invoice. This is especially handy when investigating where to post "unapplied cash".

- Multiple related accounts handled by one collector. You avoid the risk of multiple collectors calling the same customer who may have multiple accounts.

265

- Flexible and visual rules architect. If desired, collection supervisors can be empowered to change the collection rules "on-the-fly". You are no longer dependent on the vendor or your I.T. department to make rule changes.

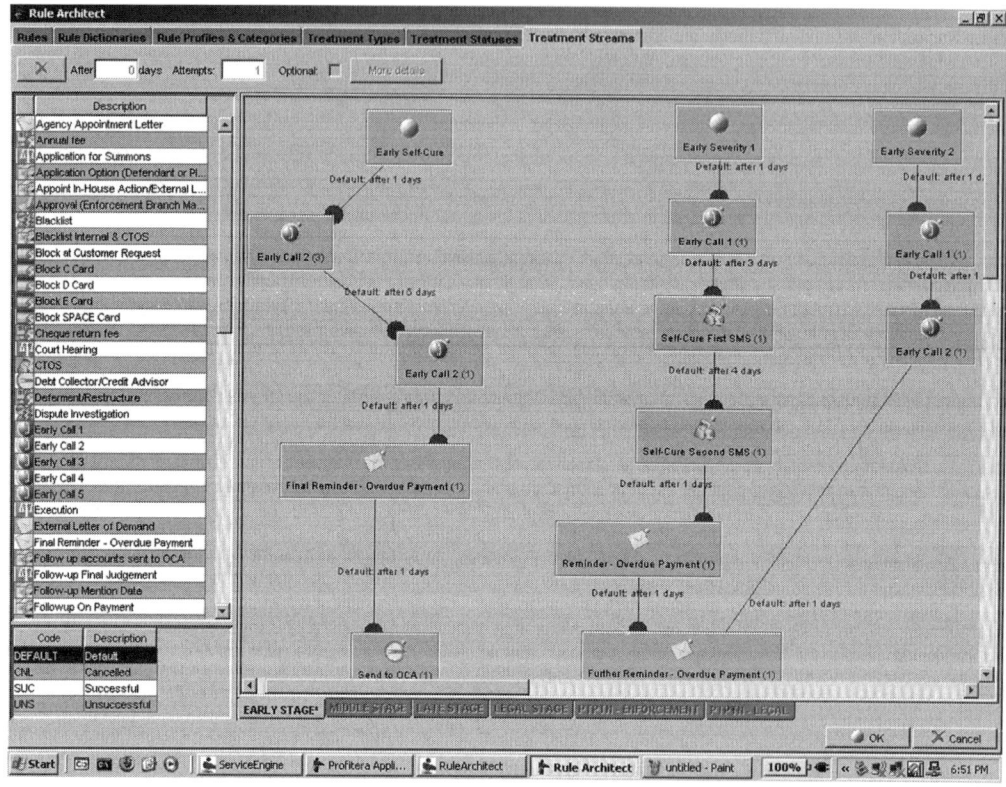

Exhibit 20.3  Rule Architect Screen

- Visual worklist manager. Collection managers can visually assign accounts to collectors through point and click buttons, instead of through complicated scripts or codes. Managers can create team or individual worklists to ensure all collectors get a fair number or value of accounts.

  The system can even route accounts by behavioral score to collectors based on their D.I.S.C. psychological profile. For example, perhaps the accounts with "bad" payment scores should route to those collectors with the highest assertiveness qualities?

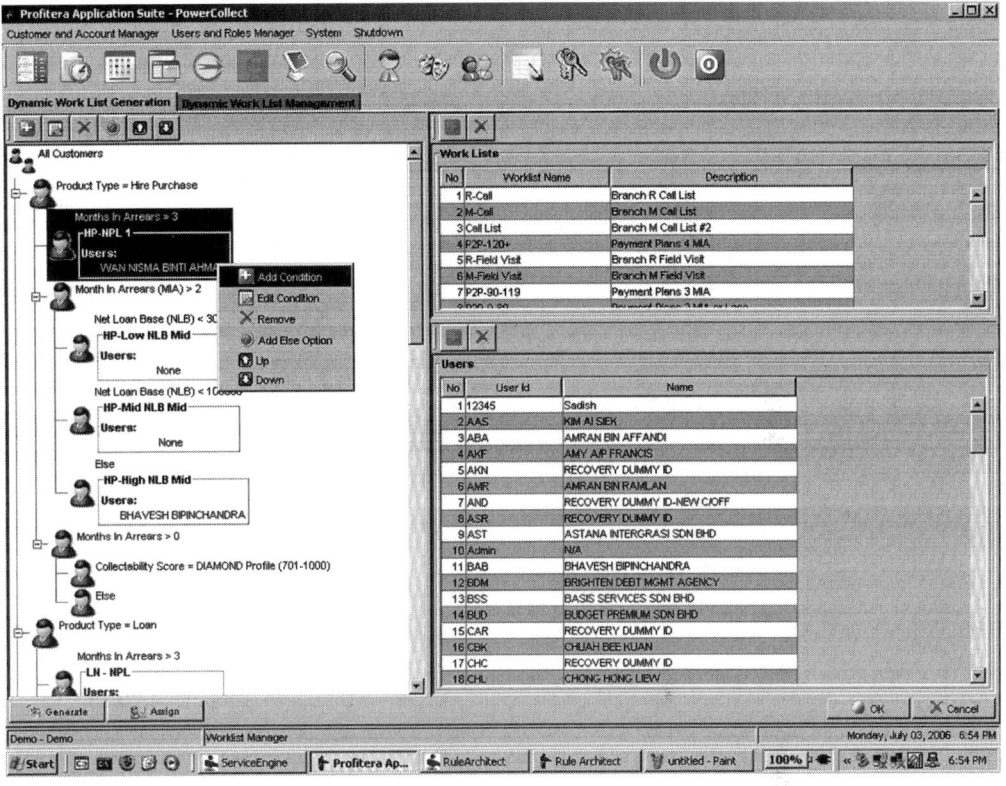

Exhbit 20.4  Dynamic Worklist Management Screen

- Auto-generation of letters, telegrams, email, and SMS messages. You can run bulk notification to your delinquent customers. You could also run batch jobs via SMS payment reminders to alert current customers about to be overdue.

- Ready-made reports. You can select from in-built reports measuring aging, flow rates, worklists, bounced cheques (NSF), promises to pay, dollars collected, and many more.

- Performance manager. You have a real time view of the performance of individual collectors, the team, the region, or department from a single console. You can make real-time decisions.

  The "incentive manager" standard feature enables an organization to easily calculate collectors' incentives according to the required KPIs.

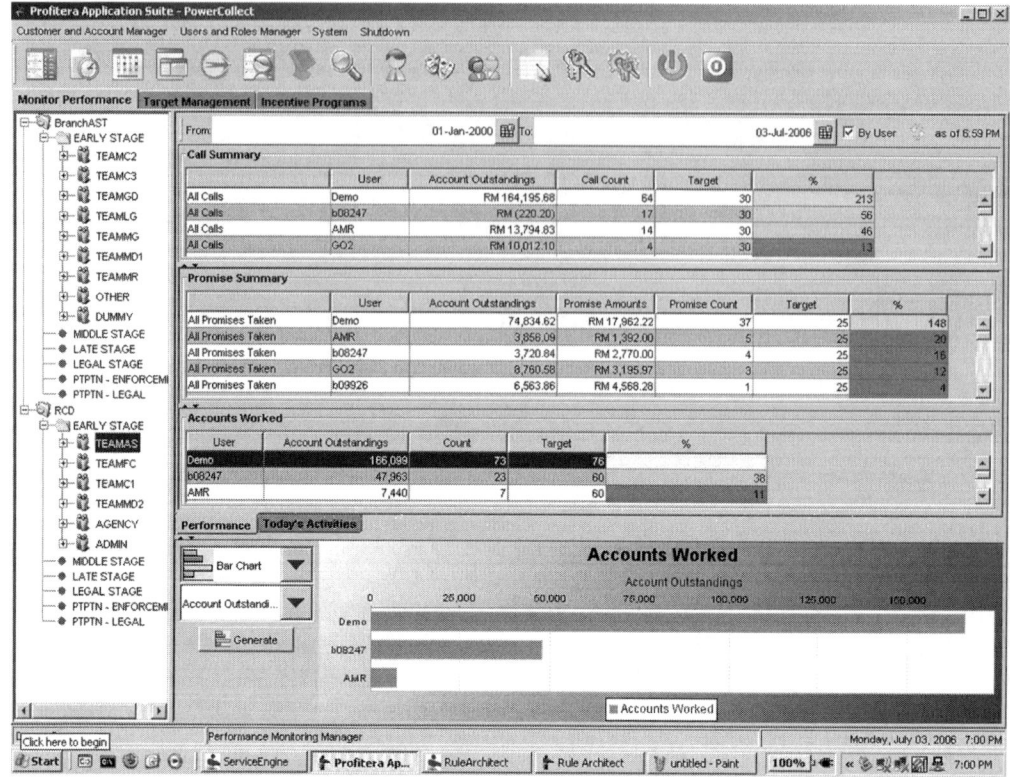

Exhibit 20.5  Performance Management Screen

- Agency and third party manager. PowerCollect allows you to track external debt collection agencies' and legal firms' performance.

For more information see <www.profitera.com>.

## *Other Debt Management Systems*

### Tallyman

Tallyman from Talgentra is another powerful, sophisticated system designed for industries that need to manage large number of accounts. Talgentra is headquartered in the U.K. but has offices throughout the world. For more information, contact them at <www.talgentra.com>

### Juris

Juris from Malaysian company Natsoft is designed for companies with large number of accounts. It has a powerful collection agency tracking engine. For more information visit <www.natsoft.com>

### volaré

Stampede Solutions, based in Malaysia, offers volaré which is geared for collection departments needing functionality at a low price. Their key clients are collection agencies. They offer flexible payment options. For more information visit <www.stampedesolution.com>

## Personal Digital Assistants (PDAs) and 3G Cell Phones

PDAs and cell phones are spreading rapidly. In fact, these two technologies are merging into smartphones. More and more groups of people are using them as prices fall. In Europe, school kids carry PDAs; while in Asia you see Indonesian tea ladies carrying cell phones.

Wireless technologies like 3G, WiFi, and WiMax will allow field collectors to check customers' payment records during their onsite visits. Repo men can check a customer's account to ensure no last minute payments were made. PDAs and cell phones are equipped with digital cameras, so field collectors can take photos or videos showing the condition of a debtor's equipment and send them back to home office.

In Asia, cell phones are being embedded with credit card information that allow users to pay by swiping the cell phone against credit or debit card readers. In the future, a lost cell phone may be as serious as losing a credit card.

## Voice Recording Systems

These systems capture all phone conversations between customers and the collectors. They're popular in the banking, brokerage, and telecommunications sectors. They store customer conversations for days or months depending on your needs. The voice conversations are saved as .wav files that can be attached to emails. I have attached one or two files to the H.R. department when a collector makes a particular inappropriate call.

However, their strength lies not in disciplining staff but in coaching them. If you want to ensure collection training sticks back on-the-job, buy a voice recording system. With such a system you can design a call management process where the collectors must follow key concepts on every call such as the 6-steps of a collection call, asking for the balance in full, and branding your company at the end of all collection calls. Call management will increase the quality of your collectors' calls since they now know what quality standard they must attain. Supervisors can play back good calls in their team meetings for all to hear and critique.

Many collectors become suspicious of these systems. They view them as "spy systems." This is unfortunate as it's in their best interest to have them. There will be times when customers complain about rude collectors, but after listening to the call, you will discover that often the collector wasn't rude at all. With the importance of Customer Relationship Management (CRM) in today's business environment, large collection call centers will view voice recording systems as an absolute necessity. Once you get one, you will wonder how you ever survived without it.

## Future Technologies

### Internet

Customers can order or purchase goods over the Web. They can also file customer service complaints. It's only a matter of time before customers file payment excuses or disputes, make payment proposals or settlements, and pay over the Web. It adds convenience to their busy lives.

By harnessing the power of the Web, collection departments can increase their customer contact points. And we all know by maintaining contact with our debtors, our chances of collecting their payments dramatically increase. Offering web options increases our customer satisfaction levels while reducing our expenses incurred each time a human makes a phone call. Our organizations save money using the Web since manually touching accounts is expensive, especially when a large percentage of our contacts are unproductive like left messages, no answers, busy signals, wrong parties, etc.

### Broadband (high-speed) Internet

Broadband Internet will likely impact phone-based collectors. With bandwidth take-up rates expanding, collectors will be able to make video collection calls over the Internet. Collectors of the future will need training in body language to read their debtors' body language, especially when receiving Promises to Pay (PTPs).

Broadband makes telecommuting an option. Employers will reduce operating expenses and employees will save time by collecting accounts from home.

### Customer Relationship Management (CRM)

CRM will play an increasing role in organizations' futures. With the customer being placed at the center of most organizations, our departments' impact and visibility should increase.

In the past, credit and debt management systems were kept separate from the rest of the organization's systems, but in the future they will be linked. For example, a collector sending a 180 day overdue account that owes RM2,300 for legal action will withhold the legal action if s/he sees

- via the CRM system – that this same customer is in the midst of buying RM2,300,000 worth of goods. Today, unfortunately, most collectors probably would send the account for legal action simply because they wouldn't know of the upcoming big sale.

With the increasing links between sales, customer service, and credit; we will see other departments making credit and collection decisions. The line between "us" and "them" will blur. As a customer, wouldn't you prefer having one point-of-contact where your credit, sales, collections, and customer service issues are handled quickly?

## Summary

- Some low and high tech tools that will increase your department's productivity are:

**Low Tech:**

☑ Headsets

☑ Fax server

☑ Automated letter generation

**High Tech:**

☑ Predictive dialers

☑ Best-Time-To-Call software

☑ Voice messaging

☑ Computer Telephony Interface (CTI)

☑ Debt Management Systems

☑ Credit and behavioral scoring systems

☑ PDA's (linked to billing or collection systems)

- New technologies that may influence our industry are :

☑ The Internet will give us and our customers more options to stay in contact. It increases debtors' convenience and reduces our operating expenses.

☑ 3G (third generation) wireless technologies that allow visual collection calls, and the sending of collection letters and bills over the smart phone.

☑ Broadband Internet connections that allow visual collection calls, and the sending of collection letters and bills over the PC.

☑ Increased usage of CRM (Customer Relationship Management) systems that link credit and collection systems with sales, marketing, and customer service's systems for a better overall view of the customer.

Again, please share with me any technological tool or prediction that you believe will impact our field: steve@servicewinners.com.

# Succeeding into the Future

**20**

*Starting a Continual Learning Program for Yourself*

*The man who is too old to learn was probably always too old to learn.*
– Henry S. Haskins

**After reading this chapter, you will be able to:**

- See the importance of staying up-to-date in the credit field.

- Understand the importance of applying knowledge to gain experience and wisdom.

- Find useful credit books, magazines and websites.

## Importance of Continually Learning

The need to continually update our skills is – at times – frightening. The number of inventions today far surpasses any other such progress in human history. Many of us feel overloaded with information.

Dr. Charles Jones of Stanford University studied the history of human progress and found the following: [36]

| Time Span | Average number of inventions per year |
|-----------|---------------------------------------|
| 5000 BC- 1 AD | 39 |
| 1801-1900 | 3,840 |
| 1901-2000 | 110,000 |

The credit field is no different from any other field. We need to continually learn and change. Our field isn't static. Our ability to learn new collection techniques and technologies will save more time, allow us to help more customers, and bring more profits to our organizations. Our ability to continually learn will also determine our own success.

Many people don't take the time to read books or magazines or browse the Internet. They usually say there isn't enough time (or

---

36   Reginald Dale, "Looking Back at Unparalled Progress", International Herald Tribune, 21 December 1999.

money) for such activities. However, their homes often have the latest home theatre systems with 101 television channels. Are we any different from our debtors? When we say, "I don't have any money (or time) to read." What we're really saying is, "I don't have any money (or time) for self-development."

The difference between a top collector, supervisor or manager to an average performer is sometimes only a couple of books, ideas or tips.

In the early 15$^{th}$ Century, nearly one hundred years before Columbus "discovered" the New World, there was another daring explorer who lived in China and sailed for his emperor. His name was Admiral Zheng He, or in S.E. Asia he's referred to as Cheng Ho. He was a Muslim eunuch and his sailing fleet was the biggest flotilla that the world would see until World War I. Zheng He had all the resources he needed at his disposal.

Columbus was an Italian sailing with minimal support from the King and Queen of the little country of Spain. Before Spain bankrolled him with meager resources, he had been rejected by the kings and queens of England, France, and Portugal. With his limited resources, he changed the world; while Zheng He's accomplishments have been largely forgotten.

A quick comparison of the two explorers' resources :

| Zheng He | Columbus |
|---|---|
| 107 ships | 3 ships |
| Longest ship was 122 m | 18 m |
| Crew of 28,000 men, women and children | Less than 100 men |

Zheng He's voyages took him to SE Asia, India, Africa and possibly the west coast of North America. These voyages helped China become the world's most technically advanced civilization at that time. In contrast, Europe was still in its "Dark Ages". When the businessman Marco Polo visited China, he marveled at the advances he witnessed. He thought no one would ever believe his tales once he returned to his native Italy.

Yet, when the Italian Jesuits visited China 150 years after Zheng He's last voyage, they found a backward power. What had happened in those 150 years for China to lose its number one position?

The first emperor who supported Zheng He had died and the new emperor decreed the exploration's costs didn't justify the benefits. Instead, he commanded that China focus inward. The fleet was left to rot, some ships were even burnt, and the voyages' records were mostly lost or destroyed.

While China was burning its ships and focusing inward, Europe was building more ships and focusing outward. Columbus' discoveries helped fuel Europe's Renaissance (rebirth). Europe became the intellectual center of the world. A power shift had happened.

What lessons does this give to credit people?:

1. **DON'T BURN YOUR SHIPS!** Keep an open mind. Exercise your brain. Welcome new ideas. Learn continuously and never be complacent. Every year you spend in collections should be a new year. If you have ten years of collection experience, it should be ten new years. Not one year repeated ten times.

   By focusing outward, you develop inward.

2. Zheng He had resources, but Columbus was resourceful. Columbus made the best of what little he had. He was highly motivated to be successful. He had a vision that the kings and queens of England, France, and Portugal couldn't deny him. He achieved excellent results with limited resources.

## *From Knowledge to Wisdom*

Wise people tend to be in short supply. A lot of people claim to be experts, but I usually find that the people who claim less actually know more. I hope you subscribe to the belief that:

*The more we know;*

*The more we discover how little we really do know,*

*And the more we need to learn.*

Knowledge is important. We hear of the "Knowledge Economy", of "Knowledge Workers", and "Chief Knowledge Officers." There's even a field of study called "Knowledge Management."

Knowledge is good. It helps us stay competitive, but knowledge without application is wasted effort as it's in the application of knowledge that we gain experience. And by analyzing our experiences we learn lessons which give us wisdom. And with wisdom we search for new knowledge.

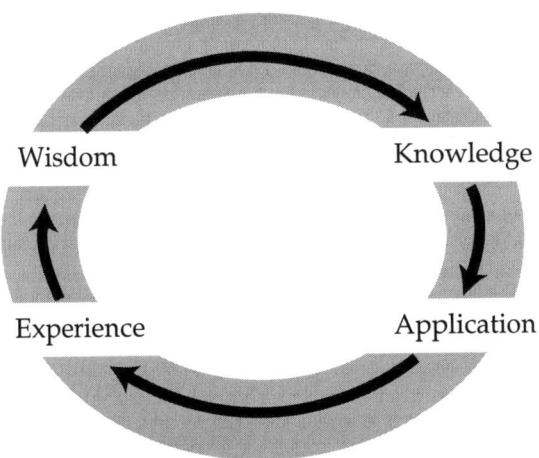

I hope this book has given you knowledge in the form of a few new ideas, strategies, and different ways of thinking that you can apply to your job.

In Chapter 1, I mentioned the primary role of a manager, or supervisor, or any employee for that matter, was to ensure their organization's survival. I suggested that the best way to do this was by helping our customers. It's by helping our customers that we generate more profits for our organizations while keeping more customers satisfied. The field of Customer Relationship Management must extend into collections.

On a recent trip back to the U.S., I met with a high-level credit executive. He had just taken a new senior position at another company. He's well-respected in the industry for maintaining industry-low bad debt figures. Over lunch, I asked him what he learned at his new employer. He said, "We left too much money on the table at (previous employer's name)."

He discovered that by watching bad debt and Days Sales Outstanding (DSO) levels so closely, although his previous company suffered miniscule bad debt losses, it lost countless millions more in revenue, profits, customer satisfaction, and asset value.

I sensed a tinge of regret.

When collections people meet, the first thing we often do is compare bad debt levels. It gives us knowledge of what others are doing, but it doesn't necessarily give us wisdom. Having low or high bad debts tells us nothing of the effectiveness of a credit or collections department. We need to go a step further. We need to analyze what the cost to the organization was in terms of profits and customer satisfaction levels by having that tight or loose credit policy.

Besides watching your organization's profit and customer satisfaction levels, I heartily recommend keeping an eye on your own career development.

## Recommended Books:

"Collect Debts and Still Keep Your Customers", by David and Martin Sher, published by Amacom- American Management Association, (1999). A practical collections book written by collection agency owners.

"Collections Made Easy", by Carol S. Frischer, published by Career Press, (1999). Tightly written with a large section on handling excuses. Legal, accounting, medical and other professional service firms will find this book especially helpful.

"Credit and Collection Handbook", by Michael Dennis, published by Prentice Hall, (2000). At 644 pages, this is a detailed, practical reference book. The later chapters on American commercial law and bankruptcy codes aren't needed by readers in Asia. The book's last few chapters are on international letters of credit and international collections.

"Credit Management: Principles and Practices", by Dr. Charles L. Gahala, published by National Association of Credit Management, (1996). This book is especially useful for those wishing to achieve NACM certification.

"Credit Professional's Handbook", written and published by the Credit Research Foundation, (1999). At 435 pages, 179 of which are glossary terms and forms, it's a comprehensive start-up book for any new credit department.

"Essentials of Credit, Collections, and Accounts Receivable", by Mary S. Schaeffer, published by John Wiley and Sons, Inc., (2002). A short, in-depth analysis of the credit field. For overseas readers, the last couple chapters on U.S. law and bankruptcy proceedings aren't needed.

"Key Management Ratios", by Ciaran Walsh, published by FT Prentice Hall, (2003). A generally easy to understand look at using ratio analysis. Mr. Walsh offers a few recommendations of new ratios over some familiar ones.

"Paid in Full", by Tim Paulsen, published by Ragnar Press, (1998). A fun, practical collections book written by a collection pro.

"Understanding Financial Statements, 6th edition", by Lyn M. Fraser and Aileen Ormiston, published by Prentice Hall, (2001). It's written in a conversational style that quickly teaches you how to analyze financial statements.

## Good Sources of Credit and Collection Information

Bank Systems & Technology Online. Good online magazine which details recent changes and challenges faced in the U.S. banking sector. It also highlights new collection technology. http://www.banktech.com/

Better Payment Practice Campaign. An interesting site that is, "Helping to effect positive change in the UK payment culture." It shares examples of credit applications, invoices, collections letters, and others. http://www.payontime.co.uk/

Business Credit Management. This informative site is geared for the U.K market. http://www.creditman.biz/uk/

CMA Business Credit Services. An extensive list of articles offering credit and collection tips. http://www.creditservices.org/articles/

Collection Advisor. This magazine is published six times a year by Recovery Advisor, LLC. It's a practical magazine that has sections for agencies and health care institutions. It also gives advice on technical solutions and management tips. http://www.collectionadvisor.com

CollectionIndustry.com. A detailed site showing the latest happenings in the field of credit from around the world. They also sell benchmarking research reports. http://www.collectionindustry.com

Collection Technology News. This trade magazine is published monthly by Royal Media Group. Subscription is $325 a year. It's geared to collection managers, agency owners, and the I.T. people who support them. http://www.royalmedia.com/sell.cfm?pub=103

Collections & Credit Risk. Published monthly by Credit and Collections World. An excellent website with selected magazine articles and "white papers" available on key credit topics. Job postings and new technologies are also included. http://ccr.faulknerggray.com

Credit Guru. A useful site with many tips. It also has a list of credit bureaus and collection agencies from around the world. http://www.creditguru.com/mainpage.htm

Credit Research Foundation. Useful research site showing DSO and aging statistics for benchmarking purposes. The statistics are from the U.S, but international readers will find the surveys interesting as a point for comparison. It also has good articles and in-depth reports. http://www.crfonline.org/

Credit Today. A trade magazine and online resource. For $279, you get 12 issues of their magazine and access to their research database. http://www.credittoday.net/public/main.cfm

Creditworthy. A useful site to get your credit department in order, especially helpful when starting up a new department. http://www.creditworthy.com/

## Credit Associations Worldwide:

### Asian Credit Associations

Hong Kong: Hong Kong Credit and Collection Management Association. http://www.hkccma.com

Malaysia: Association of Credit Management Malaysia. http://www.acmm.org.my

Singapore: Singapore Association of Credit Management. http://www.sacm.com.sg/

**Australian and New Zealand Credit Associations**

Australian Institute of Credit Management. http://www.aicm.com.au

Australian Collector Association Pty Ltd.
http://www.australiancollectors.com.au

Institute of Mercantile Agents Ltd. http://www.imal.com.au

New Zealand Credit & Finance Institute Incorporated.
http://www.nzcfi.org/

**European Credit Associations:**

Europe wide: Federation of European National Collection Associations
(FENCA). http://www.fenca.com/

Europe wide: League International for Creditors (site is in English,
French and German). http://www.lic-international.com

Ireland: Irish Institute of Credit Management. http://www.iicm.ie

Norway: Norwegian Association of Debt Collectors.
http://www.inkasso.no

Sweden: Association of Swedish Debt Collectors.
http://www.svenska-inkassoforeningen.se/In_English/

U.K.: Credit Services Association. http://www.csa-uk.com

U.K.: Institute of Credit Management. http://www.icm.org.uk/

**North American Credit Associations:**

Canada: Credit Institute of Canada. http://www.creditedu.org

Canada: National Association of Credit Management Canada.
http://www.nacmcanada.org/

Mexico: National Association of Credit Management Mexico.
http://www.nacmmexico.org/

U.S. : ACA International. An association of credit and collections professionals. Publisher of Collector magazine. ACA also has a certification
program. http://www.acainternational.org/incontent.aspx

U.S. : Commercial Collection Agency Association. An association for
U.S. collection agencies. http://www.ccaacollect.com

U.S. : FCIB: This association of executives in Finance, Credit and International Business is affiliated with NACM. It's especially useful for international readers and those involved in import / export. Although based in
the U.S., it has associations in Europe, North America and China. FCIB

also offers international credit qualifications that can be earned by passing an e-course. http://www.fcibglobal.com

U.S.: International Association of Commercial Collectors, Inc. http://www.commercialcollector.com/ScriptContent/Index.cfm

U.S.: National Association of Credit Management (NACM) is America's largest credit association. It publishes Business Credit magazine and has an archives section for members. NACM offers certification. It also sells useful books and in-depth reports. http://www.nacm.org

**Other Credit Links**

Professor John Wachowicz's website. The professor has put together the most extensive list of credit, collections and finance links I have ever seen. Part IV is especially useful.
http://web.utk.edu/~jwachowi/wacho_world.html

## *Summary*

- Knowledge without application is wasted effort. By applying knowledge we gain new experiences. From our new experiences, we gain wisdom, and from wisdom we learn the importance of continually seeking new knowledge.

- A successful collection department isn't one that achieves low bad debts at the expense of profits and customer satisfaction.

# Epilogue

### The Diaper Incident

One evening while changing our baby's diapers, my wife noticed he had a nasty diaper rash with little red bumps. We took poor Hughie to our little, neighborhood clinic. The family doctor had a quick look and pronounced, "Your boy has herpes."

Panic went through my brain. "Herpes?" I said, "Are you sure? He's only one-year's old?"

The doctor responded, "I'm sorry, yes."

She then passed us some powerful anti-herpes cream that I was afraid to put on the boy's skin. We were also charged a small fee.

After a sleepless night, the next morning, we visited a pediatrician at a private hospital. The doctor's expression was grave when I told him about the previous doctor's diagnosis. Then, as he slowly unwrapped the boy's diaper, I saw a smile break on his face.

"Oh", he said, "He's just got a yeast infection. That other doctor really misdiagnosed his condition."

The pediatrician then gave us a cheap, over-the-counter bathing solution. But his bill was a whooping three times more expensive than the other doctor's. Was I upset? No way!

The *Diaper Incident* taught me a couple lessons that apply to the business world:

Lesson #1: You get what you pay for. If you want cheap advice, you can find it. It just costs you more later.

Lesson #2: If you don't stay up-to-date in your field, you cause a lot of grief and damage to your customers. You're also considered a fool.

If your organization requires training or consulting to keep you or your staff up-to-date, please drop me a note.

## *About the Author*

Steve Coyle has collected accounts from Anchorage, Alaska to Seattle, Washington to Kuala Lumpur, Malaysia. He has collected in the banking, software, and telecommunication industries. In 1995, he arrived in Malaysia to start up the collections department at Malaysia's largest cellular phone company. That initial two-month project lasted eight years.

Steve is now a full-time trainer and consultant specializing in the credit and collections field. He primarily works in the Asia Pacific region. He is a Certified Credit Executive from the National Association of Credit Management (U.S.). He possesses an M.B.A. and a Masters in Instructional Technology. He has lived and worked in over 30 countries. He speaks a bit of French, Polish, and Bahasa Pasar (Malay).

He and his family live in a suburb of Kuala Lumpur. When not traveling on business, he and his wife, Tan Choon Ngor, keep an eye on their very active son, Hugh.

## *Contact Information*

I have tried to make this a practical book to ensure that your organization – in Asia or in the West – has an acceptable level of bad debts while achieving its profit and customer satisfaction goals. I'd appreciate any feedback you have.

Steve Coyle
ServiceWinners International Sdn. Bhd.
Kuala Lumpur, Malaysia
Email:          steve@servicewinners.com
Tel:            +60-12-2000-998
Web:            http://www.servicewinners.com

## Sample Script– Outbound: English

| Step | Phase | Script |
|------|-------|--------|
| 1 | Opening | *"Let me speak with (customer's name), please."*<br>or<br>*"Hello, Mr./Ms. (name), please"*<br><br>or for seriously overdue debtors who are hiding:<br><br>*"Hello, (customer's first name)?"* |
| 2 | After identifying customer first | *"Mr/ Ms (name), this is (your name) from ABC Company."* |
| 3 | Ask for BIF | *"I'm calling to confirm the balance of RM___ will be paid today for the (type of debt) account."* |
| 4 + | + Response | *"Great."* |
| 4 - | - Response | *"I'm sorry (repeat problem if necessary), however, you need to pay RM___ in order to help prevent (tool)."* |
| 5 | Reconfirm | *"(Customer's name), I'll note your account that you will pay (amount) by (date), correct?"* |
| 6 | *Closing | *"Thank you for using ABC Company."* |

*May be inappropriate for written-off accounts.

# Contoh Panggilan Keluar:
# Bahasa Malaysia

| Step | Phase | Skrip |
|------|-------|-------|
| 1 | Opening | *"Saya perlu bercakap dengan En / Pn ____."* <br> *"Saya hendak bercakap dengan ....."* <br> *"Saya nak bercakap dengan ....."* <br> *"Saya mahu bercakap dengan ....."* <br><br> atau <br><br> *"Hello, En / Pn____?"* <br><br> atau untuk penghutang tegar yang menyembunyikan diri: <br><br> *"Hello, (nama pertama pelanggan)?"* |
| 2 | After identifying customer first | *"En / Pn ___, saya (nama anda) dari ABC Company."* |
| 3 | Ask for BIF | *"Saya telefon untuk memastikan jumlah tunggakan sebanyak RM____ akan dibayar pada hari ini untuk akaun (jenis hutang)."* |
| 4 + | + Response | *"Bagus."* |
| 4 - | - Response | *"Saya faham masalah (ulangi masalah tersebut jika perlu), En / Pn ___, tetapi anda harus membayar sebanyak RM____ untuk mengelakkan daripada (tindakan)."* |
| 5 | Reconfirm | *"(Nama pelanggan), saya akan rekodkan pada akaun anda bahawa anda akan membayar RM____ pada (haribulan). Betulkan?"* |
| 6 | Closing | *"Terima kasih kerana berurusan dengan ABC Company."* |

# Sample Script– Outbound: Chinese

| Step | Phase | Script |
|------|-------|--------|
| 1 | 开场白 | "帮我转给(客户姓名)?"<br><br>或<br><br>"哈罗，（客户姓名）?"<br><br>或<br><br>"哈罗，（客户的名）?" |
| 2 | 确认顾客之后 | "（客户姓名）先生/小姐，我是（你的姓名）来自 ABC 公司的" |
| 3 | 要求全部欠 | "我拨电给您是要确认，您今天将会付还 RM_____ 於您的（户口的种类）户口" |
| 4 + | + 反应 | "很好" |
| 4 - | - 反应 | "我了解，（如果需要，重复客户的情况/烦恼），但是您必须付 RM_____ 的欠款以避免我们采取（行动）。" |
| 5 | 再次确定 | "（客户姓名）先生/小姐，我将记录您的户口，您会在（日期）付还 RM_____,对吗?" |
| 6 | 结尾 | "谢谢您使用 ABC 公司." |

Made in the USA